# HERMENEUTICS AS POLITICS

# ODÉON
## JOSUÉ V. HARARI AND VINCENT DESCOMBES
*General Editors*


HERMENEUTICS AS POLITICS
Stanley Rosen

FAREWELL TO MATTERS OF PRINCIPLE
*Philosophical Studies*
Odo Marquard

# Hermeneutics
# as Politics

STANLEY ROSEN

OXFORD UNIVERSITY PRESS
New York   Oxford

Oxford University Press

Oxford    New York    Toronto
Delhi    Bombay    Calcutta    Madras    Karachi
Petaling Jaya    Singapore    Hong Kong    Tokyo
Nairobi    Dar es Salaam    Cape Town
Melbourne    Auckland

and associated companies in
Berlin    Ibadan

First published in 1987 by Oxford University Press, Inc.
200 Madison Avenue, New York, New York 10016

First issued as an Oxford University Press paperback, 1989

Oxford is a registered trademark of Oxford University Press

Library of Congress Cataloging-in-Publication Data
Rosen, Stanley, 1929–
Hermeneutics as politics.
(Odéon)    Includes index.
1. Hermeneutics.    2. Political science.
1. Title.    BD241.R64    1987    121'.68    87-7945
ISBN 0-19-504908-X
ISBN 0-19-506161-6 (PBK)

A slightly different version
of Chapter 4 appears in
*Literature and the Question of Philosophy,*
ed. Anthony J. Cascardi, © 1987
Johns Hopkins University Press

2  4  6  8  10  9  7  5  3
Printed in the United States of America

# Contents

# HERMENEUTICS AS POLITICS

# Introduction

> Renan is probably the first to have been aware of the remark-
> able fact that the fascination with decadence and the appar-
> ently contradictory fascination with origins and primitivism
> are actually two sides of one and the same phenomenon.[1]

The studies presented here are unified by two closely related themes. First: the cluster of contemporary movements which we are now accustomed to call "postmodernist," although they understand themselves as an attack on the eighteenth-century Enlightenment, are in fact a continuation of that Enlightenment. Second: hermeneutics, the characteristic obsession of postmodernism, has an intrinsically political nature, which, especially in the United States, is rapidly being concealed by an encrustation of scholasticism and technophilia. As Julia Kristeva remarks:

> Academic discourse, and perhaps American university discourse in
> particular, possesses an extraordinary ability to absorb, digest, and
> neutralize all of the key, radical, or dramatic moments of thought,
> particularly, *a fortiori*, of contemporary thought.[2]

Both unifying themes are developed in the first study, in which I show how Kant is the paradigm of the internal incoherence of the Enlightenment, and hence the indispensable reference point for an understanding of the contemporary "posthistorical" condition. The Enlightenment is far from being a homogeneous phenomenon. Its fundamental structure is that of a conflict between mathematics and Newtonian science on the one hand and the desire for individual and political freedom on the other. The now-fashionable thesis of the link between scientific rationalism and domination was already well understood by Kant. If knowledge is enlightenment and science is knowledge, it follows that to be enlightened is either to endure self-ignorance or to undergo reification. In either case, the pursuit of freedom leads directly to slavery. The rhetoric of freedom that is traditionally associated with modern science loses all force as soon as it is identified as rhetoric on scientific grounds. Accordingly, science, as well as the underlying subject-object distinction that characterizes the modern epoch, is no more reasonable than any other product of the will. Indeed, if freedom is our goal, then reason is less reasonable than the imagination.

The unreasonableness of reason, and the turn to the imagination, are both illustrated in what I suggest is Kant's preparation for the discovery of "historicity" as a distinct ontological dimension. According to Kant, the understanding (*Verstand*) constitutes the world of experience, as well as scientific knowledge, which latter is marked by necessity. To the extent that there is room within experience for freedom, it cannot be "rational" in the sense of conforming with the understanding. To the extent that freedom is "rational," it must fall within the domain of reason (*Vernunft*). But reason in this technical sense has nothing to do with scientific knowledge. We cannot *know* that we are free. And there is a further difficulty. The understanding is in essence the formulation of and obedience to rules. Since there are no rules for the following of rules, or in other words, since reason is the domain of freedom, the understanding must be a spontaneous "project" (my term) of reason. But what grounds or motivates reason? I shall argue that, on the basis of Kant's texts, there is only one answer. Reason is itself constituted, or let us say constitutes itself, in accordance with the will to freedom. The upshot is that freedom both grounds, and is grounded by, reason. There is no principle of Hegelian dialectic at work here. Judged by the canons of traditional logic, which Kant accepts, his argument is invalid.

In fact, however, there is no argument here in the logical sense. The entire Kantian enterprise is justified by rhetoric. And in the specific case we are examining, Kant's rhetoric obscures the consequence of the separation of understanding from freedom as well as the subordination of reason to the will. We have to *will* that we are free, which comes dangerously close to imagining that we are free. Indeed, in the case of earthly happiness or political well-being, which for all of

Kant's terminological distinctions cannot be sundered from freedom and justice, the dominance of the will by the imagination becomes unmistakable. Kant must provide what is for all practical purposes a moral justification of political history, even while he insists on the distinction between morality and politics. History is at once produced by, and subjected to, a rhetorical hermeneutic of the imagination. To say this in another way, history is in the domain neither of nature nor of freedom. It is a self-contradictory domain of autoemancipation governed by theoretical and practical rules. In short, it is a theoretical artifact, that is to say, an interpretation or "reading" of the "book of nature" for which there exists no independent criterion of validity. This interpretation has a "transcendental" source, namely, the conditions necessary to preserve freedom. But freedom is not further justifiable; it is, as it were, the human face of spontaneity. The result is a paradox. The primacy of spontaneity makes reason (by which term I here include both *Vernunft* and *Verstand*) unreasonable because arbitrary. This is the basis for the subsequent view that reason is an artifact of history, in other words, the reverse of the eighteenth-century view that history in an artifact of reason. We thus come directly to the late-modern view, made dominant by Nietzsche and today accepted among postmodernist thinkers without any prominent exception: to reason is to interpret, because reason is itself an interpretation.

Contemporary attacks on the Enlightenment thus illustrate two main characteristics of the Enlightenment itself: the self-destruction of an exclusively or predominantly formalist rationalism, and the celebration of freedom as spontaneity. One could misunderstand the second characteristic as an assertion of the central importance of politics, but Kant's distinction between morality and politics continues to serve as the paradigm for postmodernist treatments of practice. Needless to say, in the case of some major representatives of postmodernism, the political implications or even presuppositions of the desire to "deconstruct" the modern European tradition are clearly perceived. But for deeply political reasons, they are not always passed on so clearly to the disciples. A call for the liberation of humanity from the domination of the anthropological tentacles of the Enlightenment is at once a call to anarchism, since politics as we know it is inevitably enacted by the "rationalist" state. Thus someone like Foucault, for example, who

lapsed into a flirtation with Maoism during his later years, despite the
perception that not all forms of domination are undesirable, was im-
mobilized by the contradictions inherent in his own version of Enlightenment.[3] As a decadent product of the Enlightenment, Foucault's
"value-free" commitment to a suitably modified scientism and his
complicity in the attempt to tear down "rationalist" or "bourgeois"
power structures do not constitute a serious political position but
rather amount to, or serve, a romantic identification with the outcasts
and the oppressed. Archaeological science is replaced by a genealogical
transvaluation of values, or a paradoxical, but today almost obliga-
tory, left-wing Nietzscheanism.[4]

In the initial phases of his thought, as represented by *Les Mots et les
choses,* Foucault insisted that man cannot return to his origins.[5] This
is to say that the end of the Enlightenment means the end of man, or in
other words the emergence of a postmodern human being.[6] Whatever
their disagreements on detail, Foucault and Derrida, the two most
important contemporary representatives of the postmodern attack on
the Enlightenment, agree on the "closure" of the age of metaphysics as
a necessary condition for the appearance of a new epoch, which we
may call the age of difference. Incidentally, just as Marxists quarrel
over whether the postcapitalist epoch is inevitable or is dependent
upon human choice, so too it is not clear within postmodernism
whether modernity has already and inevitably exhausted itself or
whether it requires the continuous stimulus of postmodernist rhetoric
to hasten it to its grave. On this point, too, our epoch reflects the
Kantian situation. I shall give an extended example of this situation
later in this introduction, when I come to examine the most recent
book by Jürgen Habermas.

To return to difference, it is true that Foucault's understanding of
the term is more conventional than is Derrida's. At all stages of his
thought, Foucault plainly thinks of "difference" via repression or op-
pression. As he comes closer to Nietzsche, Foucault also moves closer
to the aforementioned romantic and largely negative version of Maoism. The earlier positivism is thus inverted into negativism, that is, into
a much franker expression of rage against bourgeois society. But at no
stage of his career does Foucault illustrate the speculative madness of
Nietzsche, whereas this is perhaps Derrida's outstanding feature.

Derridean difference (*différance*) will be a main theme of the second study in this volume, in the context of a critical inspection of his understanding of Western metaphysics as Platonism. Restricting ourselves here to *différance*, we could say as an introductory approach that Derrida radicalizes Kantian spontaneity and entirely detaches it from concepts or rules. Spontaneity qua *différance* is not the transcendental ego but the primordial writer that produces signifiers rather than rules. The spontaneous Derridean signifiers themselves signify *other* signifiers—exactly as in the case of Jacques Lacan.[7] To paraphrase Wittgenstein, the world for Derrida is everything that is the text. It follows that to read is not merely to interpret, but to signify or write, and hence to produce a *different* text. The rage for difference is a direct consequence of the association between rationalist bourgeois domination and the identity and universality of mathematicized or objectified life. The celebration of difference thus pervades the most important postmodernist works of the 1960s. Particularly important for our purposes is Gilles Deleuze's *Nietzsche et la philosophie,* which appeared in 1962, five years before his own *Différence et répétition* and Derrida's *De la grammatologie.* It is thus exactly contemporary with Derrida's study of Husserl's *The Origin of Geometry.*

Deleuze interprets Nietzsche as fundamentally a thinker of difference or diversity. His Nietzsche rebels against dialectical thinking, in the sense culminating with Hegel, by substituting difference for negation and contradiction.[8] Difference is the element of affirmation and enjoyment, or the Dionysian "innocence of truth": "irresponsibility—Nietzsche's most noble and beautiful secret."[9] (I cannot resist wondering how much this statement was inspired by a reaction to the regime of de Gaulle.) Nietzsche's pivotal doctrines of the eternal return and the will to power are interpreted accordingly by Deleuze. What returns is diversity understood as the affirmative: "return is the being of difference excluding the negative."[10] Furthermore, "it is not some one thing which returns, but rather returning itself is the one thing which is affirmed of diversity or multiplicity."[11] The will to power is accordingly the interpreting and evaluating principle of qualities of force; it is genealogical; "the differential element from which the value of values themselves derives."[12] "Genealogy is the art of difference or distinction, the art of nobility."[13] Accordingly, one may infer that nobility, action, or affirmation is not properly positive or constructive, but negative and destructive.[14] Deleuze's interpretation of Nietzsche is crucial for our understanding of postmodernism. The Platonic philosopher-soldier, whose education is primarily mathematical and who remains the guardian angel of the ostensibly "liberal" Enlightenment (liberal because dedicated to freedom), leads to the tyranny of form, presence, structure, rules, and universality in the sense of the suppression of disagreement, which is itself stigmatized as "ignorance." In place of the philosopher-soldier, the postmodernist puts Nietzsche's artist-warrior: poetry replaces mathematics, difference replaces identity, and creation is unmasked as destruction.

I have suggested that the critical formulation of the contradiction inherent in the Enlightenment is to be found in Kant's unstable attempt to ground reason in spontaneity. As is already evident in Hegel's *Science of Logic,* the attempt must fail, even if it is disguised as the assimilation of spontaneity by reason. In the section entitled "With What Must Science Begin?" Hegel first criticizes those who (like Schelling) "begin, like a shot from a pistol, from their inner revelation, from faith, intellectual intuition, etc., and who would be exempt from *method* and logic."[15] We may paraphrase this observation as follows: spontaneity must be self-grounding, hence fully rational and discursive. A few pages later, in defending the notion of a presuppositionless science or an immediate beginning for logic (since a science based upon presuppositions is not self-grounding, and to that extent, is irrational or rational only relative to something ungrounded), Hegel says: "all that is present is simply the resolve, which can also be regarded as arbitrary, that we propose to consider thought as such."[16]

The arbitrary resolve to consider thought as such is the Kantian spontaneity of the will of the philosopher, who *insists* upon being rational, and so not merely logical but comprehensively systematic. This insistence is the mark of the connection between freedom and rhetoric in the Enlightenment, or in other words, between spontaneity and hermeneutics. If nature, or things in themselves, are accessible to us only through the mediation of concepts, or what Hegel more poetically calls "the terrible labor of the negative," then knowing is making. The ostensibly transcendental nature of our concepts, or the Hegelian isomorphism between eternity and temporality, is already compromised by its "genealogy" of spontaneity, or, which comes to the same thing, by its arbitrariness. When Kant's transcendental ego and Hegel's Absolute Spirit are consigned to the dustbin of history, there can be no mistaking the consequent triumph of spontaneity. As a result, theory (the contemplation of truth) is replaced by interpretation (a perspectival fiction, masquerading as a theory). All thinking is then hermeneutical. As Michel Foucault once expressed it, "the death of interpretation is to believe that there are signs, signs which have a primary, original, real existence. . . . The life of interpretation, on the contrary, is to believe that there are only interpretations."[17]

I discuss the decay of theory into interpretation in chapter 4 of the present volume. Suffice it to say here that the triumph of hermeneutics is already visible in Kant, although his rhetorical presentation of the (in the broad sense) political motivations for his critical philosophy, and hence his grounding of critique in hermeneutic, has seldom been given adequate attention. It is a much shorter step from Kant to Nietzsche than one might think. By parallel reasoning, the differences between Marx and Nietzsche are not more striking than their similarities. German critical and idealist philosophies provide us with the basis for an understanding of the typically postmodern efforts to synthesize Marx and Nietzsche.

By the same token, they enable us to understand cases like that of T. W. Adorno, in whose *Negative Dialectics* one finds a Marxism blunted (ostensibly refined) by an anti-Enlightenment aestheticism which, in its tacit equation of creation and destruction, and its consequent celebration of diversity, sounds as though it had been inspired by Deleuze's study of Nietzsche. Adorno's negative dialectics is intended to serve the cause of reconcilement between things and concepts, which are forced together, and hence into contradiction, by traditional dialectical thinking. Reconcilement is accomplished by dismantling "the coercive logical character of its own course." In other words: deconstruction. "Reconcilement would release the nonidentical, would rid it of coercion, including spiritualized coercion; it would open the road to the multiplicity of different things and strip dialectics of its power over them."[18]

Adorno rightly notices, and rejects, "a propensity of all Enlightenment: to punish undisciplined gestures."[19] In the *Dialectic of Enlight-*

*enment,* written with Max Horkheimer, he makes this point as an attack on the implicit positivism of the Enlightenment. "For the Enlightenment, whatever does not conform to the rule of computation and utility is suspect. . . . Enlightenment is totalitarian."[20] It is totalitarian because "it confounds thought and mathematics."[21] Horkheimer and Adorno see part of the problem, but they apparently miss the subterranean connection between mathematical tyranny and spontaneous freedom. If mathematics is coextensive with reason, there is no reason to employ mathematics. Reason is itself already spontaneous. It is therefore no higher, but no lower, than negative dialectics.

The aestheticism of neopositivist science—"a system of detached signs devoid of any intention that would transcend the system,"[22] like Foucault's interpretations of interpretations, or Lacan's and Derrida's signifers that signify signifiers—is a consequence of what Adorno calls "reconcilement," but which we may recognize as the continuous hermeneutics of a postrationalist age. One thing is true: as a quondam Marxist, Adorno does not press his negativism to the point at which nature is entirely assimilated by concepts.[23] Within the domain of what Adorno would call neopositivism, we find statements like this one from a leading "analytical" philosopher, Hilary Putnam: the picture of a univocal correspondence between what is inside and what is outside the brain "leads to the metaphysical fantasy of a 'ready-made world', with self-identifying objects, 'built-in' structure, essences, or whatever . . . ."[24] In its place, Putnam goes on to assert "a *human* kind of realism," which is essentially a belief in knowing which language games are being played, plus "a lot of empirical information."[25] He does not seem to notice that language games and empirical science are already conceptualizations, and hence (in the broad sense of the term) "formalizations" of the world. Even further, they are historical products, artifacts, or spontaneous interpretations. Is there any wonder that postmodernism has begun its inexorable advance through the corridors of our leading departments of philosophy?

Horkheimer and Adorno may be given full credit for spelling out the tyrannical and positivist elements in the scientific Enlightenment. We can understand the force of their critique of the suppression of human nature by the administered life. But what would they recommend in its place? It is obvious that negative dialectic will not help. Nor can we take seriously the erotic liberation recommended by Herbert Marcuse. In order to find the response of the Frankfurt School to the problem of the Enlightenment, and so its recommendations for the return from the postmodern wasteland (in which the everyday world is regarded as a metaphysical fantasy) to a legitimate modernity, we must turn to Jürgen Habermas. A recent publication, *Der philosophische Diskurs der Moderne,* provides us with a pertinent text. In it, Habermas treats the developing crisis of the modern age from Hegel to the latest spokesmen for postmodernism. There is much to be learned from the first 343 pages of this book, and much with which I agree. But our present concern is with chapters 11 and 12, in which Habermas summarizes his familiar solution to the problem raised by the dialectic of Enlightenment.

Habermas tells us that the modern doctrine of subjectivity has an intuition of freedom and emancipation, but it ironically perverts this intuition into self-repression and objectification. Furthermore, the expressivity of the individual, when articulated by the categories of the subject-object distinction, turns into a loss of self as well as "narcissistic anxiety in face of the loss."[26] The story of modernity is thus one of the self-thematising and self-reifying scientism of modern subjectivity.[27] "The paradigm of *Bewusstseinsphilosophie* is exhausted." To this point, we recognize the position of Horkheimer and Adorno. But Habermas goes beyond criticism to advocate a theory of linguistic intersubjectivity. Once again, it is not entirely clear whether Habermas claims to present an analysis of how human society has always functioned or a recommendation as to how we are to understand ourselves henceforward. The problem arises because Habermas is not simply making recommendations for a new social policy. He purports to be giving a true account of the "ontological" and semantic structure of society. If the account is correct, then why has modernity led to an impasse, if not actual shipwreck? On the other hand, if the account must be accepted as true by a society *in order for it to work,* the question of objective or scientific truth arises. How do we know that Habermas's "theory" is not in fact a perspectival hermeneutic of human existence that, like any rhetorical doctrine, depends for its effectiveness on persuasion rather than truth?

The problem faced by Habermas is thus exactly the problem of Marxism. A theory that depends upon human choice for its effectiveness is validated by that choice, and not by a correct explanation of history, society, or the ostensibly theory-neutral laws of "communicative reason." When Habermas does make a theoretical statement about communicative reason, he describes it in terms like these: "the performative engagement of participants within interactions, who coordinate their plans for activity in that they make themselves understood to one another about something in the world."[28] I suggest that this is a platitude. It is true, but empty, and one may accept it without being required to take a step in accord with Habermas's more specific social and political doctrines. The statement just cited is a correct description, for example, of Nazi Germany. No doubt Habermas would reply that this shows its theoretical soundness, but we do not require theories telling us how to cross the street or that the best way to communicate with people is by speaking to them.

Needless to say, this is not Habermas's last word. He goes on to insist upon the purely procedural, nonreligious, and nonmetaphysical nature of communicative reasoning. In other words, Habermas is here offering a theoretical account of human society, not a program for social action. By "procedural," he means that the linguistic nature of intersubjectivity provides a measure for communicative reason, namely, a procedural concept of rationality. This concept contains as its elements propositional truth, normative correctness, subjective truthfulness, and aesthetic suitability.[29] Again, it is not clear whether this is a scientific description or a hermeneutical recommendation. In either case, Habermas is engaging in the same "objectification" of rationality that has been practiced by modern philosophies of subjectivity. This is not a process, incidentally, to which I am objecting. It is not easy to see how one could present *any* account of rationality without attempting to analyze the components of sound reasoning. Presumably Habermas believes himself to have avoided "objectification" because he includes normative correctness, subjective truthfulness, and aesthetic suitability in his concept of rationality. But this is not enough. In the first place, Habermas is not the first person to have seen these various aspects of rationality. The point is that to see them, and thereby to distinguish them, is already to objectify. But second, his theoretical articulation of the elements is conventional; it fails to consider, for example, whether a nonreifying account of rationality would perceive a unifying characteristic that is concealed by the objectifying procedure of distinguishing separate functions. Finally, the theory says nothing about what constitutes normative, subjective, or aesthetic truth.

How can these three types of truth be made compatible with propositional truth? Habermas's syncretism is silent on this point as well. He does tell us that the normative content of *Vernunftkritik* must come from "the rational potential dwelling within everyday praxis."[30] The reader cannot fail to ask: *What* rational potential? If normative content comes from what a society regards in its everyday praxis as normatively correct, then Habermas's theory serves merely to confirm our prejudices. If it comes instead from propositional truth, then Habermas relapses into positivism, if not something worse. And similar objections could be formulated with respect to the two remaining elements of the concept of rationality. In sum: everyday praxis is precisely what led in the sixteenth and seventeenth centuries to modernity and the crisis of self-consciousness. On the other hand, concentration upon the linguistic structure of social interaction, apart from the dangers of objectification, may provide interesting information to the science of linguistics, but it furnishes nothing with respect to the correct organization of society or the most fundamental political problems. To give just one example, the theory of speech-acts may be adopted by monarchists as well as by socialists.

Habermas is quite mistaken in regarding his conception of communicative reasoning as "metaphysically neutral." This is clearly impossible, since the theory consists of an eclectic selection of elements from theories already propounded by the most influential thinkers of the past two hundred years. It is neutral, if at all, only in the sense that the elements cancel each other out. But even this cancellation is a consequence of adherence to the major themes of modern subjectivist metaphysics. The point can be made in an especially telling way by noting Habermas's assertion that there is no totality in the Hegelian sense. Instead, he says, there is a sharp distinction between the life-world, namely, the cooperative accomplishment of communicating actors, and the interpretations by these actors of all aspects of their common lives.[31] It follows that every kind of hermeneutical doctrine will manifest itself among the actors, exactly as has happened in the course of the modern epoch. Furthermore, according to Habermas, the theoretical structures of the life-world consist of traditions, groups, and the process of socialization of coming generations.[32] In other words, the structures of the life-world *are themselves interpretations* that generate unending interpretations.

Another way in which to bring out the emptiness of Habermas's theory of communicative reason is to note that it is rooted in a doctrine of intersubjectivity. If subjectivity is replaced by intersubjectivity, then surely objectivity is replaced by interobjectivity. Does this not mean simply that objectivity is replaced by subjectivity? To make the same point in another way, everything depends upon what is meant by the prefix "inter." Like the moderns whom he criticizes, Habermas gives what is essentially a linguistic interpretation of "inter." Since his linguistic doctrine is an internally incoherent brew of positivist objectification and historicist subjectivism, Habermas has in effect done nothing more than to smuggle all of the modern epoch into his notion of "inter" or "communication."

In an earlier work, *Knowledge and Human Interests,* Habermas concludes an often interesting historical analysis of his modern predecessors with the following contentions: "The achievements of the transcendental subject have their basis in the natural history of the human species." These achievements are fundamentally linguistic. "What raises us out of nature is the only thing whose nature we can know: *language.*"[33] He goes on to say:

> From the beginning philosophy has presumed that the autonomy and responsibility posited with the structure of language are not only anticipated but real. It is pure theory, wanting to derive everything from itself, that succumbs to unacknowledged external conditions and becomes ideological. Only when philosophy discovers in the dialectical course of history the traces of violence that deform repeated attempts at dialogue and recurrently close off the path to unconstrained communication does it further the process whose suspension it otherwise legitimates: mankind's evolution toward autonomy and responsibility. My fifth thesis is thus that the unity of knowledge and interest proves itself in a dialectic that takes the historical traces of suppressed dialogue and reconstructs what has been suppressed.[34]

Habermasian deconstruction is reconstructive or positive. The natural science of language replaces classical theory or modern ontology in the process of liberation, according to which we may communicate in an unconstrained manner. Habermas thus repeats the dilemma of the Enlightenment, even as he endorses its goals. An "objective" or "procedural" linguistic science, in fact linguistic sociology, is employed to guarantee complete discursive freedom. But this is impossible, for two reasons. First, the use of linguistic sociology, an instrument of Enlightenment, objectifies the speaking subject, eliminates "error" (incorrect modes of speech), or enforces its own conditions of rationality. Second, to the extent that linguistic sociology succeeds, against its regulatory ("procedural") nature, in allowing unconstrained dialogue, it sanctions the radical multiplicity of interpretations that characterizes the very crisis Habermas seeks to avert. The union of knowledge and interest, or of nature (science) and history (hermeneutics), is a self-contradictory theoretical construction. In political terms, *there is no liberal solution to the aporia of the Enlightenment, because liberalism (and a fortiori socialism) is itself the crystallization of that aporia.* The incoherence of unrestrained interpretation both reflects and intensifies the arbitrariness or spontaneity of the discursive structure of communicative reason. In saying this, I have no intention of precluding liberalism. What I object to is the delusion that there is a liberal theory of liberalism which is free of the intrinsic aporia of liberalism.

The doctrines of Habermas, like those of his colleague K. O. Apel, are a fashionable and well-meaning attempt to circumvent the exhaustion of modern philosophies of subjectivity and thereby to continue with the goals of the Enlightenment in a coherent, self-consistent manner. Their method is a friendly eclecticism that sacrifices nothing. Unfortunately, this amiability leads to the loss of everything.[35] I would almost be willing to say that I prefer the straightforward and clearheaded approach of Maoism. The only way in which to carry through the Enlightenment to something like a comprehensive and coherent conclusion is that taken by Alexandre Kojève, and even he had to buttress his Stalinism with the exoteric mask of Hegelianism in order to give a veneer of intellectual respectability to his political program. It is only a slight overstatement to say that the only point on which Kojève was a genuine Hegelian is one which holds equally good for

Hobbes. The Enlightenment, carried through to its logical conclusion, means the suppression of opposition, or a discourse that is "homogeneous" in its acceptance of a single universal criterion of rationality. Habermas and Apel earn our admiration for their unwillingness to succumb to postmodern nihilism, but the value of their work lies in their historical analyses; they are not radical thinkers but professors. We are shocked and repelled by Kojève's Stalinism, but we can learn something important from the manner in which he articulates it. I have therefore included a lengthy study of the man who is furthermore the *éminence grise* of the last two generations of French thinkers.

This study, contained in chapter 3 of the present volume, takes the form of a comparative analysis of the doctrines of Kojève and of Leo Strauss. Whereas both practiced esotericism, they did so in the "modern" rather than the "ancient" manner, with sufficient clues to, and explicit statements of, their actual views to enable us to determine these views with satisfactory textual documentation. Strauss's fame as a theoretician of the right parallels Kojève's influence on representatives of the dominant "progressive" branch of late modernity. A study of their work, which intersects, sometimes explicitly, at certain points, has much to teach us about the political nature of hermeneutics. It also enables us to formulate with unusual clarity the problem underlying the Enlightenment: the quarrel between the ancients and the moderns.

The most effective way in which to introduce the quarrel between the ancients and the moderns is to say that it turns upon a fundamental difference of theology. The ancient philosophers rejected the warnings of the poets, as exemplified in Pindar's admonition: "do not strive to be a god." They differed from their modern colleagues, however, with respect to the nature of divine praxis, a term we may somewhat anachronistically apply to the ancient thinkers in its modern sense of a combination of theory and production. The classical philosophers, in particular those of the Socratic school (which Leo Strauss sought to continue), understand by praxis the construction of a cosmos in which there is an exoteric separation of *theoria* and *poiesis*. The modern philosophers who trace their lineage back to English doctrines of power and utility (and whom Kojève, despite a heavy veneer of aestheticism, continued to represent), accept no such distinction in their exoteric or political teaching. The quarrel between the ancients and the moderns, as it was played out in the exoteric debate between Strauss and Kojève, has its inner or esoteric meaning in the question *quid sit deus*?

From this standpoint, my study of Strauss and Kojève can be taken as a companion piece to the contrast between Emmanuel Levinas and Jacques Derrida. Strauss and Kojève, and Strauss as much as Kojève (once we put aside Strauss's exoteric flirtation with Hebraic tradition), are atheists who wish to be gods. Levinas and Derrida present us with two different versions of the dilemma faced by the philosophically corrupted members of the Hebraic tradition. Levinas, like a mystical counterpart to Maimonides, is forced to employ philosophy in order to deconstruct reason. Up to a point, Derrida is engaged in exactly the same enterprise, but with this crucial difference: There is no God in Derrida's anticosmos, but only the Talmud. And since there is no God, the Talmud is not the Talmud.

Whichever side one takes in this complex theological debate, one will be sure to engage in something that is serious (to employ a Platonic distinction that Derrida makes much of). I want to close this introduction by assuring the reader that, despite my criticism of postmodernist thinkers, I feel the force of their enterprise, and recognize the sense in which I am one of them. I ask them only to grant me that the distinction between postmodernism and modernism is absurd. It will follow directly that the quarrel between the ancients and the moderns, which can be fought out only by moderns, once it is understood in properly theological terms, cannot possibly be explained as the struggle between *parole* and *écriture*. In other words, we shall make no serious advance until we understand that what has been called "the history of the metaphysics of presence" is a vulgar religious myth which cannot be taken seriously by seriously playful theologians. At the beginning of the *Phaedrus,* Socrates tells us that he has no time for demythologizing, as he is too busy attempting to discover his own nature. In the late twentieth century, when a greater degree of frankness is required by the greater degree of corruption, we must publicly reject this instance of Socratic irony in favor of the genuine Socratic leisure. To do this is in no sense to desert modernity for antiquity. It has to be remembered that the antidote for historicism is not surrender to the disease itself. By the same token, our need for leisure will leave us no time to chatter about reification or logocentrism. We do not wish to achieve notoriety among humans at the expense of being excluded from the company of the gods.

# 1

## Transcendental Ambiguity:
## The Rhetoric of the Enlightenment

The modern age has been characterized since its inception by a contrapuntal structure of daring and inquietude. The daring is best illustrated by the mathematical enthusiasm of Descartes and his progeny. Daring casts its own shadow: terror. In Pascal's words, "the eternal silence of these infinite spaces terrifies me."[1] The secular infinity of the modern universe brings with it a modern conception of the experience of time. To cite Pascal again, "we never care about the present time." And so "the past and the present are our means; the future alone is our end. Hence we never live, but we hope to live." Pascal thus introduces one of the central themes of the modern age: the absence of the present. This theme is intrinsic to Kant's speculations on history, which, as we shall see, is for him populated by human beings who, in Pascal's words, "continuously dispose themselves to be happy," and hence inevitably never achieve that goal.[2]

Kant, the great synthesizer of the Enlightenment, is famous for his injunction *sapere aude*. The element of inquietude in his version of Enlightenment is less well known, because Kant's inquietude is concealed by a rhetorical mixture of hope and technical ambiguity. More specifically, Kant's great modern predecessors attempted to regulate Cartesian daring with one form or another of classical political prudence. Kant claims to reject the accommodation of theoretical frankness to prudential considerations. In so doing, he seems to provide a

historicopolitical counterpart to the Enlightenment project of unlimited scientific progress.

However, Kant is led to restrict the scope of scientific knowledge in
order to preserve the possibility of freedom and morality. At the same
time, he distinguishes between morality and politics, which leads in
turn to a bifurcation in his explicit doctrine of freedom. Politics is
neither scientific nor (in the proper sense of the term) moral. Moral
freedom is obedience to the moral law that reason legislates for itself.
Political freedom is the preservation of justice and tranquillity, which
allows the individual to pursue worldly happiness.

Science is knowledge of natural necessity, whereas morality is a
condition of the free will. The consequence of Kant's distinction in this
regard is that there can be no knowledge of morality. Politics is motivated by natural inclination, which seeks self-interest and the gratifica-
tion of the passions. As a consequence, whereas it might be said, or
rather hoped, that political progress tends toward a conjunction with
morality, we can never know this. On the other hand, politics cannot
be simply identical with natural science, since it is clearly a matter of
prudential calculation or "cleverness" (*Klugheit*) and therefore concerns the contingent particulars of everyday life. Otherwise stated, if
politics were determined by nature, it would be impossible to speak of
freedom or responsibility. There would be no basis for hope.

On the basis of this brief preliminary sketch, we can infer two
reasons why Kant turns to speculations about history. First, the separation of knowledge and morality on the one hand, and of morality and
political or empirical existence on the other, may leave room for the
possibility of freedom in the moral sense, but this concerns our existence in the next world. It provides no explanation of how morality is
to regulate science in this world. Human freedom in this world requires not merely the regulation but the transcendence or mastery of
nature. It is not enough to prevent the epistemological encroachment
of scientific reasoning upon morality. Science must also be forced to
submit to the human will.[3]

The second reason is that Kant is deeply convinced of the farcical
nature of human existence as it is normally perceived, and wishes to
defend "providence" from the charge that our life in this world is
nothing more than misery and injustice. Whereas he cannot offer us

worldly happiness, Kant wishes to justify our misery and to encourage us to act on the basis of hope, in order to contribute thereby to the very condition that all human beings desire.

History, which is fundamentally political, is essentially distinct from both knowledge and morality. In Kant's technical terminology, history cannot be deduced from a transcendental ground. It is literally *ground-less*. Otherwise put, since there are no synthetic a priori political or historical judgments, history is also nonrational. As a groundless phenomenon, history constitutes an "ontologically" distinct domain. As a nonrational one, it cannot be the subject matter of rational philosophical analysis and argumentation. Instead, we must have recourse to rhetoric and to hope when speculating about history. And finally, to the extent that history is natural, it is incompatible with freedom or inaccessible to decisions of the human will.

We may combine the remarks of the previous paragraph in the assertion that Kant discovers the modern conception of history as an ontologically independent dimension within which other ontological dimensions are somehow unified. He anticipates the nineteenth-century discovery of historicity. Second, Kant conceives of history in a fundamentally nonrational or transrationalist manner. Third, he prepares the late nineteenth-century view, exemplified by Nietzsche, that "Being" is intrinsically historical and irrational. Fourth, Kant radically lowers the status of political prudence, or *phronesis;* his initial identification of history with politics leads in both the short and the long run to a depreciation of politics. The next step is the concealment of the political nature of history by attempts to go beyond both rationalism and nonrationalism, or to discover a "new" kind of thinking that is appropriate to the peculiar nature of history. This new thinking, in keeping with the radical contingency of history, takes on the character of poetry. This is, of course, not to say that Kant intended to do these things. But he did them nevertheless.

Taking a still broader standpoint, we may say that Kant is both the critical paradigm of the internal inconsistency (and hence the "fruitfulness") of the Enlightenment and the indispensable reference point for an understanding of the late-modern attack on the Enlightenment which has come in our own decade to be known as "postmodernism." I shall argue in the course of this book, with respect to Kant in particular, that postmodernism is in fact a *continuation* of the Enlightenment. The first indispensable point of contact between Kant and late or postmodernism is the anticipation of historicity. I shall argue that there are two more, equally indispensable points of contact. For the moment, I merely name them: the transformation of philosophy into global hermeneutics and the introduction of the rhetoric of frankness. What I mean by these points will be made clear in due order.

# II

*Was ist Aufklärung?* In 1784, thirty-three years after the publication of the *Encyclopédie,* Kant addressed the Germans with this rhetorical question. I shall suggest that this question, to which Kant's comprehensive teaching is addressed, requires an equally rhetorical answer. Everything turns upon the first principle of Kant's thought: the unquestioned desirability of freedom. Unfortunately, freedom is an ambiguous first principle. Like any first principle, it cannot be deduced from some higher ground. It also suffers from the serious disadvantage that anything at all can be deduced from it. From the outset, it is evident that the defense of freedom is necessarily rhetorical.

Let us examine the relevant details of Kant's comprehensive procedure. We begin by a brief contrast between Kant's and d'Alembert's reply to the question "what is Enlightenment?" D'Alembert speaks of "the order and linkage of human knowledge"[4] and of the eighteenth-century transformation of science.[5] According to d'Alembert, "the tableau of our actual knowledge [*nos connaissances réelles*]" constitutes "the history and the eulogy of the human spirit; the rest is nothing but fiction or satire."[6] Kant (if not entirely consistently) was also in favor of scientific progress. Nevertheless, he does not identify it with Enlightenment, which he defines instead in political or historical terms. He thereby comes very close to identifying the Enlightenment with what is for d'Alembert "nothing but fiction or satire."[7]

D'Alembert shares the Cartesian confidence in our ability to distinguish between fiction and science. I would not go so far as to say that Kant lacks this confidence. Nevertheless, one of the main consequences of his so-called Copernican revolution (an expression not actually employed by Kant) is to transform science into a *fiction* in the literal sense: something not simply arranged but *formed* by human intelligence. As we shall see, this is necessary for Kant's defense of freedom. We should not overlook the fact, however, that Kant simply radicalizes an implication of modern natural science since Descartes, if not before that.

In reflecting upon the difference between d'Alembert and Kant, it is worth considering briefly Kant's relation to Rousseau. Rousseau attempts to combine a modern conception of science with an ancient conception of political virtue. This in turn leads him to retain the Baconian doctrine of the advisability of restricting the public dissemination of certain scientific results. Rousseau's classical bent keeps him from separating politics from morality. But this is not to say that he accepts the classical conception of freedom. When Rousseau distinguishes between public virtue and private perfection, he shifts from morality to what may be concisely designated as the aesthetic sensibility.[8]

In the first *Discourse,* Rousseau argues not so much (if at all) that morality is intrinsically more noble than science, as that science is dangerous to morality and hence to politics. Kant's view is noticeably different. He holds that nothing is higher than morality (a good will); in addition, as we have already seen, he separates morality from politics. Rousseau's doctrine of the aesthetic sensibility holds no interest for Kant. In his teaching, private perfection cannot be acquired by an extrapolitical existence. It must be pursued within social intercourse, in political life, and hence within the mainstream of history. Even the philosopher-scientist, who is relatively detached from active political life, is a citizen and, as a teacher, an official of the state. He thus has political responsibilities in a theoretical *and* practical sense.

Kant's political philosophy does not take the traditional form of the articulation of the best regime. What one may call Kant's "concrete" political recommendations are always subordinate, both explicitly and implicitly, to his overall interpretation of human freedom and rationality. No doubt the same could be said of the traditional political philosophers, and yet there is a fundamental difference between them and Kant. Kant's hermeneutics of freedom drives him toward a speculative or rhetorical doctrine of history. Kant's political "ideal" is inseparable from his doctrine of infinite historical progress.

Before we articulate the details of Kant's reflections on history, it will be necessary to say a few words about the major theoretical hypothesis of his philosophy. I shall say just enough about this to serve the purposes of the present investigation. We need to see more clearly why freedom holds both a central and a deeply ambiguous position in Kant's version of the Enlightenment. This insight in turn will explain why Kant's comprehensive philosophy is equivalent to a hermeneutics of human nature and, by extension, why postmodernism is essentially Kantian. We shall be in a position to see the line of development from Kant to Nietzsche, whose principal doctrine is well formulated by Jean Granier as follows: "Being [*l'Etre*] is always and necessarily Being-interpreted [*l'Etre interprété*]."[9]

# III

One may distinguish three main senses of freedom in Kant, of which only two are explicitly stated by him. The first and least important is political freedom.[10] The second and best known is moral freedom. The third and least known, because never (to my knowledge) mentioned by Kant, is the freedom to choose or to reject the Copernican revolution. This third sense is by far the most important. The difference between the second and the third senses will emerge from an inspection of two crucial technical terms in Kant: spontaneity and autonomy. In order to explain these terms, it is necessary to say a few words about the hypothesis of the transcendental ego.

Kant argues that if we wish to explain both causal necessity in nature and moral freedom, a fundamental shift in our comprehensive intellectual perspective is required. Instead of allowing the intellect to conform to an ostensibly independent nature, we require that nature conform to the intellect. Kant claims in the first *Critique* that mathematical propositions and physical laws are patently necessary, which would be impossible if we did not ourselves furnish the component of necessity by the act of conceptual thinking. We note in passing that if this claim is replaced by the denial of the strict necessity of mathematics and physics, there is no further need to accept the Copernican revolution for the sake of moral freedom. Curiously enough, the advent of the view that mathematics and physics are fictions, and so contingent or perspectival, brought with it the corollary that moral laws are also contingent or perspectival. Instead of being preserved, moral freedom was replaced by what I call "the necessity of contingency."

But let us remain with Kant. Acceptance of the need for the Copernican revolution brings with it the hypothesis of the transcendental ego, or a set of logical conditions by which a thinking and sensing being such as ourselves both constitutes the world of nature in space-time and leaves "room" for the possibility of moral freedom. Such freedom has its agency outside of space-time, yet it must manifest itself within space-time. This is one of the most obvious points of difficulty for Kant's doctrine and has been much discussed. We merely note it.

The transcendental ego possesses two intellectual faculties, which he calls *Vernunft* and *Verstand*. Both faculties are "spontaneous" and "autonomous," albeit in different senses of the terms. *Verstand* produces concepts spontaneously; these unify sensations into objects of experience, which are also possible objects of scientific knowledge.[11] *Vernunft* produces the idea of a spontaneous, extraworldly cause of a series of conditions within the spatiotemporal world, namely of itself as initiating moral action within the world. It thus supplies the Idea of Freedom "as a capacity of absolute spontaneity," which *Verstand* requires, but of which it can provide no examples (since the knowable is always antecedently conditioned *within* the world).[12]

Of special importance to us is Kant's statement that *Vernunft* "creates for itself . . . the Idea of a spontaneity which can begin to act from itself."[13] It does so because it *requires* such an Idea in order to sustain the initial hypothesis. In other words, the creation of the Idea of the spontaneity of *Vernunft* is not the same as, but the condition for the possibility of, the exercise of moral spontaneity in the creation of moral law (and hence in the exercise of moral freedom). Kant does not "know" in advance, by an inspection of human experience, that *Vernunft* has this spontaneous creativity. Exactly like a theoretical physicist (or Cartesian mathematician), he *constructs* theoretical entities that serve his purpose. There is no empirical confirmation of Kant's hypothesis, however, since what counts as experience, and also as confirmation, is created by our acceptance of the hypothesis. Kant acts not like a humble empirical scientist but like a world-maker or god.

Spontaneity, as a causal agency, is autonomous. It acts as an expression of self-produced law. Otherwise it would be merely chaotic.[14] But the production of laws is not the same thing as obedience to these laws. If they were the same, spontaneity would be transformed into necessity, and freedom of the will would be impossible. As a consequence, although Kant either does not notice this or remains silent on the point, *the laws are themselves spontaneous.*

Spontaneity is a necessary presupposition of moral (and indirectly, of political) freedom. As the spontaneous "theoretical" activity that creates whatever technical concepts it requires, it is an expression of freedom in the third sense: namely, the freedom to accept or to reject Kant's interpretation of human nature. When therefore Kant says at the beginning of the second *Critique* that freedom is "the cap-stone of the entire construction of a system of pure, even of speculative reason,"[15] he may be understood in two senses. Within the edifice of pure reason, moral freedom is no doubt the capstone. But the foundation from which Kant constructs the edifice of his system is freedom in the third sense.

Spontaneity is the "ungrounded ground" of the transcendental ego. Freedom in the third sense means that we are free to accept or to reject the worlds of knowledge and morality as "defined" by Kant. As a consequence, these worlds are radically contingent. We are free to posit chaos as the primeval condition. This is in fact the step taken by Nietzsche, who gives no coherent explanation for his decision; but we may at least partially understand it as a consequence of Kantian spontaneity, itself disseminated through the history of philosophy in the nineteenth century.

Spontaneity is also the presupposition of the transformation of philosophy into hermeneutics. It is the historical antecedent of chaos, but also of Jacques Derrida's currently fashionable *différance.* Whether we start from the free activity of the subject or from the random production of self-deconstructing world structures by chaos, the net result is the same. In either case, Being is an interpretation. Strictly speaking, the postmodern attack on subjectivity is nonsense; *I* must read the text produced by chaos, and to read is to interpret. The fact that I am also free to interpret myself does not do away with the need for a point of reference in each new interpretation. Without a point of reference such as the self-conscious reader, talk about writing says nothing, and nothing recognizable as reading takes place.

## IV

Thus far I have explained two of the three major ways in which Kant is paradigmatic for an understanding of postmodernism as a continuation of the Enlightenment: the discovery of historicity and the transformation of philosophy into hermeneutics. I turn now to the third: the invention on a global philosophical scale of the rhetoric of frankness. The rhetoric of frankness plays its primary role in the dimension of philosophical politics.

Rhetoric is the art of persuasion. As such, it may of course employ scientific evidence and logical argumentation, but it is not bound to the use of these devices. We may distinguish between two kinds of rhetoric. The first sanctions lying, in the specific sense of pretending to believe what one does not believe and not to believe what one does believe. The second does not sanction lying in this specific sense and, indeed, states frankly that it does not know what it does not know; in other words, it identifies its hypotheses as distinct from the arguments to which they give rise. This type of rhetoric freely asserts that it will assume what it needs in order to preserve a case it deems worth making. Kant practices this second kind of rhetoric.

Let us turn to Kant's own discussion of rhetoric (although he does not use that term). It occurs in a neglected section of the first *Critique*, entitled "The discipline of pure reason with respect to its polemical use."[16] The section itself falls under the more general heading "The Transcendental Doctrine of Method." The general heading is misleading for our purposes, since it gives the impression that method, including the polemical use of reason, will be deduced from a transcendental ground. But this is not the case, except in the limited sense that an injunction against lying may be derived from Kant's moral philosophy. However, the case of lying plays no major role in the section we are about to examine. The rejection of lying instead serves, whether intentionally or not, as a kind of distraction from the actually pivotal issue of the polemical use of pure reason. Let us see how this is done.

In the text under study, Kant discusses the natural human disposition or inclination "to hide one's true sentiments, and to make show of certain assumed ones, which one holds to be good and respectable." He does not merely refer here to the withholding of certain truths from public circulation, a procedure that was endorsed by men of the stature of Bacon and Rousseau and to which Kant himself had no objection, as we know from a letter to Mendelssohn.[17] Instead, Kant has in mind a more extreme form of the accommodation of truth to political expediency, as for example the noble lie of Socrates' just city. Following Leo Strauss (and before him, Nietzsche), we shall call this form of rhetoric "esotericism."

Unlike certain contemporary scholars who have confused ignorance for incredulity, Kant does not deny that many of his predecessors practiced esotericism. He allows that the natural inclination to do so has not only civilized but also moralized us to a certain degree. However, this inclination

> serves merely provisorily, in order to bring the human race out of savagery [aus der Rohigkeit]. . . . But later, when genuine principles have been developed and have entered into the art of thought, then such falsehood must be ever more strongly combatted; otherwise, it corrupts the heart and does not allow good sentiments to arise, thanks to the rank growth of the weeds of decent appearance.[18]

In order to clarify the sense of this passage, we make a slight detour back to the essay on Enlightenment. Kant develops his motto of the Enlightenment, "dare to know," in such a way as to make clear that daring is a function of the free will. And he does this without any technical discussion of his doctrine of moral freedom and the good will. Instead, Kant says that Enlightenment is the exit by the human race from self-imposed immaturity (Unmündigkeit) or from the failure to exercise the "resolve and courage" (der Entschliessung und des Muthes) required to make use of one's own understanding, without the assistance of others.[19]

Since man's immaturity is his own fault, he must be free to take the steps necessary for eventual maturity. If the process were natural, it would be irrelevant both to use terms of praise and blame in speaking of it and to attempt to encourage human beings to initiate it. A further ambiguity of Kant's position is that, though resolve and courage would seem to be moral terms, they are employed with respect to

historical or political action. Kant could of course reply that resolve
and courage initiate a historical process that points us toward the
infinitely distant convergence of morality and politics. But this does
not meet the objection that, on Kantian grounds, morality is not and
cannot be directed toward self-interest or worldly happiness.

I believe that this problem is avoided if we take resolve and courage
to be practical or historical rather than moral virtues. This coincides
with the distinction between history and morality and at the same time
leaves open the possibility of an infinitely distant convergence between
politics and morality. It also makes much clearer the link in Nietzsche
and Heidegger between resolve and courage on the one hand and
historicity or the production of a world perspective on the other.

Furthermore, if we identify resolve and courage as peculiarly historical virtues, this also sustains the Kantian distinction between nature
and freedom, which is needed in order to make sense of Kant's conception of history. According to Kant, the same passions or expressions of
natural necessity that in the short run prevent political stability will in
the long run, thanks to what I would call "the cunning of history,"
establish that stability by their inner dialectical development. Kant as
it were mediates between Hobbes and Hegel by making natural inclination (passion and desire) the engine of historical progress.[20] But natural progress is compatible with a community of clever devils. It leaves
no room in itself for either historical or moral freedom.

By separating resolve and courage from the natural dialectic of passion and desire, our distinction does leave the required room. One
cannot remove every vestige of inconsistency from Kant's doctrines.
But my proposals make sense out of Kant's immediate distinctions;
they allow us to see how Kant is moving toward the elaboration of a
conception of history that is neither knowledge nor morality but the
medium for the synthesis of the two. The following passage from an
essay by Emil Fackenheim is relevant at this point:

> [Nature] confines herself to posing the problem to be solved; she
> does not solve it. Man himself both must and can give the solution.
> He must give it, because nature does not give it, and because the
> problem, unless solved, will destroy him. He can give it because,
> already free in the choice of means, he can free himself from the
> despotism of natural ends.[21]

In order to engage the correct historical virtues, Kant must employ rhetoric. Still more specifically, he must counter the pre-Enlightenment rhetoric of caution with a rhetoric of daring, that is to say, of frankness. Without wishing to deny the great difference between the tone and intentions of Kant and Nietzsche, one may nevertheless say that the first sets into motion a type of rhetoric that is carried to an extreme by the second. If we now return to the text from the first *Critique*, we see that esotericism cannot be simply condemned. It is not possible to say that esotericism enforced the condition of immaturity that Kant seeks to remove. Whereas this is true to a degree, maturity also depends upon the development of scientific knowledge and political culture. Only when these have reached the proper stage of development is it legitimate to shift from the rhetoric of caution to the rhetoric of frankness. Kant believed that his was such a time. It was a time in which one could begin seriously the task of subordinating the mastery of nature as means to the carrying out of purposes that man has set himself. To quote one more time from Fackenheim (who is himself paraphrasing the third *Critique*): "cultural freedom is the freedom to transform nature; but the freedom of discipline consists in the emancipation from nature."[22] What Fackenheim calls the freedom of discipline, I describe as an application of the third sense of freedom.

We are now ready to return to the discussion of the polemic of pure reason in the first *Critique*. Kant is in the process of rejecting the rhetoric of caution. This does not mean that he is about to publish hitherto suppressed scientific truths; rather, he wishes to institute a new conception of the relation between science and historicopolitical activity. It would not be going too far to say that Kant wishes to produce a new kind of human being, one who is mature rather than immature. He therefore proceeds in his methodological text by formulating the procedure that he in fact follows in his historicopolitical writings. But the procedure is such that it cannot be "formulated" in the manner of a twentieth-century treatise on methodology. Kant instead employs the rhetoric of frankness to recommend the rhetoric of frankness.

Kant goes on to apply the distinction between concealment and frankness to the utterances of speculative thought. Nothing can be more harmful to the interests of our "insights" (*Einsichten*) than to communicate with one another "mere falsified thoughts" (*blosse Gedanken verfälscht einander mitzuteilen*), "to conceal doubts which we feel contrary to our own assertions, or to give a veneer of certainty to grounds of proof which do not actually satisfy us."[23] We note that this has no bearing on cases in which the invocation of resolve and courage is required in order to validate the entertainment of subsequent arguments and proofs. To be satisfied with one's hypotheses and to defend them with a polemical rhetoric is not the same as to convert them into scientific or logical deduction.

Kant continues: the procedure of giving a veneer of certainty to our proofs when they do not actually satisfy us may seem to be prudent, permissible, and praiseworthy if it is due not merely to private vanity but to the desire to protect the common people from politically dangerous subtleties of reason. "In this regard, I must think that there is nothing more evil in the world than to combine furtiveness, dissimulation, and deception with the intention of preserving a good thing."[24]

"I must think" (*sollte ich denken*): is this a heartfelt reference to the categorical imperative? Certainly not without elaborate qualifications, since Kant has just granted the contribution made by esotericism to civilization and morality. Without that contribution, Kant would have had no audience for his praise of frankness. In other words, we are now at a moment of transition, *itself produced not simply by historical circumstances but by Kant's will to change those circumstances*. Despite his objections to political revolution, Kant, like every genuine philosopher, is himself a revolutionary thinker. He wishes to reject the world "produced" by his predecessors in order to establish his own regime. Opposition to revolution comes only after the establishment of legitimacy.

Kant makes this almost explicit with his next assertion: "I therefore presuppose readers who do not want to hear of righteous things being defended unrighteously." The readers, of course, are not the unphilosophical many, but those who are capable of understanding, or of supposing themselves to understand, the *Critique of Pure Reason*. There is no question that Kant invokes morality in justifying his presupposition concerning his audience. But philosophers like Bacon and Rousseau were not advocating unrighteousness; their conception of morality differed from Kant's. We must be clear about this crucial point. If it is argued that the discussion of polemics is nothing other than an application of Kant's moral doctrine, it remains true that Kant has offered no theoretical justification of that doctrine as yet. His "moral" rhetoric is just that—rhetoric, and extremely simple or popular rather than philosophical or prudential rhetoric.

## V

In order to bring out the exact nature of Kant's procedure, it is once more necessary to juxtapose our passage from the first *Critique* with the essay on Enlightenment. In the former text, Kant continues with the assertion that he opposes deception in the case of "pure speculation" (*blosse Spekulation*), namely, "the weighty questions of God, immortality of the soul, and freedom."[25] This leaves open the possibility that some form of deception may be permissible in nonspeculative matters. Nor should we forget that, according to Kant himself, there can be no knowledge, and hence no "grounds of proof," concerning God, immortality, and freedom.

In the essay on Enlightenment, the following passage bears upon our immediate concerns: "The public use of one's reason must always be free, and this alone can bring mankind to Enlightenment; the *private use* of reason may however often be very narrowly restricted, without otherwise hindering the progress of Enlightenment."[26] As the context shows, Kant means by "public" not politics but the function of the scholar before the entire literate world. By "private" he means the function of a state official or some civil servant (which would include university professors).

Exactly as in the first *Critique,* Kant attempts to make learning and science public, or transpolitical, whereas politics is relegated to the sphere of the private. He thus very nearly inverts the procedure of Rousseau, for example, for whom science is to be kept as the private activity of such "preceptors of the human race" as Bacon, Newton, and Descartes.[27] As we shall soon see, however, Kant's ultimate opponent is Plato. Kant's objection to Plato is not that he founds the metaphysics of presence but that he practices and advocates what might be called discursive absence.

Kant advocates freedom of speech with respect to speculative matters. He perhaps implies, but does not state, that freedom of speech (something different from prudential lying) is to be encouraged in the case of scientific knowledge. On the other hand, he more than implies that restrictions upon frankness in political (i.e., private) affairs are to be imposed. For example, Kant opposes revolutionary conspiracies (as distinguished from cases in which they occur naturally) because they require lying. But he only equivocally excludes the right to lie on the part of the state official who is responsible for the preservation of the legal order.[28]

In general, Kant allows speculative reasoning in public about the totality of human experience, and hence about political affairs, but he does not allow disobedience to the law. The untenability of this distinction is evident in the case of religion. Again, theoretical criticism of religious beliefs in public is permitted, even by the very pastor who is charged with enforcing those beliefs.[29] On the next page, Kant says that no political association has the right to interfere with Enlightenment. This certainly entails that religion will not merely be subjected to public "theoretical" criticism but that it will be brought "within the bounds of reason alone."

Kant's doctrine entails a restriction of freedom for orthodox believers, a restriction to which he gives the euphemistic name of "Enlightenment." Those readers who are in sympathy with a rationalist "religion" should bear in mind that the issue is by no means restricted to religion. Enlightenment is impossible without the extirpation of ignorance and superstition. Unfortunately, one man's light is another man's darkness. As a consequence, Enlightenment depends upon a restrictive political rule, or the employment of enforced purification, with or without force of the vulgar sort, but always by means of rhetorical polemic. This point will assume considerable importance in a later chapter. It is also critical for our understanding of Kant.

I said a moment ago that the ultimate opponent of Kant's historico-political rhetoric is Plato. Let us now make this explicit. Kant opposes the conception of politics, typical of the immaturity of the race, according to which the mass of human beings are regarded as cattle or sheep who require to be tended by shepherds of superior intelligence. In an obvious reference to Plato's Republic, Kant speaks of these shepherds as "guardians." Thus far, Kant says, "only a few" have succeeded in cultivating and freeing their intellects, that is, in reaching the point at which they would be amenable to ending the state of primitive laziness and cowardice in which the guardians have kept the human race.[30]

Despite the immaturity of the human race, some few members have managed to free themselves sufficiently to disagree upon the desirability of continuing the politics of caution. Kant's position here is reminiscent of the view of Montesquieu and other thinkers of the Enlightenment, who regarded religion as an invention of the few to regulate the many. To come directly to the point, if this regulation is abolished, the result is not so much unlimited scientific progress as unpredictable political change. The complexity of Kant's doctrine is evident from the fact that he favors a mixture of progress, hence change, and regulation. It is easy enough to say that Kant desires orderly or law-abiding progress. But this is like trying to mix oil and water.

In short, Kant does not seem to have thought through the political implications of unrestricted speculative freedom. Similarly, there is no clear analysis of the incompatibility of free scientific discussion and political order. But that Kant, whether consistently or inconsistently, favored political enforcement of *both* Enlightenment and political stability is unquestionable from the texts.

To come back to the guardians, it follows from Kant's presentation that the intellectual freedom of "a few" who are outside the guardian class will not suffice to bring about Enlightenment. There must be disagreement within the guardian class as well (something that Socrates takes great pains to avoid). In other words, the guardians must themselves be "enlightened." How will this occur? Those few who think for themselves (or who have arrived at Kant's view of the matter) will no longer accept the Platonist presuppositions of the other guardians. They will spread anti-Platonism among the masses even while attempting to "persuade" their fellow guardians. In other words, they will engage in revolution. There is no other way to shift from one philosophical world to another, from one hermeneutic of human nature to another. To characterize the revolution of the guardians in Kantian terms, it will be for the sake of their own worth and "for the calling of each man to think for himself."[31]

The guardians become Kantians when they arrive at the conclusion that they cannot respect themselves if they do not live in a "rational" or "enlightened" society. They must therefore respect the "calling" of each citizen to respect himself in turn. Kant's position may therefore be understood, not merely theoretically but historically as well, as the midpoint between Platonism and Nietzscheanism. Kant's attempt to mix oil and water, or freedom and regulation, partly conceals the fact that his doctrine of freedom is a transcendental version of Nietzsche's doctrine of radical uniqueness or creativity. Differently stated, the doctrine of the transcendental partly conceals the fact that Kant's actual first principle, spontaneity conceived as freedom, legitimates Nietzsche's first principle of health understood as creativity.

In the case of Nietzsche, each person who exemplifies the philosophy of perspectivism asserts his uniqueness in the very act of becoming Nietzsche's disciple. In the case of Kant, my "calling" to respect myself or to legislate for myself turns out to be the expression of my respect for Kant, and for his right to legislate or enforce by the will of his interpretation of human nature my "right" to self-legislation. Whereas the same argument may be applied in good conscience to the case of Christians, Kant is patently not a Christian at all. The use of Christian elements to give rhetorical plausibility to their political doctrines is a commonplace among modern philosophers.

Our concern here, however, is not with the details of Kant's rationalist religion. The main point is to see how Kant uses rhetoric to enforce a global philosophical revolution. The obstacle to Kant's deification is also inferrable from our reflections upon the required revolution of the guardians. It is a radicalized version of the theological problem of the proliferation of sects. Contrary to the official rhetoric of the Enlightenment (which Kant, as a disciple of Newton, still shares), whereas there may be one comprehensive truth, there is no single *interpretation* of the truth. We have no reason to assume that the guardians will achieve a unanimity of interpretation. On the contrary, the very disagreement that Kant postulates as the precondition for his own revolution gives us grounds for assuming the opposite.

# VI

Even in the course of his technical writings, Kant often reveals the copresence of a rhetorical dimension. One common device is to employ political and juridical metaphors. In the passage on the polemical use of pure reason, Kant asserts that reason must submit itself to critique in all of its undertakings, for it has no dictatorial powers and "its verdict is always nothing but the agreement of free citizens." Furthermore, each citizen must be permitted to express without hindrance not merely his objections "but even his veto."[32]

The apparent meaning of this metaphor is as follows: critique is both judge and jury. Differently stated, the citizens are philosophers or practitioners of reason; they submit their efforts to the judge or critique. But the verdict of critique is at the same time the verdict of reason, namely, the agreement of the aforementioned philosophers. The net result is that critique is *not* independent of the free use of reason. And to say that this use is free is to say that each philosopher is free to disagree with his colleagues.

This passage provides us with a good example of Kant's style. Without lying, he nevertheless says what he means in so obscure a manner that it becomes visible only to a careful analysis of his rhetoric. Let us continue our analysis. Kant goes on to say that reason, in its dogmatic or nonmathematical employment, must present itself with diffidence, and indeed with a complete renunciation of dogmatic authority, to a higher judge.[33] What precisely does this mean?

"Dogmatic" presumably refers to the speculative use of reason with respect to God, freedom, and immortality. But why should reason renounce dogmatic authority in its dogmatic exercise? How could it renounce such authority? Certainly scientific knowledge cannot be the judge in question. One might wish to respond that the higher judge is here morality, but this answer, to say nothing else, depends upon what Kant means by "nonmathematical" reasoning. This in turn might shift the sense of "dogmatic."

We bear these questions in mind and continue. When reason has to deal not with the censure of a judge but with the claims of a fellow citizen (*Mitbürger*), then it may justify itself "*kat'anthrōpon,* which secures it against all injury, and acquires an entitled possession that need fear no foreign pretensions, even though it cannot be sufficiently proven *kat'alētheian.*"[34] In other words, if there is no higher judge, namely, critique or reason, but only the opinion of a fellow citizen, then ad hominem arguments for the sake of self-preservation are permitted. Since one's fellow citizen can only respond with ad hominem arguments of his own, what is required here is polemical rhetoric rather than rational in the sense of scientific or logical demonstration.

We cannot avoid the attempt to explain what is meant by "non-mathematical" reasoning in our passage. Elsewhere in the first *Critique*, Kant draws a technical distinction between the mathematical and the dynamical categories of *Verstand*, that is, between two senses in which pure concepts are applied to the understanding of possible experience. The *mathematical* deals with intuition as pure form (space and time); the *dynamical* treats of the existing object or the content of intuition.

> The principles of mathematical employment will therefore be uncon-
> ditionally necessary, that is, apodictic. Those of dynamical employ-
> ment will also indeed possess the character of *a priori* necessity, but
> only under the condition of empirical thought in some experience,
> therefore only mediately and indirectly.[35]

In other words, the "dynamical" use of reason (which synthesizes categories with sensations) depends for its conviction upon antecedent experience.

If this is what Kant means by "nonmathematical" in conjunction with "dogmatic," then we can attribute the following sense to our passage. Whenever the authority of reason depends upon the posses-sion by its addressees of the appropriate experience, it is entitled to make its case in a manner that will be persuasive to the actual experi-ence of the given person. Kant's formulation is reminiscent of Socrates' description of philosophical rhetoric in the *Phaedrus*, where we are also instructed on the details of persuasion *kat'anthrōpon*.

Kant's "higher judge" might not seem Socratic, but further reflection shows us otherwise. It could be thought that the higher judge is the hypothetical person of more experience in a sense relevant to the spe-cific issue. In the present context, it must be the philosopher whose grasp of the comprehensive situation is superior to ours—that is, here, to Kant's. But plainly Kant recognizes no such philosopher. He puts the point in an ambiguous metaphor because he is restricted by appropriate "modesty," that is to say, considerations of rhetorical effectiveness.

We are all on the same footing, or fellow citizens, in matters of this sort; this is the modest or un-Socratic surface of Kant's rhetoric. In fact, however, Kant means that we are all on the same footing in quite another sense: namely, of being able to protect Kant's own teaching from any possible attack. Reason is entitled to secure its authority by ad hominem argumentation when that authority cannot be scientifically or objectively enforced. This is quite Socratic or Platonic. In the first *Critique,* Kant is the voice of reason. He is therefore entitled to employ ad hominem arguments, and thereby to become our enlightened guardian who will free us, or instill in us the proper resolve and courage to free ourselves, by use of the appropriate rhetoric. It is thus an extremely interesting consequence of our analysis that Socratic or Platonic rhetoric is not entirely distinct from the rhetoric of frankness.

We must now clarify what Kant means by "dogmatism." In the preface to the first *Critique,* Kant defines "dogmatism" as the attempt to arrive at philosophical knowledge "from concepts alone."[36] In the passage on polemic, he says:

> By the polemical use of pure reason, I understand the defense of its assertions against their dogmatical denials. Here it does not come down to whether its assertions might not perhaps also be false, but only to this, that no one could ever assert the opposite with apodictic certitude (or even with greater likelihood).[37]

This statement makes it seem as if our "fellow citizens" but not we ourselves are employing dogmatical reasoning. But this is of course not what was said directly above. In fact, the polemical defense is as dogmatic as the denials it opposes, unless one makes it explicitly clear that one is defending speculations about God, freedom, and immortality, and so arguing "hypothetically" and rhetorically. Kant both does and does not do this. In other words, in order to see the underlying rhetorical structure of Kant's thought, we have to put together the passages from the section on methodology in the first *Critique* with the discussions of freedom, spontaneity, autonomy, moral freedom, and the liberation of the human race from immaturity.

Kant concludes the paragraph under immediate inspection with his favorite legal metaphor. "Whereas our title to these possessions may not be sufficient, it is fully certain that no one will ever be able to prove the illegality of this possession." This amounts to saying that we ourselves avoid the use of dogmatical reasoning only in the sense that we defend hypotheses that can be neither proved nor disproved. The attempt to persuade others to adopt philosophical ideas inferred from concepts by means of rhetoric rather than scientific or logical argumentation may fairly be named "dogmatic" or "polemical" rhetoric.

Kant is entirely explicit on the hypothetical nature of speculative assertions concerning God and immortality, although he omits to mention freedom here. He is quite certain that human beings will never discover "certain demonstrations of the two cardinal assertions of our pure reason: that there is a God, and that there is a future life." But he is "apodictically certain" that no one will ever be able to assert the opposite "with the least likelihood, let alone dogmatically."[38] I believe that freedom is omitted here because Kant takes it to be a fact, namely, an immediate consequence of the fact of the moral law.[39]

Two connected points follow. The first we already know: the cardinal assertions of pure reason lie outside rational knowledge and are therefore dogmatic assertions of a rhetorical kind. Second: since God and the soul are beyond all possible experience, when we dogmatize or speculate about them, not only are we not engaging in a mathematical use of reason, but we are also not engaged in a dynamical use. The parenthetical addition of "nonmathematical" as a gloss of "dogmatic" at B767 thus turns out to be misleading, even though it is true as far as it goes.

We can restate Kant's meaning more explicitly as follows. God and the soul are not possible objects of experience. But there is another kind of experience, which we may call "nonobjective," that is accessible to at least some human beings. This experience leads neither to knowledge nor to transcendental deduction but to speculation that is more or less likely. The degree of likelihood is ascertained by the degree of support the given speculation provides for Kant's overall hypothesis. As Kant puts the point in the passage on polemics: "it remains sufficient for you, in the presence of the strictest reason, to speak the justified language of a firm belief, even though you must give up at the same time the language of knowledge."[40]

Kant goes on to advocate a comprehensive freedom to rational speculation "in the domain of pure Ideas."[46] We are entitled to infer that this freedom is comprehensive; it extends to those who hold a totally different conception of human nature, hence of freedom and morality, than does Kant. The domain of the polemical use of pure reason is the domain of speculation, hence of either dogma or rhetoric, and a fortiori of ad hominem arguments. It is the domain within which philosophers debate the relative merits of their comprehensive teachings. Thus we have shown that the discussion of the polemical use of pure reason is entirely in accord with the consequences of Kant's conception of freedom, spontaneity, and autonomy.

# VII

I want next to focus attention on Kant's treatment of happiness, especially as it intersects with the speculations on history. Kant's attitude toward happiness, both in this world and the next, is one of suspicion. In general, he regards it as a temptation that leads the person to deviate from his duty. He is therefore led to argue that human beings do not regard happiness as the highest good. That this is not persuasive is recognized by Kant himself, as for example when he says that the summum bonum, namely, virtue, becomes the "total and perfected good" only through the addition of happiness.[42] Nevertheless, Kant insists that we must *deserve* to be happy, or that virtue is the condition for happiness—in the next world.

Not only does virtue not cause happiness in this world,[43] but history is incompatible with happiness at least until that moment in the infinite future when morality and politics coincide. Kant makes this point in a variety of ways—for example, in connection with purposiveness. Purposiveness is a regulative ideal that we require in order to understand certain aspects of nature, but it is not itself a knowable, and in that sense rational, element of nature itself. Mechanism and purposiveness must "no doubt" coalesce in a higher principle, but such a principle belongs to the supersensuous domain and can never be known.[44]

For this reason, we cannot know that human life is tending toward a happy fulfilment. Otherwise put, human beings cannot rest content with the possession and enjoyment of anything, and they have no stable idea of happiness, present or future. Kant therefore rejects happiness as the goal of historical existence and replaces it with cultural perfection.[45] He thus prepares the way for Hegel's insistence that world-historical individuals are motivated, not by happiness but by self-satisfaction. This last is Hegel's version of what Kant calls "duty." Hegel narrows the point to world-historical individuals. In the late nineteenth century, Nietzsche still concentrates upon the "superman", or outstanding exemplification of the will to power. But his celebration of radical originality and perspectivism is widened in our own century by Heidegger to encompass the "authentic" individual (*Dasein*). It is not, I think, by chance that Kant speaks of resolve (*Entschliessung*) and Heidegger of resolution (*Entschlossenheit*).

By replacing happiness with culture as the goal of worldly existence, Kant initiates the age of the intellectual, and hence the alienated intellectual. He asserts that "splendid misery" is the necessary historical destiny of the human race,[46] thereby echoing Rousseau's statement in the first *Discourse* that Enlightenment, although "a great and beautiful spectacle," can never make us happy.[47] Whereas Kant gives a higher political role to culture than does Rousseau, he agrees with Rousseau in distinguishing it from happiness. Although Kant states that the highest end is morality, whereas Rousseau distinguishes between political morality and private aesthetic experience (not to be confused with intellectual culture), both deny the characteristic thesis of the Enlightenment. For neither does contemplation or theory give to man his highest value.[48]

For Kant, man gives worth to himself through the free acts of a good will. He must do something, or act spontaneously, and hence autonomously, in order to be a final end or purpose (*Zweck*).[49] We must repeat that, as so acting, the person is not a political agent. "The perfect accordance of the will, however, to the moral law is *holiness*, a perfection of which no rational being of the sensuous world is capable at any moment of his existence. Since it is nevertheless required as practically necessary, it can only be found in an *infinitely continuing progress* toward that perfect accord," which must be assumed "as the real object of our will."[50]

When we dispose our will in accord with the moral law, what we aim at is perfection or holiness, not political self-interest or the satisfaction of desire. Action does not make us happy in this world, and it must be left as an ambiguous possibility whether it makes us happy in the next. For we cannot avoid noticing that the real object of our will must be *assumed:* it is a hypothesis. Indeed, this hypothesis "is practically possible only under the presupposition of the immortality of the soul."[51] It is therefore a *double* hypothesis.

Nevertheless, Kant does not deny us the right to search for happiness in the political domain. This is after all what is crudely achieved by the satisfaction of natural inclinations. Whereas the moral law is alone worthy of our respect,[52] Kant is enough of a political realist to make the following acknowledgment: "Each person is permitted to search for his happiness along the path that seems good to him, as long as he does not violate the freedom of others to strive after a similar end, which is compatible with the freedom of each man according to a possible common law."[53]

We should not give more importance to this acknowledgment of political freedom and the right to pursue happiness than it merits. In the first place, we know from other texts that this right is in vain, since misery, not happiness, is our historical lot. Second, despite his distinction between politics and morality, Kant is unable to resist the temptation to conceive of history in a way that is obviously (if inconsistently) moral.

One of the clearest discussions of the relation between politics and morality occurs in an appendix to the essay on Eternal Peace. Kant says there that it is the a priori universal will of a folk that establishes such principles of moral politics as this: "a folk ought to unite in a state according to the exclusive legal conception of freedom and equality; and this principle is grounded, not upon cleverness [*Klugheit*] but upon duty."[54]

There is then for Kant no theoretical quarrel between morality and politics; one is tempted to say that this is because they have nothing to do with each other. Kant admits a subjective quarrel between the two,[55] but this quarrel leads to the political primacy of "cleverness" in the collective attempt by free persons to seek their personal happiness. "Politics says, 'be ye as wise as serpents,' to which morality adds (as a limiting condition) 'and innocent as doves.' "[56]

The impossibility of dovelike innocence is taken into account elsewhere by Kant, for example in the essay on Universal History, in which he interprets the permanent opposition at the personal level of natural desires as "the unsocial sociability of men" or as the engine that drives the human race toward its complete development. The hypothetical achievement of the condition of universal peace depends upon a kind of mechanical equilibrium of mutually antagonistic states.[57] Kant does not expect human nature to change during the unending progress of history. Human beings will be protected from one another by the very passions that endanger them.

As a result, moral progress is restricted to the race and is not extended to the individual human being.[58] The virtuous man is obligated to assume "that since the human race's natural end is to make steady cultural progress, its moral end is to be conceived as progressing toward the better." Otherwise, "in the long run," the dream of life "becomes a farce."[59] We see here Kant's tendency to connect culture with morality despite his more fundamental distinctions. This is no doubt due not merely to his own deep respect for moral virtue but to his desire to give some tincture of the possibility of happiness to historical existence. However, what is required to validate these self-interested speculations is "a justification of nature—or better, of providence."[60] But no such justification is possible.

In the third *Critique,* Kant connects a belief in God with the notion of purposiveness, itself required for the justification of nature, and hence for the possibility of historical happiness in the infinite future. He says there that God is required, not for the validation of moral laws (this is accomplished by our respect for the law) but for aiming at the final purpose in the world, which will be brought about by the moral law.[61] As we have seen, however, purposiveness is itself a human hypothesis. Kant comes close here to saying that God is a human creation.

He comes still closer in the second *Critique,* where he calls it not merely a permissible hypothesis but a postulate of practical reason, to hold that God exists: "the righteous man may well say, 'I *will* that a God . . . exist.' "[62] This postulate is connected to the moral law, apparently in contradiction with the passage just cited from the third *Critique.* In the second *Critique,* Kant holds that the moral law is a fact of reason that everyone knows.[63] It should be unnecessary by now to insist upon the unsatisfactoriness of this claim. Apart from its empirical weakness, the claim rests upon Kant's fundamental hypothesis about the nature and content of the moral law, and so upon the doctrine of spontaneity and autonomy, which, as we have seen, are hypothetical assertions to be enforced by rhetoric, not by empirical evidence or transcendental deduction.

It looks very much as though Kant continues to share the classical philosophical desire for happiness or, to say it in another way, as though he shares the philosophical tendency to self-exaltation. In this quite unnoticed way, there is indeed a link between Plato and modern thought, but it has nothing to do with the metaphysics of presence. As Socrates says in the *Philebus*, "the wise all agree, thereby exalting themselves, that intellect [*nous*] is king for us of heaven and earth."[64]

Kant would no doubt deny my imputation to him of a subterranean link between philosophy and happiness. In a previously cited text, Kant makes a statement about virtue and happiness that he might insist applies also to the philosopher's duty to exercise his speculative abilities:

> it can in no way be said that every state I *prefer* to all others is regarded by me as happiness. For I must first be certain that I do not act contrary to my duty; only then am I allowed to look toward such happiness as I can make compatible with my morally (not physically) good state.[65]

To this I would reply: If I conceive it my duty to philosophize, then in my own case the conflict between morality and happiness is resolved. But there can be no transcendental ground from which to deduce such a duty. It is a consequence of the spontaneity that *produces* the transcendental ego as an instrument in the actualization of philosophical purposes.

# VIII

From a Kantian standpoint, the Enlightenment of d'Alembert is defective on two counts. It restricts the engine of human progress, and the essential significance of human life, to the domain of mathematical science, and it is implicitly an interpretation of freedom that leads to domination and even to tyranny. One may prefer Kant's version of the Enlightenment because it attempts to preserve freedom and so belief from the debilitating encroachment of mathematical necessity.

But Kant's version is also defective, and at bottom on d'Alembertian grounds. Kant in effect identifies rationality, in the sense of the instrument of knowledge, with mathematical thinking, hence with universality and necessity. Practical reason or the Aristotelian *phronesis* is reduced by him to *Klugheit,* or worldly cleverness, the instrument of self-interest.

Kant has no serious doctrine of political rationality. The identification of history and politics, as we have seen from more than one angle, leads to the rendering nonrational of both. This is one of Kant's most terrible legacies to late modernity. To put the same point in another way, Kant's excessively rigorous morality, in which respect for the law is at the same time humility toward oneself,[66] is contradicted by the daring intrinsic to his rhetoric of frankness. It thus leads paradoxically to a self-destructive transcendence of the self, as is especially obvious in the postsubjectivist epoch.

One does not have to be a partisan of the ancients, but merely a thoughtful modern, to see the disastrous consequences that follow upon the separation of theoretical from practical eros. If rationality is equivalent to mathematical reasoning, then morality is meaningless. Talk about a sense of duty deteriorates sooner or later into the sectarian defense of what comes to be regarded as *Schwärmerei*—to use Kant's own word for Platonism.[67]

The heart of the matter is already evident in Kant's appeal to his contemporaries to exercise resolve and courage, in order to achieve autonomy of reason (in the broad sense of the term). In the twentieth century, resolve and courage are invoked as responses to the absence, or to the impossibility, of rational autonomy, and so they function as the pivot of anti-Enlightenment rhetoric. So too the latest descendants of d'Alembert have lost his conviction that mathematical and experimental science constitutes the history and the eulogy of the human race. What has gone wrong? The history of Europe after Kant suggests part of the answer. If reason is identified with science, then resolve and courage are unreasonable.[68]

Part of our answer is illuminated by another look at Rousseau, the first great critic of the Enlightenment, who is at the same time the grandfather of Romanticism. In a way that is misleadingly reminiscent of Nietzsche and Heidegger, Rousseau opposes the Enlightenment from the standpoint of classical antiquity. Unlike Nietzsche and Heidegger, however, he takes his bearings by Socrates. More specifically, Rousseau praises classical virtue, not archaic poetry. To the extent that Nietzsche and Heidegger are disciples of Rousseau, they follow the author of *The Reveries of a Solitary Promenader*, not that of the political discourses.

We have already seen Rousseau's "Baconian" attitude toward the arts and sciences. Let us add here that Bacon's scientific priests, Rousseau's great preceptors, and Kant's guardians are modern, partially enlightened versions of Plato's philosopher-kings. Even in the case of Kant, there is a discernible tincture of classical reticence, due to Kant's fear of pleasure as well as to the need to preserve morality from knowledge. Unfortunately, the mixture of daring and prudence advocated by Plato's Eleatic Stranger[69] becomes excessively volatile when modern science replaces classical wisdom. Daring triumphs over prudence and flirts with madness.

In the nineteenth century, after the (for us) symbolic deaths of Hegel and Goethe (in 1831 and 1832), scientific enthusiasm predominates for the most part over prudence. Consider the two great revolutionaries of the left and right, Marx and Nietzsche. Marx unites scientific materialism with the new wisdom of economics in order to dissolve the ideology of the bourgeoisie. Nietzsche, also decisively influenced by scientific materialism, employs the aristocratic science of philology rather than the vulgar science of economics, again with the intention of destroying bourgeois Europe.

It remains for a third great scientific materialist, Freud, whose outlook is decisively shaped by nineteenth-century thought, to replace enthusiasm not with reticence but with a sober and manly (i.e., resolved and courageous) political despair. It is in Freud much more clearly than in Nietzsche that one sees the fundamentally pessimistic, even nihilistic, consequences of modern science. Nietzsche's daydream of the superman is replaced by Freud's doctrine of wish fulfillment. Even more drastically, the will to power is unmasked as the death wish.

Contemporary philosophy is thus affected by four distinguishable lines of force emanating from the modern European Enlightenment. First, there is the conception of a moderate scientific progress, regulated by political prudence, which is thus still regarded as a legitimate, nonmathematical form of rationality. But this line of force appears to be unstable. It bifurcates into the pure scientific enthusiasm of eighteenth-century French thought and the ambiguous teaching of Kant, who replaces prudence with the historical dialectic of the passions. Finally, there is the radical rejection of scientific optimism, a rejection in which the Enlightenment turns on itself but with the aid of scientific weapons. Scientific clarity thus reveals the political destructiveness of scientific truth. The Kantian thesis of the salutary consequences of human passion is replaced by the Freudian thesis of the self-destructive consequences of human passion.

Scientific daring, itself a form of philosophical eros, or what Socrates calls divine madness, is thus intrinsically at odds with political prudence. When detached from prudence, madness becomes human, all too human, and never more so than in the posthumanist generation. When the science of grammatology replaces the sciences of economics and philology (not to mention the still stricter Muses), the foundations are dissolved, and unending progress decays into unending signification. The referent of a signifier is merely another signifier. Or, as Michel Foucault puts it, what is needed today is to think discontinuity, difference, "to dissociate the reassuring form of the identical," for after all, "we are difference."[70] Contemporary philosophy thus presents us with the mad spectacle of a sick man consulting two surgeons, each of whom insists that to be cured, he must be hacked to pieces.

The fate of the Enlightenment in our time allows us to infer with confidence the following two conclusions. First: advances in mathematics and the experimental sciences do *not* yield moral or political progress. On this score, Rousseau was certainly correct. Second: advances in critical philosophy lead neither to the salvation of morality nor to metaphysical progress. On these two points, Kant was certainly wrong. To this I would add a third conclusion that is perhaps not so obvious as the first two. The so-called Platonism of the modern epoch, as it is defined by Heidegger and his successors, is a phantasm. Whatever we may think of the results, Plato's guardians, having been partially or totally enlightened, are replaced by the tribunes of the *vulgus*.

These remarks are not intended as a rejection of the Enlightenment.

I agree with Nietzsche's more sober admiration for the "liberating and clarifying utility" of the Enlightenment and with his judgment that it must be purified, not simply rejected.[71] In order to engage in such a purification, however, one must have an accurate diagnosis of impurity. Only then, to continue with the medical metaphor, do we reasonably entrust ourselves to the surgeon. The legitimation of modernity (to borrow the title of Hans Blumenberg's important book) requires something more than the assertion of the independence of modernity from the (essentially classical) past. Self-assertion is not the same as purification.

According to Blumenberg, "the concept of the legitimacy of the modern age is not derived from the accomplishments of reason, but rather from the necessity of these accomplishments."[72] By "necessity," Blumenberg apparently means the consequences of self-assertion. According to Blumenberg, the modern age is not a secularized version of Christianity; it has produced itself. Blumenberg derives the license of self-assertion from an interesting interpretation of Leibniz. By analogy with Leibniz's principle of sufficient reason (*Prinzip des zureichenden Grundes*), Blumenberg poses a concept of "sufficient rationality" (*einer zureichenden Vernunft*).

Reason is as it were sufficient unto itself on Leibnizian grounds, as Blumenberg makes the case, thanks to the assumption that this is the best of all possible worlds. On this assumption, "one can in principle deduce the answer to any conceivable question." Again, in Leibniz, "everything is aimed at the goal of realising the omnicompetence and independence of reason."[73] In one last citation, "the modern age does not have recourse to what went before it, so much as it opposes and takes a stand against the challenge constituted by what went before it."[74]

Blumenberg's thesis, then, is that modernity, the second overcoming of gnosticism,[75] is effectively autonomous with respect to the past, except in the negative sense just quoted. He thus confirms my own account of spontaneity as the first principle of modernity. Blumenberg seems to go even beyond Kant, since his own legitimation of modernity is compatible with the subsequent claim of postmodernity to an analogous spontaneity. With his conception of "self-assertion," Blumenberg "secularizes" Kant's doctrine of spontaneity, or transforms it from the ungrounded ground of the transcendental into the human grounding of a historical epoch.

Blumenberg's legitimation of modernity is the necessary consequence of the self-assertion of spontaneity. Despite his greater learning and sober thoughtfulness, Blumenberg stands on common ground with the prophets of postmodernism. His defense of the independence of modernity thus helps us to understand the continuity of the internally inconsistent self-justification of Enlightenment. But this defense forces us to wonder about the legitimacy of an ungrounded self-legitimation. And it serves to rehabilitate the very thesis that Blumenberg attacks—namely, that the modern age is a secularized version of Christianity. Is not self-assertion the mark of man become like God, master and possessor of nature? Or is it the mark of Satan?

I may now conclude this section of my investigation. Kant, as I have tried to show, anticipates postmodernism on three fundamental points. First, he distinguishes history from both knowledge and morality, thereby preparing the doctrine of historicity as an independent ontological dimension. Second, the subordination of rationality to spontaneity leads directly to the transformation of philosophy into hermeneutics. Third, Kant, for all his reticences, is the father of the modern rhetoric of frankness. It is true that on this point he seems to be anticipated by writers like Rousseau and the Marquis de Sade. But it is Kant who furnishes the medium by which such a rhetoric is transmitted into philosophy.

Postmodernism has no more rejected Kant than Kant rejected the Enlightenment. We are now living through the rhetorical frenzy of the latest attempt of the self-contradictory nature of Enlightenment to enforce itself as a solution to its own incoherence. It remains to be seen whether this is merely the continuation of the farce of existence or whether there is a way in which to combine prudential sobriety with self-contradiction. It is not enough simply to say with Walt Whitman: "Do I contradict myself? Very well then I contradict myself. I am large. I contain multitudes."

# = 2 =

## Platonic Reconstruction

What is the difference between speech and writing? This is the point of orientation for the extravagant discourse (spoken and written) of Jacques Derrida, the most prominent contemporary opponent of the Enlightenment. In his dispensation of darkness, Derrida is a paradigm for a multitude of lesser antiluminaries. One cannot quite say that they shine in his reflected brilliance without sacrificing what I believe is a valid metaphor. Perhaps it would be better to think of Derrida's disciples as consequences of what he himself calls "the trace." To quote the master: "the trace is in effect the absolute origin of sense in general. But this amounts to saying, once more, that there is no absolute origin of sense in general. The trace is the *différance* that opens appearance and signification."[1]

To say that sense originates in *différance* is still something of a euphemism, since what in fact originates is an endless sequence of signifiers signifying other signifiers. The trace, or *différance,* is a kind of postontological yet fecund *nihil,* or a posttheistic version of what Hegel called "the terrible labor of the negative." In a word, for Derrida, it is not God who illuminates the darkness, but the darkness that produces such light as there is. So too, at least in the United States, Derrida spawns his progeny, ostensibly opposed by the last vestiges of analytical philosophy, but at a deeper level strengthened by their common heritage in the conception of ontology as grammatology. "Deconstruction" is then like calling to like, or a radical secularization of destiny.

Very well, then, darkness is indispensable and inexpugnable. But we may justify the reservation that it is not sufficient by pointing to Derrida's hermeneutical intensity, which is not without its own luminosity. The playfulness of the great deconstructor cannot conceal the bitter seriousness with which he attempts to remove what he regards as the misunderstanding of self-consciousness. Derrida continues the Nietzschean attempt to purify the Enlightenment by a destruction of bourgeois civilization. To this task, he brings the ontological portentousness of Martin Heidegger: the articulate Parisian wit is too often dulled by the garrulous bourgeois professor. This, I think, is the contradiction in the heart of Derrida's esprit; it is this that mitigates, although it does not suppress, the value of his writings.

As has been pointed out by others, there is a strain of the Talmudist in Derrida (for me, not his least attractive feature). But only a strain, I would regretfully insist: the Talmud conceals a serious teaching beneath its playful clarifications. Underneath the Derridean playfulness (which, as I shall later suggest, is not playful enough), one finds instead a seriousness that is in search of a doctrine, but that is not serious enough, and that therefore dissolves whatever it touches. Just as Derrida's attack on the Enlightenment is itself a consequence of the Enlightenment, so I find his deconstructive mania to be not Talmudic but an inversion of the Protestant ethic of work as salvation. For Derrida, the terrible labor of negativity is the posttheistic version of salvation. The motto of the modern age is that we understand only what we make. For Derrida, we understand only what we deconstruct. Derrida is an ontological Freud.

When construing the Talmudic component in Derrida, one should recall his debt to Emmanuel Levinas.[2] The following passage from Derrida's appreciation of Levinas helps us to take our bearings with respect to the errant disciple's central concern, and also to make the transition to Plato:

> Moreover, how could Hebraism belittle the letter, in praise of which Levinas writes so well? For example: . . . "To love the Torah more than God" is "protection against the madness of a direct contact with the Sacred" [*Difficile Liberté*]. The aspect of living and original

speech *itself* which Levinas seeks to save is clear. Without its possibility, outside its horizon, writing is nothing. In this sense, writing will
always be secondary. To liberate it from this possibility and this
horizon, from this essential secondariness, is to deny it as writing,
and to leave room for a grammar or a lexicon without language, for
cybernetics or electronics. But it is only in God that speech, as presence, as the origin and horizon of writing, is realised without defect.
One would have to be able to show that only this reference to the
speech of God distinguishes Levinas's intentions from those of Socrates in the *Phaedrus;* and that for a thought of original finitude, this
distinction is no longer possible. And that if writing is secondary at
this point, nothing, however, has occurred before it.[3]

In Levinas's interpretation of Judaism, God is both the life beyond
the presence of Being, and hence the presence of speech—to Himself,
and the *deus absconditus* or the absence, not of Being, but of what is
beyond Being, that may safely be approached only through the obliq-
uity of (as Derrida might put it) the "trace" of His voice, the written
accounts of His laws—by us. But what of the remark about Socrates?
On one point, Derrida is certainly correct. There is no pagan god in the
Platonic dialogues who plays an ontological version of the living Hebrew God. The Platonic Socrates, and above all the *Phaedrus,* replaces
the creator God with the political Olympians whose task is to tend the
cosmos, not to make it. The deity who plays the central role, however,
is Eros, who neither speaks nor writes, nor is the unity of life and
discourse; instead, his primary function is to guide us upward to the
nonliving and nonspeaking Ideas.

I am not engaged here in an exercise of hairsplitting. Derrida's
radical oversimplification of the difference between Levinas and Socrates is quite indicative of his oversimplification of the *Phaedrus* and,
more generally, of Plato's account of writing. Without Jehovah, there
would be for the Jews no writing at all, but merely scribbling. Plato
has no analogue to Jehovah to begin with; instead, he has himself.
Whereas Jehovah is the author of the universe, Plato is the author of
the dialogues, and so too, as we shall see, of Socrates.

Let us come at this point from a different direction. As understood
by Levinas, and, I think, correctly, there is no ontology in Judaism.
Derrida finds in the Platonic dialogues the ruins of a failed ontology. I
think this is wrong, and in showing why, I shall be making use of

purified or "reconstructed" fragments of evidence supplied by Derrida himself. The difference between Judaism and Platonism is nevertheless obviously crucial. The Jew approaches God in the fulfillment of the Law. This fulfillment is a mystery, not a logical construction, not even a logical paradox, because the Law is not *logos*. The mystery is that whoever believes in and fulfills the Law is present in the absent God. It is therefore a Greek misunderstanding of Torah to regard it as writing in the Derridean sense of the word, just as it is a Christian misunderstanding of Jehovah to regard Him as in principle a *deus absconditus*. The Hebrew letters are transformed by faith into divine speech as surely as bread and wine are transformed for the orthodox Catholic into the flesh and blood of Jesus. And here one might make a Derridean comment that the letters are no less life than the flesh and blood. It is madness to attempt to approach God directly, namely, by circumventing Torah, not out of respect for writing as the "trace" of the absence of God, but because Torah is precisely the proper manifestation of the Creator to His creatures. The attempt to approach God directly is a revolt against the distinction between creator and creation, or the attempt to achieve the promise of Satan ("ye shall be like God"), only by substituting *parousia* for knowledge of good and evil.

*Parousia* is not ontology. It is not discursive, hence no more speech than writing. But it is, or would be, the discharging of the hypotheses of ontology, hence what one might almost call the *deconstruction* of ontology by the fulfillment of its promise. In the Platonic dialogues, there is again no ontology (no discursive *logos* of Being). Socrates encourages the madness of a silent and direct approach to the Ideas; indeed, he refers to this erotic ascent as "divine madness." We shall look carefully at the details of this encouragement later; I hope thereby to show that Derrida's central insight into Plato is also a profound (and therefore fruitful) misunderstanding. Speech is a consequence of whatever success we may obtain through divine madness; it is not the medium of that success. To anticipate, Derrida is quite mistaken to associate speech in Plato with a metaphysics of presence and to infer from this association an ontological meaning in Socrates' criticism of writing. Speech, more specifically *human* speech, is as much a mark of absence as is writing. Derrida fails to appreciate the significance of the fact that *logos* means neither speech nor writing in Plato's vocabulary and hence that it can be used in a secondary sense for either the one or the other. The distinction between speech and writing that Derrida finds in Plato (although, as we shall see, he also denies that it is there) is imposed onto the text by a contemporary or post-Kantian incapacity to detach oneself from language, from the sign as signifier, not of a being (to say nothing of Being), but of another signifier.

The man of religious faith regards it as madness to attempt to become a god. The pagan philosophers, especially those of the Socratic school, thought otherwise. To the Hebrew at least, speech (Torah) is the certain sign of the presence and absence of God, and hence of the difference between creator and created. It is this speech that enforces the distinction between writing (commentary on Torah) and scribbling (philosophy and postphilosophical deconstruction). To the pagan philosopher, certainly to the Socrates of Derrida's prooftext, the *Phaedrus,* the crucial difference between speech and writing is political, not ontological. Nevertheless, the distinction between speech and writing has something to do with the philosophical inversion of the religious interpretation of madness. At the risk of seeming to propound a paradox, I want to maintain that human speech is superior to human writing because it is closer to silence. (The reason for the qualifying "human" will appear shortly.) By this I mean two things. First, in addressing human beings, as Socrates points out in the *Phaedrus,* the speaker knows when to keep silent, whereas writings do not. Second, writing is "garrulous" precisely for the reason that Derrida prefers it to speech. Writing, as it were, cannot stop talking, because, as the "trace" of absence, it has no idea where it is, and in fact, as detached from the guidance of speech, it is *nowhere.* But this is not to support the thesis that the excellence of speech is to keep talking in the illumination of the presence of Being. Speech is the living presence, not of Being, but of the speaker to himself, of intellect or *Geist,* not of form. And *Geist* is accessible to itself only as myth: so at least Socrates teaches us in the *Phaedrus.* If I, as the "receptivity" of form that must necessarily be formally indeterminate, am present to myself *as* speech, then speech is "formally" the presence of absence.

As soon as we put the point in this way, we understand how close Aristotle's doctrine of the passive intellect is to Plato, despite the former's dislike of myth. It is the mistake of modern epistemology and the "philosophy of mind" to think that I can be present to myself as a formal structure, namely, the artifact of epistemological analysis. On the other hand, one can say that it is the peculiar insight of late modern Continental linguistic philosophy to have developed, but also to have narrowed, the Aristotelian notion of man as the talking animal, in such a way as to allow of the following conclusion: the closer I come to formal structures, and the more I talk about them, the more I conceal them—that is, the more I replace the web of forms or Ideas by the web of concepts or linguistic constructions. I think that, when properly stated, this is a sound insight. It is properly stated, however, only when contrasted to the vision of forms as well as to the listening to the soul *as* speaker. To take only the second case: if I bespeak the world, I do not bespeak speaking. This was Kant's crucial insight, except that he lost it by transforming it into an artificial construction in its own right: the transcendental ego. The greatest barrier separating Kant from Plato disappears as soon as we recognize that transcendental doctrine is a myth and also that to recognize it as such is not to abolish the psyche but to return it to itself.

The ontological or constructive impetus of speech is precisely what makes ontology impossible, or "uncovers" it as *poiēsis* and *technē.* This is the sound core to the modern maxim that we know only what we make. Speech, the presence of the living intelligence, is able to silence itself: to commune, or to strive to commune, with the silent Ideas in the silence of pure *noēsis*. The living intelligence thus disappears as it approaches the vision of the Ideas: it "loses itself in thought." Silence triumphs over speech with the cooperation and consent of speech, "illuminated" by divine erotic madness. But for this reason, *parousia* is not ontology. The most one could say is that the "traces" of ontology begin to differentiate themselves in the linguistic space left vacant by the absence of *parousia*. If the contours of this linguistic space are given an anticipatory shaping by the departure of the forms, the imprint is not sufficient to provide us with ontology. As contemporary mathematics testifies, it is not even sufficient to provide us with an eternally valid logic.

To come back to Derrida after this necessary digression, that he is not a genuine Talmudist follows trivially from the fact that he is not a Jew, not in the sense of Levinas. For Derrida, the partisan of original finitude, of the origin as differentiation, hence of an infinite sequence of finite writings, it is indeed the case that nothing has occurred before writing. There is no divine life antecedent to writing. As Derrida says in another text, "Life must be thought of as trace before Being may be determined as presence."[4] However, he is also not a genuine Socratic, not because he rejects or deconstructs Platonism, understood as the metaphysics of presence, but because he does not know that this has already been done by Plato, with the assistance of a Socrates grown young and beautiful.[5] And this in turn, I suspect, is because he has been prevented by the legacy of Nietzsche, Freud, and Heidegger from following the Socratic maxim: "know thyself." He has mistaken this maxim as an injunction to ontological epistemology, or the reification of being. Derrida, who apparently identifies the self with the modern doctrine of subjectivity, which he believes himself to have deconstructed, has on his account, no self. As a consequence, he has no knowledge.

## II

At the beginning of his commentary on the mythical account of the origin of writing in the *Phaedrus,* Derrida has this to say about the presentation by Theuth of his invention to Thamus, the divine ruler of the Egyptians:

> God the king does not know how to write, but this ignorance or this incapacity testifies to his independent sovereignty. He has no need to write. He speaks, he says, he dictates, and his word suffices. Whether a scribe from his secretariat then adds the supplement of a transcription or not, this consignment is essentially secondary.[6]

The first thing to be said is that not all gods are the same. Derrida is not sensitive to theological difference, as we saw previously in his discussion of Levinas. The God of the Hebrews is of course not the same as the god of the philosophers, and neither of these should be assimilated to the Egyptian deities. For Jehovah, who is a creator, to speak *is* to write: divine speech constitutes itself as the world, of which Torah is the living essence. (I note parenthetically that Kant replaces Jehovah by the transcendental ego, and the rules of *Verstand* for Torah.) Second, Derrida has not quite grasped the significance of the fact that Theuth, the inventor of writing, is also an Egyptian god. Neither Zeus nor his divine subjects need to write. The point being made here by Socrates is therefore not primarily that of the distinction between the royal god and the other deities.

What we want to know is why writing is assigned to an Egyptian god. It is true that the Egyptians were the older people and hence that their gods may be said to antedate the Greek gods. But this explains nothing; the Muses, for example, are Greek, not Egyptian. Socrates could easily have assigned the invention of writing to Hermes, the intermediary between gods and mortals, about whom we will have something further to say below. Much more illuminating is the fact that the Egyptians were famous for their excessive piety, to which the extraordinary number of their gods testifies, and to which Plato alludes elsewhere.[7] The attribution of writing to an Egyptian god thus carries a doubly religious significance, which is entirely in keeping with the double emphasis of the *Phaedrus* on myth and politics. The relatively brief passages on diaeresis, which Socrates praises as a necessary adjunct to philosophical rhetoric, are themselves subordinated to political employment, as I will show later.

Derrida does not make these distinctions. Despite his often extraordinary eye for the significant detail, not to mention his exorbitant taste for the superfluous complexity, Derrida's deconstructive hermeneutics is not attentive to the written text in its own terms, largely because he denies the significance of the author's intention. Instead, he hurries to identify Thamus, "the king who speaks," with the (ontological) *father* who rejects his son, or the offering of his son; "the father suspects and always supervises writing."[8] From here it is an easy step "to the permanence of a Platonic scheme that assigns the origin and the power of speech [*parole*], and precisely of *logos,* to the paternal position." For Derrida, this is a "structural constraint" by which "platonism" (behind which hides Plato), "which imposes all of Western metaphysics in its conceptuality," has transmitted the ambiguous understanding of writing as a *pharmakon:* a remedy that is also a poison.

It is entirely invisible to Derrida that by his own interpretation, what he calls "platonism," and hence Western metaphysics, is not Greek but Egyptian. All the more appropriate his own ambiguous loyalty, which

we may call a *pharmakon,* to the Hebrews. The ostensible quarrel
between Greek metaphysics and postphilosophical deconstruction is in
fact a *gigantomachia,* or theological war, between the Egyptians and
the Jews! Plato was then not an ontologist, but an Egyptologist.[9] Does
Derrida unconsciously conceive of himself as Moses? If so, he shares
this illusion with most leading philosophers of the modern epoch. In
the same passage, Derrida asserts that "the origin of the *logos* is *its
father.*"[10] If this were to be given a Greek rather than an Egyptian
interpretation, we should have to insist that Thamus is not the father
of *logos* in its critical Platonic sense, namely, as truth, reason, or
proportion, but rather of speech—and not even of speech as an imitation of or supplement to *logos,* but rather of speech as poetry. For
there is no *logos* among the Egyptians. Unfortunately, there is also no
poetry of the correct (Hebraic or Greek) sort.

Let us step away for a moment from the Derridean text, which is not
so much a "web" (*textus*) as a "mesh" (*macula*), and hence, by a
genuine etymology, a "spot" or "stain" (even the trace of a deconstructed net). The Hebrew God both speaks and writes; in His divine
activity, there is no distinction between speech and writing. The Egyptian gods speak and write, but they distinguish between these activities. The Greek gods speak but do not write. This, I suggest, puts us in
touch with the correct theological paradigm by which to understand
the fundamental distinction posed by the *Phaedrus:* the distinction
between Socrates and Plato. Socrates is a Greek god who speaks but
does not write. Plato is neither an Egyptian nor a Greek but, if we may
playfully modify an observation by Clement of Alexandria, a Hebraic
philosopher,[11] who is present as absent in written dialogues that are
in fact his monologues, intended as a philosophical Torah for human
beings. Two related points: the dialogues do not create the original
world, but they reorder it into an intelligible cosmos. Second, as a
philosophical Torah, they require a philosophical Talmud. The law
requires interpretation. As in the case of the Hebrew Talmud, the
interpretation is rescued from fantasy by the "pretheoretical" accessibility of the world.

Within a purely Greek perspective, we may make our point by
alluding to the well-known quarrel between poetry and philosophy.
From Homer through the lyric poets, the emphasis is upon the differ-

ence between gods and mortals. As Apollo warns Diomedes in the *Iliad* (V, 440ff.), "Ponder, son of Tydeus, and draw back; do not hope to be equal to the gods in thinking, since the family of the deathless gods and of mortals who walk on earth is never the same." There is no need to multiply citations here;[12] it will suffice to mention Pindar: "but if anyone tends his wealth in a healthy way, by being bountiful with his possessions and by winning good report, let him not seek to become a god."[13] In the Socratic tradition especially, but more generally among the philosophers (Empedocles, Pythagoras), this advice is disregarded.[14] As Aristotle puts it in his straightforward prose, the theoretical life, "which produces nothing from itself besides theorising," is "higher than the human life. Not *qua* human will one live it, but he will achieve it by virtue of something divine in him. . . . If then the intellect is divine in comparison with man, so is the life of the intellect divine in comparison with the human life."[15] The great myth of the soul in the *Phaedrus* makes it unmistakable that, for Socrates, the philosophical life is most divine (see 249a1–b1 and 256a5–c7).[16]

To be sure, Aristotle is even more explicit than Plato, nor am I attempting to suppress the difference between them. To the contrary, this difference is intrinsic to Aristotle's criticism of Plato, and thus to his decision to give up the dialogue form for the treatise or lecture. Aristotle does not merely love or pursue wisdom; like Hegel, he regards himself as possessing it.[17] He thus denies the assertion of Simonides that "god alone can have this possession." Contrary to the poets, "it is not possible for the divine to be jealous, and in accord with the proverb, 'poets tell many lies.' "[18] From the Aristotelian standpoint, Plato is still too close to the poets. It would take us too far afield to explore this point. Allow me to leave it at the following suggestion. Aristotle's break with Plato is closely connected to a diminution by the former of the value or importance of the specifically human, and hence, of what Plato calls in the *Laws* the "playful."[19]

We cannot, however, understand Plato by adopting the Aristotelian standpoint. I cite him in order to deepen the portrait of Plato's implicit thesis (which, by the nature of playfulness, he would not make explicitly). From what one could somewhat misleadingly call a psychological perspective, Aristotle's representation of himself as divine is a radical simplification of Plato's poetic evasiveness. As I am arguing throughout this investigation, Plato is entirely too evasive for Derrida's net. The contradiction—if that is the right word—of Socrates' criticism of writing by its appearance within a writing is not a testimony to Plato's "parricide" or externally compelled autodestruction. It is rather Plato's testimony, which we may consider as monologue or dialogue, as speech or writing, a testimony to the difference between himself and Socrates.[20] Socrates is not, as he himself believes, an example of the divine, and hence unproductive, theoretical viewing described explicitly by Aristotle and poetically by Socrates in his myth (which he attributes to the poet Stesichorus). He is, as we may call him, a sterile voyeur of the erotic madness of others, but is himself neither divinely mad nor a divine voyeur.

The great specialist on eros is himself erotically deficient. He is loved by others but himself loves no one, as Alcibiades reveals in the *Symposium* (222a7–b8). If this is right, and it is apparently challenged only once in the Platonic corpus (*Charmides* 155d3–e2), then Socrates is incapable of taking the necessary first step in the erotic ascent that he himself describes in the *Symposium* and the *Phaedrus*. Socrates is incapable of philosophical pederasty because he is incapable of pederasty.[21] Derrida thus vitiates the brilliance of his equation of the criticism of writing (spilling the seed in vain) with a criticism of pederasty by attributing it to Plato instead of to Socrates.[22] We may adopt his terms to correct his thesis. The pederast Plato does *not* contradict (or unconsciously deconstruct) himself: he contradicts the unerotic Socrates.

I said previously that the distinction in the *Phaedrus* between human speech and writing is not ontological but political. We must now explain the qualifying term "human." First, I note that, in general, for Plato, "political" is virtually synonymous with "human," and hence with "playful." In addition, when gods play with the human, the result is divine play.[23] It is therefore not merely playful, but serious as well. Second, whereas the distinction between speech and writing is indeed playful, at a deeper level, *there is no distinction between speech and writing in the Phaedrus*. But this is not the identity that Derrida himself notices at *Phaedrus* 276a5–8. To state the correct conclusion at the outset: speech and writing are the same as imitations of the divine *logos*, but they differ in their political function. As what one might call the divine *logos* itself, speech and writing are again the same. But this sameness is not the same as its political identity within difference.

To proceed more consequentially, there is indeed a "reversal" here of the function of the argument, as Derrida asserts.[24] But Derrida takes Socrates' reference, here and elsewhere, to the *logos gegrammenos* (the *logos* in letters) as support for his inference that "writing is not an independent order of signification; it is weakened speech, something not completely dead."[25] This is true for two reasons. First, and for our immediate purposes not of central importance, speech is the mark of thinking, and is therefore more "alive" than writing. Once we put aside the entire Platonic web of playful seriousness about speech and writing, there is no reason to deny that writing fulfills an essential role in the rendering precise of speech. That is a platitude, and it has no bearing on the concerns of the *Phaedrus*. Second, and directly relevant, writing is the "weakened" form of the living law. It cannot be adjusted to the individual citizen, and it must be "supplemented" by the speech of equity.

In order to appreciate the deeper level of the discussion in the *Phaedrus*, we remind ourselves that the writing-down characteristic of the human inscription of human speech is not the divine writing-down of the divine *logos*. Remarkably enough, Derrida himself warns us of this distinction: "writing in the soul is not a writing that breaches, but only a writing of transmission, of education, of demonstration, or at best, of dis-covering, a writing of *alētheia*. Its order is didactic, maieutic, or at any rate elocutionary. Dialectical."[26] But this citation requires further study. We must first note the important equation by Derrida of writing as truth (*alētheia*) with writing as pedagogy or elocution. This is, of course, a demotion of truth. Derrida does not tell us what he means by "writing that breaches" (*une écriture de frayage*), but he ought to mean what could be called the theological identity of speaking and writing. It follows that the aforementioned reversal is not a self-contradiction but a signal of complexity. Using Derrida's own expression, but not his intention (and on Derridean grounds, his own intention is irrelevant), writing that takes place "within a problematic of truth" is, when viewed from the exterior (from the perspective of a god), not the writing-down of "truth" in the pejorative sense but poetic speech that provides an interpretation of the "everyday" or "pretheoretical" world, and so that constitutes the intelligible cosmos, but not, to repeat an earlier warning, in the sense of the Kantian transcendental ego.

We have to emphasize the initial similarity between Kant and the reading I suggest of Plato in order to defend ourselves against it. The Kantian world is not a divine revelation or a philosophical poem; it is not an interpretation to be confirmed or denied by a pretheoretical inspection of the world of human experience. The Kantian world, as constituted by the transcendental ego, is on the contrary the unique world of human experience. There is no "other" world, pre- or posttheoretical, to which it can be compared. Hence, all interpretations are of, and subordinate to, the transcendentally posited structure of intelligibility. As we saw in the preceding chapter, interpretation arises within Kant from his consideration of history, and so, of course, from the human defectiveness of the transcendental philosophy. In Plato, however, if there is transcendental activity, it is "poetic," and hence itself requires interpretation. Whether or not we obey the voice of a god depends upon the persuasiveness of divine rhetoric.

This said, I come back to the Platonic reversal. Speech, understood as what Derrida calls *alethic* or pedagogical writing in the soul, is the interior of divine *logos*. Within the interior of divine *logos,* the distinction between speech and writing has political but neither ontological nor theological significance. It is a speech assigned to human beings, for the care of human beings, by a god. As soon as we understand it to be assigned speech—and how could we fail to understand this, since the words are assigned to Socrates by Plato?—the Derridean distinction between the interior and the exterior has to be radically revised. Human or assigned speech and writing are not themselves a legitimate expression of the distinction between the interior and the exterior, as Derrida believes is the case for Plato. *Both at once constitute the interior* of the Platonic monologue. As a direct corollary, it is not Plato's intention that the interior be superior to the exterior. To the contrary, the exterior is superior to the interior.[27] I now repeat my previous assertion that the dialogues constitute the Platonic Torah and hence that they require a Talmudic interpretation. In a sense, Derrida's own interpretation entirely transcends the "interior" interpretations of traditional philology because it is, in a way perhaps unnoticed by Derrida, exterior to the text as a text. Derrida, however, wavers on the surface of the cosmos: the motion of genesis unsteadies his view of the difference between Plato and Socrates.

## III

Talmudic hermeneutics is not philology. We shall state our conclusion in the middle, in good Talmudic form. What, then, is the difference between speech and writing? Answer: none, or in other words, silence. Otherwise put, speech and writing differentiate silence: they are the origin of difference, and hence of *différance*. Derrida, of course, believes the contrary, because, like all linguistic (post-) ontologists, he takes language or writing to be its own origin. Posthuman writing originates in nothing: "if writing is secondary at this point, nothing, however, has occurred before it."[28] Divine writing of the Hebraic kind is the same as speech; it produces the world. Platonic writing interprets the world as a cosmos.

But the question returns: What is the difference between human speech and writing? And the reply is once more: nothing. The question returns because it has been incorrectly posed. What we ought to have asked for is the difference between the nothing of silence and the nothing of *différance*. And this in turn leads to the question of why gods create. The question cannot be asked of Jehovah, since His every reply is itself a creation. One may give, of course, the answer that Jehovah creates because of His goodness. But this is merely to repeat the assurance of Genesis 1. We are told there that at each stage of the creation, God saw it to be good. The act of creation is itself identical with speech; for example, "And God said, 'let there be light.' " This is precisely what I mean by the identity of divine speech and writing. But the approval of interpretation is silent: God *sees* (ראה) that it is good.

What then is the difference between Genesis and the major myth of the *Phaedrus*? On one point, they agree; the viewing of the divine is silent. The difference is that, within the myth of the *Phaedrus*, there is no creation or production. The soul, as directed toward the Ideas, is silent. However, the book of Genesis, as a writing, is posterior to the speech of creation it records. The speech of the *Phaedrus*, as a Platonic writing or monologue, *is* the speech of creation. Platonic monologue orders the cosmos after a silent vision of the good, which transforms the pretheoretical understanding of the world. In Genesis, on the contrary, the vision of goodness is posterior to discursive creation.

The most evident inference from these facts is that, in the Hebrew tradition, goodness is relative and posterior to creation, hence to the will of God, whereas in the Platonic tradition, creation is relative and posterior to goodness. Human beings must take Jehovah's word for His goodness, and hence for the goodness of His creation. In the case of Plato, they can see for themselves (if they have eyes to see). But they must do so silently, and this is their *imitatio dei*. Derrideans, however, cannot look, and they cannot be silent. This is a necessary consequence of the primacy of writing, or of nothing as prior to the secondariness of writing.


## IV

According to Derrida, "platonism," or "the dominant structure of the history of metaphysics," is "played out in the play between two writings. Whereas all it wanted to do was to distinguish between writing and speech." Derrida bases this assertion upon the previously discussed passage of *Phaedrus* 276a5–8. Speech, as writing in the soul, is on this basis unable to distinguish itself from writing in letters external to the soul. Consequently, the *Phaedrus* does not so much condemn the bad (external) writing as prefer one writing (the good or more vital, because ensouled, version) to another. Derrida correctly observes that it is

> remarkable here that the so-called living speech is suddenly described by a "metaphor" borrowed from the same order as that which one wishes to exclude, from the order of its simulacrum. Yet this borrowing is rendered necessary by that which structurally links the intelligible to its repetition in the copy, and the language describing dialectics cannot fail to call upon it.[29]

Within the dialogue, Socrates does not comment explicitly on this metaphorical reversal of the apparent point to his criticism. Derrida takes it as a necessary consequence of language itself, that is, of primordial writing, within which the fraternal distinction between human speech and writing can only be expressed in terms of the structure that binds them together. Writing is the copy or simulacrum of speech for Plato, but, on Derrida's account, the "structure" of copying is itself writing.[30] The form or Idea is accordingly a product of *différance*. The "aneidetic" *pharmakon*, "the difference of difference,"[31] is "the prior medium in which differentiation in general is produced, along with the opposition between the *eidos* and its other; this medium is *analogous* to the one that will, subsequent to and according to the decision of philosophy, be reserved for transcendental imagination. . . ."[32] In other words, Derridean writing is the radicalization of sophistry,[33] with which Plato equates the "bad" writing in the *Phaedrus*.[34]

What can traditional or philological hermeneutics say against this interpretation? It can, of course, reject what Derrida himself proudly identifies as hermeneutical *excess,* a method that from the outset is intended, or compelled, to "slip away from the recognised models of commentary."[35] Unfortunately, without some analogous excess, philology has nothing with which to counter, let alone replace, Derridean excess. In the exercise of its own proud moderation (which, to tell the truth, is normally honored in the breach), philology can do nothing but read the text aloud, guarding against even an inflection of the voice that might "read" something into the text; or at best it might define the metaphor as a metaphor—in other words, engage in tautology. As is more likely, it can preserve a dignified silence, which comes to the same thing: nothing.

Philology becomes significant only as the handmaiden of philosophy. Since Derrida takes his stance outside of philosophy, within the exigency of *différance,* we do not "refute" him when we ourselves take our bearings by the philosophical question of the Platonic dialogues, and in particular of the *Phaedrus:* how can a human being become a god? The extent to which we are able to accommodate our own hypothetical excess to a greater number of passages in the Platonic corpus than Derrida, or to give a more precise account of Derrida's own proof texts than he does, will be of interst to philologists, or at least to philosophically sympathetic philologists, but surely not to Derrida. What one can, I think, legitimately say to him is that, after all, on the principles of deconstruction, there is *no* valid or uniquely true interpretation of a philosophical text. Not only, then, is mine as "good" as his (no better and no worse), but it is better to the extent that Plato is entirely superfluous to his own enterprise. Derrida has not, and cannot have, proved that *his* interpretation is sound or that Plato has been deconstructed by the radical exigency of *différance*. Whereas I in turn cannot "prove" the "excessive" dimension of my interpretation (any more than any other interpreter who goes beyond reading the dialogue aloud), I can link it to the text and to a Platonic question. I can give evidence, and I can turn Derrida's own observations into evidence. In Derrida's case, this is impossible. There is no Derridean evidence, because each signifier signifies merely another signifier. The rejection of the metaphysics of presence is a two-edged sword. *Écriture* is the name of the double absence of the signifier and the referent.[36] As such, it is the sword that chops off the hand of the Derridean writer. If the world is a text written by *différance,* it is a tale by an idiot, a nonsubjective subjectivity or idiot savant, hence a tale full of sound and fury, signifying nothing. As Derrida himself asserts, the concept is a signifier.[37] Thus writing is the possibility for the signifier to repeat itself "without the truth presenting itself at all."[38] Evidence is presence, and in Derrida, nothing is entirely present—nothing in its entirety but absence.

This had to be said. Now let us take a look, with a clear conscience, at some pertinent Platonic texts. In the *Theaetetus,* Socrates explains discursive thinking (*dianoeisthai*) as the soul conversing with itself, and speech (*logos*) as the clarifying of *dianoia*. The same definition is given by the Eleatic Stranger in the *Sophist*.[39] It might seem that, if we are permitted to collate passages from separate dialogues on this point (like a good philologist), these texts, taken together with *Phaedrus* 276a5–8, establish that talking aloud is always the same as *dianoia*. But the inference is invalid. The *Theaetetus* and *Sophist* define *dianoia* as speech and epistemic speech as *dianoia*. It is then possible for a nonepistemic speech to be inscribed in the soul in a way other than the inscription of epistemic speech. Exactly the same situation obtains in the *Phaedrus,* where the *logos* contrasted by Socrates with writing is "the one which is written with *epistēmē* in the soul of the one who knows." Phaedrus emphasizes the point by repeating it more elaborately (the written word is the image of the spoken word of the knower). "Altogether so," Socrates confirms (276ff).

In a passage we have already cited, Derrida indicates that he has noticed something of this sort. Writing in the soul is not "writing that breaches" but didactic and maieutic writing, the writing of truth.[40] He rightly connects this to a more general consideration of the intrinsic limitations of dianoetic *epistēmē*, which I shall consider in a moment. But he does not seem to notice that there is, as it were, a pregnant absence here, about to fill itself up with a poetic *epistēmē*, to say nothing of the silence of noetic perception. Derrida is apparently deaf to two kinds of speech in Plato: the speech of poetry or myth, and the speech of silence. He attends to the myths, of course, but he does not hear them. Having been stunned by the Heideggerean doctrine of the metaphysics of presence or vision, he is deaf to the function of hearing or listening in Plato, just as he silently reinterprets silence as writing.

Derrida does not understand that his own account of the "reversal" in the Socratic argument, together with the ensuing restriction of the criticism to didactic writing, limits the scope or significance of his own deconstruction of the ostensible Platonic preference for speech. He understands that speech is already a mark of absence but not that this is precisely why Socrates defines speech in terms of writing. Hence he does not understand (despite his evasive use of "platonism") that *there is no metaphysics of presence in Plato.* In the alternative formulation, there is no ontology in Plato, because Plato regards ontology as impossible. What we find instead is a daydream, couched in a mixture of mathematical and poetic rhetoric, of ontology; better, we find a rhetorical praise of eidetic phenomenology. Let us see how this is done.

## V

Derrida has two main theses. The first is that Plato prefers speech to writing. The second is that this preference is deconstructed by the exigency of *différance*. Derrida is presumably not especially impressed by the principle of noncontradiction. We philologists, nevertheless, must insist that the second thesis is contradicted by his admission that Plato does not criticize writing *tout court*, but a certain kind of writing. Not let us move backward to the first thesis, assisted by our interpretation of the second, which illuminates, rather than follows from or explains, the first.

According to the first thesis, writing, the favorite son of *différance*, is the hand of Esau within Jacob's coat. In Derrida's own terms, for Plato, speech is preferable to writing because it is fully alive, invigorated by the ontological sun, hence present to the truth as presence, as *eidos* or visible form. On the other hand, the dialogues show that "any *full, absolute* presence of what *is* . . . is impossible." Even further, the *Sophist* supports the conclusion that "if truth is the presence of the *eidos*, it must always, on pain of mortal blinding by the sun's fires, come to terms with relation, nonpresence, and thus nontruth."[41] Stated with maximum concision, Derrida holds that language dilutes or conceals presence with absence. The Platonic dialogues, thanks to "the absolute invisibility of the origin of the visible," are "a structure of replacements such that all presences will be supplements substituted for the absent origin."[42]

As we have seen, Derrida's two theses are rooted in the antecedent hypothesis that Plato is a failed ontologist in the Heideggerean sense of the term. The emptiness of this hypothesis can be shown in a preliminary manner. Derrida's account of the metaphor of the sun in Plato is based upon a conflation of two misreadings. He infers from the use of the sun metaphor in the *Phaedo* and *Republic* that the origin of Being (already a Heideggerean term) is invisible. The actual situation is different. In the *Phaedo*, Socrates tell us that he turned away, not from the origin of Being (or being), or from being as presence, but from physical things, from physics to *logos* (99d). In the *Republic*, Socrates does not say that the origin of being is invisible (if it were, he could hardly have compared it to the sun); instead, he declines to discuss it with Glaucon in direct terms (VI, 506d6–e5).

There are two different suns here, and their conjoint message is non-Derridean. The shift from physics to *logos* cannot be completed by a superordinate shift from "physiology" (accounts of natural beings) to "ontology" (a *logos* of the origin of beings). The origin of being is not invisible; it is unspeakable—and not merely to Glaucon. This is not an allusion to a secret teaching, for it is no secret in the dialogues that there is no ontological teaching. To the contrary, philosophy, narrowly understood, is throughout a silent vision of beings, the hyper-uranian beings of *Phaedrus* 247c3 or the "greatest forms" of *Sophist* 254d4. These forms can be seen and named, but as soon as we try to state more definitely their properties and relations, we stumble into self-contradiction. I will give one example here from the discussion in the *Sophist*. The pure forms *being* and *same* are said to be distinct; yet we cannot speak or think of *being* as distinct, except by thinking of *being itself*, and hence as the *same* as itself. The impossibility of thinking or speaking of being apart from sameness is not countered by the "abstraction" of *sameness* from *being*. The need to abstract is already a sign that we cannot conceive them to be actually (or as the Stranger might put it, in their *dynamis*) independent.

This little example is enough to indicate what happens when we insist upon developing an ontology. Either we produce "abstractions," or conceptual artifacts, or else we weave together these abstractions into a dialectic of the Hegelian sort, not analytical but synthetic or speculative, in which each formal element is a moment in the Concept. In both cases, we are exploring constructions of thought, not of Being. It should be emphasized here that, within its own domain, analytical discourse is quite adequate to its task. I do not see that this is acknowledged by Derrida, for whom discourse and writing as such is continuously deconstructing or differentiating itself. Derrida's conception is thus a kind of inverted Hegelianism. Concepts, instead of coming together into a totality, are continuously falling apart into a multiplicity. But this is nonsense. If we take them as distinct disciplines, geometry, algebra, logic, or set theory do not deconstruct themselves. Whether on Platonic assumptions or those of post-Gödelian postmodernism, the proof of the incompleteness of a formal system containing the arithmetic of the natural numbers is a formal proof. Formal mathematics cannot by definition be separated from its form. Whether mathematical beings are in fact concepts is quite another matter. The point is that mathematics, or analytical discourse in general, goes wrong when it attempts a comprehensive synthesis. It goes wrong when it attempts to replace, or to assimilate, synoptic vision.

Let us summarize: *dianoia* cannot produce ontology for two reasons. First, the elements of analytical discursivity, and hence the beginning as well as the end of analysis, are not themselves accessible to analytical discursivity, except in the sense that to name is to "analyze" on the basis of an antecedent discrete vision or perception. Second, the results of analytical discursivity are radically incomplete in themselves. They do not fit together into a coherent account of the whole. To give the outstanding example, there is no analytical discourse about the personal soul. For this reason, analytical discourses must be completed by poetry.

At this point, it might seem that, after all, we are tipping our hat to Derrida. For there is surely no unique poetic completion of philosophy. But this does not lead to deconstruction. Mathematics and the rest of analytical discourse remains what it is, regardless of poetic completion. The perception of forms guides every type of discourse; even deconstructionists can see what they are saying. And the stabilities of pretheoretical or everyday life, although they are not philosophically complete, remain intelligible in their own terms without philosophical completion.

The distinction between analytical and poetic discourse, then, does not "cancel" or dissolve either of its two terms. Furthermore, just as the Platonic dialogue unifies the two types of discourse, so we may illustrate concretely the unification as a celebration of mathematical imagination. I refer to the *Timaeus*. In this dialogue, the passage running from 28c5 to 29d3, when taken in conjunction with 59c5–d3, lends support to some previous conclusions, as well as supplying us with a transition to a further result. The mathematical tale of genius is itself a poem or "likely myth" (περὶ τούτων τὸν εἰκότα μῦθον) in which the technical details of the story derive their significance, and thus their unity, from an assumption we have met before. "If then the cosmos is noble [χαλός] and the demiurge is good [ἀγαθός], it is clear that he looked to the eternal," that is, to the eternal paradigm that is comprehensible by intelligence. The demiurge, we may here simply assert, is not a Hebraic creator-god but the principle of the intelligibility of the constitution of the cosmos, the goodness of which is subordinate to the eternal paradigm. Thus, even if understanding the structure of the cosmos is a constructive or productive activity of the discursive intelligence (here, of the intelligence of Plato), intelligibility is posterior to the gazing upon goodness or eternity. This is not annulled even though what we can say as a consequence of this gazing (*theoria* in its original sense) is always a likely story. "For we must remember that I who speak and you who judge have the human nature" (29c8–d1).

In the passage just scrutinized, discourse about genesis is associated explicitly with human speech. Since the discourse is comprehensive, or about the cosmos as a whole, it is also mythical. The later passage (59c5–d3) provides a third point. "When someone, for the sake of recreation, puts aside *logoi* concerning the beings that endure forever, and acquires a blameless pleasure from likely [stories] concerning the beings of genesis, he will produce a moderate and sensible play [παιδιὰν] for his life." The discourse about genesis is also playful. In modern science, mathematics replaces myth to the extent that it gives a form to the likely, which is subject to empirical manipulation. But no one who has studied the history of cosmology, and especially its most advanced stage, will dare to say that thinking about the cosmos as a whole has freed itself from myth.

The *Timaeus* puts mathematics to a mythical, human, and playful use. This is because the topic is genesis rather than eternity. We are, of course, interested here in the Platonic distinction, and not in whether eternity is actually accessible to human beings. There is a passage in the *Laws* of which Derrida makes much, and we may employ it to obtain a further result. The passage occurs in book VII (803b3ff). The Athenian Stranger says that "the affairs of mortals are not worthy of great seriousness, although it is necessary to be serious about them; and that is not a fortunate thing." I interpose the following remark. It is necessary for gods as well as for mortals to be serious about human affairs, because gods would not be gods unless they were "worshipped" by mortals. Whatever may be its resolution, the master-slave dialectic applies to the relations between the divine and the human, as well as to that between humans. And without question, it applies to those humans who aspire to be gods, or to give them their political name, philosopher-kings. To continue now with the passage from the *Laws,* the Stranger goes on to observe that

> one must treat seriously the serious, but not what is not serious, and that by nature god is worthy of an altogether blessed seriousness, whereas man, as we said previously, has been constructed as a kind of plaything of god [θεοῦ τι παίγνιον], and this is truly the best thing about him. Every man and woman should follow along in this

manner and, playing the noblest games, live such a life, the opposite
of what is now thought to be the case.

Derrida provides an extensive quotation of this passage, from which
he infers that the impossibility of ontology requires Plato to regard his
dialogues as games, "the best, the most noble play."[43] Again: "Plato
plays at taking truth seriously."[44] But "play is always lost when it
seeks salvation in games."[45] Up to a point, Derrida attributes this
playfulness to Plato's consciousness of the lack of seriousness of his
own venture. At a deeper level, however, Plato is subject to the compul-
sion of writing itself in its double form:

> What law governs this "contradiction," this opposition to itself of
> what is said against writing, of a dictum that pronounces itself
> against itself as soon as it finds its way into writing, as soon as it
> writes down its self-identity and carries away what is proper to it
> *against* this ground of writing? This "contradiction," which is noth-
> ing other than the relation-to-self of diction as it opposes itself to
> scription, as it *chases* itself (away) in hunting down what is properly
> its *trap*—this contradiction is not contingent.[46]

And so on. In short, Plato's playful writings are produced by what
Derrida presumably regards (although not on Platonic grounds) as the
*serious* identity of diction and scription. The attempt to oppose speech
to writing thus itself produces writing.

Derrida in effect accuses Plato of aristocratic irony and a deep cyni-
cism based upon the recognition of the impossibility of ontology. At
the same time, he assures us that Plato was fundamentally an ontologist who attempted to construct a metaphysics of presence. Even if we
grant the doctrine of the necessity of unconscious autodeconstruction,
this fails to explain the contradiction attributed by Derrida to Plato's
conscious self-interpretation or motivation. Differently stated, it is
scarcely plausible that Plato was nothing by intention but a metaphysician of presence, since he certainly wrote, not just the passages that
look to Derrida like a metaphysics of presence or its failure, but the
poetic or dramatic *context* that renders these passages playful. In fact,
the writing of the presumably serious passages is enough to render
them playful. The thesis of the unconscious self-deconstruction of the
metaphysics of presence is contradicted by the twin facts of the dialogues as writings and by Derrida's own interpretation of them. If

Derrida's account of Plato is right, then it is obvious that Plato knew what he was doing, *regardless* of the additional exigencies of *écriture*.

The same interpretation, however, shows us that Plato could *not* have been essentially a metaphysician of presence, failed or successful by his own criteria. Were this the correct understanding of Plato, then he would have written not dialogues but metaphysical treatises. Metaphysicians of presence are not playful. One is tempted to cite the example of Aristotle as decisive on this point. By my interpretation, however, the dialogues become intelligible as theological, and consequently political, documents. On the face of it, it is a fallacy of hermeneutical perception to read Plato as though he were Rabelais, or (to put it bluntly) a man who would waste his time composing satires in order to amuse himself and to become famous. There is no doubt that Derrida has a keener perception of aristocratic playfulness than those professional scholars who parse the "arguments" extracted from the dialogues by disregarding the precise nature of the documents they believe themselves to be studying. Unfortunately, Derrida seems to have a tin ear for theology; I mean by this that, very much like a bourgeois professor or technologist, he does not know what it means to wish to be a god.

Socrates opposed diction to scription and wrote nothing. Derrida has entirely failed to explain why Plato plays at being an author. The first step is to see that the dialogues are written for *our* salvation. Nevertheless, I would not rule out the possibility that they were also written for Plato's salvation. But that possibility cannot even be noticed when formulated in Derridean terms. If it is a god's salvation to provide a revelation, and at least in this sense, a cosmos, this hardly proves that play is lost when it seeks salvation in games. Derrida's conception of being "lost" is, ironically, Christian. It is rooted in a deep disappointment at the presumed absence of the truth of the presence of Christ. If there is no God, then there is nothing but *différance*, i.e. nothing. This is Nietzsche with a vengeance, a Nietzsche without any sense of Zeus as the "playing lad" (παῖς παίζων), as Heraclitus puts it. For Derrida, on the contrary, "writing and speech have thus become two different species, or values, of the trace."[47] There is nothing playful about this, but neither is there anything serious here. Where there is only *différance*, there is no difference.

# VI

Plato is serious as a god, not as an ontologist. Ontology, like postontology, is a suitable occupation for professors. Gods speak—and thereby also write—in different ways to different mortals. Their most important speeches are revelations granted to their prophets. What looks to me very much like typical Enlightenment antitheological ire is no doubt the reason why Derrida trivializes prophecy and thus misses the importance of hearing in the dialogues. Whether for this reason or another, there is no doubt that Derrida has nothing to say about divine madness: this is an outstanding lacuna in his reading of the *Phaedrus*. In sum, an excessive concern with *eidos* vitiates Derrida's account of the Platonic doctrine of the soul.

In the *Republic,* immediately preceding the poetic discussion of the soul, Socrates remarks to Glaucon that blind men may take the right road (VI, 506c7). They are guided by those who see, and this is accomplished by the voice. The blind man is a traditional paradigm for the prophet, whose ear is opened to aural representations of the divine *logos* even as his eye is closed to the metaphysics of presence. I suggest that we may apply a distinction to representations or images that is introduced for that purpose by the Eleatic Stranger in the *Sophist* (235c8). Icons are images that correctly duplicate the measures and proportions of their originals; phantasms alter the original measures and proportions in accordance with human perspective. The odd situation then arises that icons produce inaccurate perceptions, whereas phantasms, despite their intrinsic inaccuracy, produce accurate perceptions. A prophecy, whether visual or aural, acquired through divine madness, is a phantasm of a complex totality having no determinate formal structure. The three main examples of such totalities in the Platonic dialogues are the cosmos, the polis, and the personal soul. In these cases, phantasms are mandatory if anything true is to be said, because there are no correct measures or proportions to be derived from the originals. An iconic or correct representation of an absence of a definite measure or proportion, or of the presence of continuously changing measures and proportions, is a contradiction in terms. In other words, an accurate image of inaccuracy must itself be inaccurate.

The soul is regularly said to be divine in the Platonic dialogues.

More precisely, the soul contains divine elements that permit it to desire, and in an attenuated sense to possess what is truly divine in an unmitigated manner. The soul is divine, not merely to the extent that it is capable of seeing the divine beings, but as it participates in the divine *logos*. Does the soul have an Idea? For our purposes, we can leave it at Socrates' own formulation in the *Phaedrus* (246a3ff.). To describe the Idea of the personal soul (not the world soul or principle of change) would require an entirely divine and lengthy discourse. "But as to what it is like, this is a human and lesser matter." So the likeness of the soul conveyed by the Stesichorean (heard) myth, is a phantasm, an accommodation to human perspective, and as such, a game.[48]

This, incidentally, should be obvious from the fact that it is addressed to Phaedrus, an admirer of Lysian rhetoric and a person of an inferior nature. But the game, like Phaedrus, is interior to the dialogue. To present a playful account of the soul is not to suppress the fact that the soul is divine, and hence a serious matter. The phantasm that is the dialogue *Phaedrus* must therefore, in order to yield its serious meaning, be seen from the exterior. Within the phantasm, this is represented by the ascent of the best souls to the roof of the world. But the representation is doubly fantastic, since what we see on the roof of the world is not the soul but the hyperuranian beings. One may infer from Socrates' silence on the point that there is no Idea of the soul.

At the same time, it can easily be shown that there are also no icons (accurate images) of the Ideas. Consider first the following passage from the *Symposium*. Early in her instruction of the young Socrates, Diotima explains to him that the power of Eros, a great daimon intermediate between the divine and the mortal, is "to interpret [ἑρμηνῦον] and convey the things from humans to gods, and the things from gods to humans: from the one, needs and sacrifices; from the others, orders and recompense for the sacrifices. As it is in the middle, and so is filled up with both, Eros thus binds together the whole to itself" (202d11–e7). According to Diotima, then, Eros produces a whole by *incorporating* the divine, which is in this way rendered intelligible to us. Eros here plays the role of Hermes and consequently stands for the accessibility of divine speech. We can apply this directly to the divine speech of Plato, whose philosophical eros produces the dialogues, and in *this*

way, namely, through phantasms accommodated to the human understanding, makes possible a poetic discourse (which may include mathematical elements) about the Ideas. As within the whole, the Ideas are
accessible to an erotic hermeneutic only. However, the case is exactly
the same if, as the *Phaedrus* claims, they are beyond the whole. Only
this time, Eros has been promoted to the status of a god, no doubt in
accord with the greater difficulty of the task.[49]

It must be emphasized that, even in the *Phaedrus,* there is no complete perception of the Ideas. Only the best of the eventually human
souls, through much (speechless) striving, are at last able to stick their
heads up through the roof of the cosmos and to look at the hyperuranian beings. They gaze upon these beings with difficulty, because of the
inarticulate fuss made by the horses just below the surface (248a1–
b5). To this we may add that the revolution of the world of genesis
will inevitably both blur and render multiply perspectival the soul's
view of the beings fixed overhead. The same must be said of our
interpretations of a Platonic dialogue. Seeing the Ideas is like stargaz-
ing, not astronomy. Interpretation of the dialogues is Talmudic, not
philological. The passage just cited brings Socrates very close to
Heidegger, and thus to Derrida. But there is a critical difference.
Whereas the hyperuranian beings are visible only as recollected from
the change of historicity, they are themselves neither historical nor
projections of protosubjectivity. And this is the difference between
silence and speech; silence is the appropriate response to eternity,
whereas speech generates history. Otherwise put, the attempt to describe the Ideas produces analytical or poetic artifacts, and these are
the "displacements" of Being as presence to which Derrida refers.

Within the dialogues, then, taken as writings, the *parousia* of vision
is announced, but also displaced, by the function of hearing. Recollec-
tion takes place through the instrumentality of myths, of *dialogues,*
which the Platonic interlocutor has in the first instance heard and in
the second instance speaks to us. He has heard it from the ancients,
who stand closer to the origins than we do, or from a poet, who in turn
has heard it from the Muses.[50] The Socratic *daimonion,* of course, is a
voice, not an *eidos* or vision. This is why there is no "transcendental
deduction" of the Platonic Ideas: all discursive analyses are grounded
in silent visions. Even in the *Sophist,* the favorite dialogue of the

unerotic ontogrammatologists, the greatest kinds or pure forms of being—rest, change, sameness, and otherness—are not introduced through conceptual definition: they are pointed out as obvious, as taken for granted. "We say, do we not. . . ." The function of speech here is not to ground a philosophy of linguistic analysis but to rule it out. We are being directed to listening as the testimony of the obvious: of seeing.[51]

In the *Phaedrus*, Socrates says that the soul is mantic, and prophecy is associated with Eros at the beginning of the Stesichorean myth.[52] But there is an ambiguity in the nature of prophecy that turns upon the relation of speech to silence, which becomes the fundamental opposition as soon as we grant the intrinsic sameness of writing and speech. Derrida never sees this, because for him, the primordial nature of writing makes silence impossible. And this is why there can be no difference in Derrida between writing and reading. Derrida cannot read at all, because reading requires a moment of silence in which we *see* the text. For Derrida, however, seeing is already writing; hence reading is a displacing or rendering absent of the text. It is the replacement of the absent original by another, different text, which is in its turn implicitly absent, implicitly replaceable, but *never legible*. Derridean writing thus becomes a satire on Eros, which is continuously changing its shape. Yet the Derridean soul, because of the absence of a divine gift, is neither erotic nor mantic.[53] His madness (if that is the right term) is postmodern, hence neither divine nor human.

Prophetic or divine madness originates in vision and silence. This is why the soul is almost entirely silent in the ascent to the hyperuranian beings, and the exception proves the rule. Conversation occurs between the mythical parts of the soul only when they debate whether or not to have sexual intercourse with a beautiful youth.[54] At the same time, prophetic vision produces speech: the discourse of revelation, as spoken to us, via Phaedrus, by Socrates. The vision is instantaneous;[55] in the imagery of the *Phaedrus*, it punctuates the moments of the revolution of cosmic genesis. The speech, however, is temporal; perhaps one could say that it is human temporality as such. The Platonic dialogues, then, are indeed "texts," that is, a web of speech and silence, but as speeches, they are artifactual phantasms of the truth, produced in the full seriousness of divine play and requiring "correction" by the reader through the use of the laws of psychic perspective, or in other words, through an erotic hermeneutic.[56]

## VII

Derrida has correctly identified the deficiencies of human *logos,* when this is directed toward ontology. In my opinion, he is also right from a Platonic standpoint, but not for the reason he thinks, in associating human *logos* with sophistry and grammatology.[57] The continuous changes of genesis require a corresponding art of noble sophistry, called just now erotic hermeneutic. Therefore ostensible ontologies are indeed grammatologies, namely, rules of discourse. The grammatologist believes that he is awake at last, after the long dream of the metaphysics of presence. In the *Theaetetus* (201d8), however, the attempt to describe the elements of knowledge is referred to as a dream. In the *Republic* (VII, 533b6), Socrates says that mathematicians are men who dream that they are awake. In the *Timaeus* (52b7), the mathematical physicist refers to (what we now call) space as a dream. References of this sort could easily be multiplied: in general, one could say that only god is wise, presumably because only god is genuinely awake. Humans must rest content with philosophy, or the dream of wisdom.[58]

We require only the briefest reminder of the nature of dialectic or diaeresis (not necessarily synonyms) in order to be persuaded of its dreamlike character. In general, it should be said that we find much inspiring propaganda in the dialogues for what has impressed many as a science of forms, but no instances of its detailed application. To summarize the propaganda, the heart of the operation is to see pure forms, then to count their constituent formal elements, to divide complexes into their constituents and accordingly to gather phenomenal instances under the appropriate type, to discern whether the forms possess an active or a passive power, and to ascertain how formal elements do and do not combine.[59] Sometimes the operation begins with beings chosen from everyday life (like the sophist, the statesman, or, as in the *Philebus,* the ox); sometimes it is intended to proceed exclusively with pure forms. In all cases, the logistical or calculative operations presuppose a noetic perception of the forms themselves (for even in the case of everyday things, we must first perceive their form before we can divide it accurately). In all cases, then, there is a disjunction between seeing and articulating.

We must insist upon the fact, which has been misunderstood by many, including Derrida, that the counting and measuring of Platonic dialectic, if we take it seriously as a direct description of formal structure, is a *phenomenology*, not an ontology. It becomes an ontology, in a sense reminiscent of Cartesian *ordo et mensura*, only when we regard it as poetic, that is, not as straightforward myth but as *conceptual construction*, another species of *poiēsis*. Dialectic produces ontology in the sense that ontology is a human construction. If on the other hand arithmetic is divine, it is nevertheless true that numbering, and hence division and collection, are ontologically neutral with respect to what is numbered. These operations fulfil with indifferent reliability any intention, and the application of any paradigm, within any perspective.

We therefore grant that Platonic *ordo et mensura* culminates in the production of artifacts. Nevertheless, they are images of originals. Similarly, discursive analysis (scription or diction) is, as Derrida rightly asserts, infected with nonbeing.[60] It is correct to say that writing cannot bring forth "the *alētheia* of the *eidos*."[61] But Derrida also says that

> dialectics is always guided by an intention of truth. It can only be satisfied by the presence of the *eidos*, which is here both the signified and the referent: the thing itself. The distinction between grammar and dialectics can thus only in all rigor be established at the point where truth is fully present and fills the *logos*. But what the parricide in the *Sophist* establishes is not only that any *full, absolute* presence of what *is* . . . is impossible, not only that any full intuition of truth, any truth-filled intuition is impossible; but that the very condition of discourse—*true or false*—is the diacritical principle of the *symplokē*. If truth is the presence of the *eidos*, it must always, on pain of mortal blinding by the sun's fires, come to terms with relation, nonpresence, and thus nontruth. It then follows that the absolute precondition for a rigorous difference between grammar and dialectics (or ontology) cannot in principle be fulfilled.[62]

This is a crucial, and culminating, passage in Derrida's essay, and we have seen part of it before. Once more we agree with his contention that dialectic, or analytical discourse, cannot fulfill itself. The reason, however, is that phenomenology is no more a science than is ontology. Descriptions, even of pure forms, vary with the perspective or intention of the phenomenologist. We also note once more that Derrida cannot distinguish between silence and speech. The *eidos* is for him "a signified and a referent" because he is himself already ensnared in the web of linguistics. A truth-filled intuition is not the same as a truth-filled *logos*. Were there no "true" in the sense of genuine intuitions, then there would be no possibility of intelligent speech, since the criterion for the distinction between two speeches would itself be a speech, thereby giving way to the infinite regress that we may as well call grammatology.

One does not, therefore, come fully to grips with Plato by showing that there is no difference between ontology and grammar. This may be brought out by a comment on Derrida's connection between the "parricide" and the problem of nonbeing. In the *Sophist*, the Stranger reports on Parmenides' injunction against saying that nonbeings are (237a2ff.), or more generally against pronouncing "the altogether not" (τὸ μηδαμῶς ὄν). He goes on to say that it is not possible to think discursively or indeed to express in any way through *logos* "non-being taken apart by itself" (238c8–10). Nevertheless, in a later section, preparatory to developing his own analysis of nonbeing, the Stranger requests that Theaetetus not suppose him to be turning into a kind of parricide (241d1). He does not assert that he is about to commit parricide; instead, he puts us on our guard against this appearance, even though it will be necessary to interrogate or "torture" the saying of Parmenides. This becomes entirely clear at 257b3–4, where the Stranger enunciates the cardinal point of his own analysis: "Whenever we say 'non-being' we do not speak of something opposite to being, but only other."

There is, then, no parricide. The Stranger in efffect obeys Father Parmenides (although both must mention "the altogether not" in order to state the injunction against stating it). He shifts to a different interpretation, according to which "not" means "other." Derrida's elaborate discussion of the problem of writing in terms of the father and the son is thus misconceived; unfortunately, it plays a pivotal role in his interpretation, and thereby spoils some of his keenest insights. In particular, the death of Socrates cannot be equivalent to the parricide against Parmenides for two reasons. First, there is no parricide. But second, Socrates is not Plato's father: *he is Plato's son,* a fictional character in a drama, a Socrates grown young and beautiful.[63] Derrida is accordingly doubly mistaken in his conclusion that "writing is parricide" for Plato.[64]

The altogether not can enter into rational discourse only through the phantasm of its name. The honoring of Parmenides' injunction in fact shows conclusively that there is no ontology in Plato, since we cannot think the "otherness" of being simply by asserting "other." But no contradiction ensues from our thinking it, so long as we make no attempt to capture it in a contradiction-free discursive analysis. And in fact we must think it, if only to avoid it in discourse. It is coordinate to the unspeakable *parousia* of the *eidos.* If we were to develop this point, it would lead us to a criticism of Western metaphysics as the consequence of the failure of the Eleatic Stranger to murder his father. But although the inability to attend to the altogether not is indeed partly explicable by what Derrida calls the metaphysics of presence, such attention does not do away with the coordinate role of presence. Any speech about Being must also begin with Nothing, as Hegel does in *The Science of Logic.* However, to consider this would take us too far afield. Suffice it to say here that the altogether not stands between *parousia* and discourse like a hellhound that can be placated only by magic: by a *pharmakon.*

Plato is vindicated if we understand him to be employing the Eleatic Stranger to make exactly this point. The *pharmakon* is discursivity itself, which replaces the original (nothing) by its phantasm (otherness), or, in still more vulgar terminology, by negation. Thus each thing is, in itself, other than all others. Accordingly, the "not" within "otherness" (precisely because of the technical failure to eliminate the original) is *disseminated* (a good Derridean word) throughout all of language, which thus fails utterly to resolve the problem of sophistry. On this point, Derrida and I are in accord.

We disagree, however, on the general explanation of this fact. Inside every inside is a trace of nothing—but *not* a trace of writing. Derrida is

wrong to say that writing opens up the series of oppositions domi-
nated by "inside/outside."[65] To the contrary, writing is itself constituted by the trace of "not" within its every positive stroke. It thus
images the ultimate ontological mystery of being and nothing. The
"not" is indeed a *pharmakon;* it poisons epistemic discourse, but it
makes possible the remedy of poetry, of the phantasm that succeeds in
conveying an accurate perception precisely because it is *not* the original, not accurate. Derrida understands this far better than those of his
critics who shake the Laputan rattle of clarity in his ears, but he does
not understand that he is himself, in his anti-platonism, a Platonic
trace.

# VIII

Since writing in the full Platonic sense produces a cosmos, it can hardly
be equivalent for him to pederasty, or the spilling of the seed in vain.[66]
To the contrary, it is Socrates, who does not write, but who is also not
a pederast, whose seed is sterile.[67] The Platonic dialogues distinguish
between carnal or human and psychic or divine pederasty; another
name for the second type is "correct pederasty."[69] In the *Symposium,*
this is associated by Diotima with production in the soul, but not with
"external" writing. In the *Phaedrus,* "correct" or philosophical pederasty has no connection at all with production, and hence none with
writing. To write is to fertilize the garden of letters; putting to one side
the question of whether it is playful or serious, writing is heterosexual
reproduction. I do not deny the comparison of erotic ascent to purified
pederasty, but this is not a basis upon which to accuse Plato of
phallocentrism. Even correct or purified pederasty suppresses the phal-
lus. But within the cosmos, writing, especially in the form of philosophical rhetoric, is political. The polis is not pederastic but heterosexual. Psychagogy knows no restrictive covenant for the exclusion of
females.

Derrida is of course aware of the connection between politics and
the discussion of writing in the *Phaedrus.* He regularly dilutes politics
into morals[69] or pedagogy,[70] however, and he has apparently not
seen at all correctly the connection between politics and the relation of
the sexes on the one hand and philosophy on the other. He misses the

heterosexual link between politics and Plato's two favorite metaphors for philosophy: weaving and hunting. The women sit home and weave while the men are out hunting. For the polis, both are necessary. This has its philosophical corollary in the double nature of the Socratic soul, which is both male and female. This is visible throughout the *Phaedrus*. Socrates compares himself and Phaedrus to young girls, to Bacchae, and to those who are possessed by nymphs.[71] The dramatic locale of the dialogue suggests an analogy between the pair Socrates-Phaedrus and the maiden Oreithuia, whereas Eros is cast as the ravishing Boreas.[72] And in the *Phaedrus,* as elsewhere, Socrates employs the female oath, "by Hera!"[73]

Socrates, whose teacher on erotic matters is a woman, and who claims to have studied oratory with Aspasia, describes himself in the *Theaetetus* as a midwife or now sterile female who assists youths in their effort to give birth to psychic progeny.[74] He thereby accentuates the female dimension in correct pederasty. Let us not forget that, according to Callicles in the *Gorgias,* Socrates looks like a pederast to the nonphilosopher; this confirms the revelation of Alcibiades in the *Symposium*.[75] The philosophical or manic soul is not pederastic in the vulgar sense, but Bacchic.[76] This points the way to a deeper understanding of the philosophical transformation of pederasty in the *Phaedrus;* the love of masculine beauty requires purification by the female element in Eros in order to become love of the beautiful soul. This is entirely compatible with the thesis that pederasty represents in the dialogues the transpolitical dimension of philosophical Eros.[77] We must not forget that Eros, to speak with Freud, is "polymorphous" or polyeidetic, and not a simple, unilinear force. From the broad political perspective, Eros is not only the origin of the city but also the source of its destruction (as Socrates warns in the *Republic* VIII, 546a1–b3).

We can now understand why, on the one hand, the *Phaedrus* begins with an exit from the city, and, on the other, it is dedicated to an essentially political discussion of writing. Eros is the middle term: it takes us up to heaven, but then back to a reflection on political rhetoric. This is why the dialogue is called *Phaedrus*. Phaedrus is a devotee of Lysias, against whom, together with those like him, the Socratic criticism of writing is addressed. Men of Lysias's rhetorical stamp are advised to give up writing. No such recommendation is made to Isocrates, whose soul Socrates praises: "by nature, there is something of philosophy in the man's intelligence."[78] This exemplifies the earlier remark by Socrates that it is not shameful to write; it is shameful to write and to speak (λέγειν τε καὶ γράφειν) shamefully and evilly.[79] There is then a shift to writing nobly in general, but this does not break the link with politics, as is plain from the context. Phaedrus has never heard of nonpolitical uses of rhetoric; that is, he has never heard of political rhetoric in the broad or Platonic sense of psychagogy.[80] He is not particularly able in abstract discussion and requires a paradigm to make things vivid. Socrates complies with a metaphorical description of "every *logos*": it ought to be like a living being.[81]

The psychagogic or political function of writing requires it to accommodate its discourse to the nature of each reader. This is, of course, a political requirement that writing cannot fulfill. The political dimension is not, as Derrida holds, "the first accent" of the discussion;[82] it is the fundamental and comprehensive accent. Philosophical rhetoric is inseparable from political rhetoric: from the public appearance of philosophy. Even Socrates' treatment of dialectic is linked with the political: the technical, as opposed to the "empirical" speaker, must have knowledge of his subject matter, and hence of the nature of the addressee, in order to accommodate the first to the second, in order to impart to the soul of the addressee "the desired persuasion and virtue."[83] We should therefore not be surprised when Socrates later compares the playful writing of serious men to farming for the amusement that is derived from gazing upon beautiful plants, which are the memoranda of just, beautiful, and good things. Nothing is said of truth.[84] The plants, I suggest, are not merely the political writings but the citizens they engender. For Phaedrus, writing is, as Socrates describes it, an altogether beautiful game, "telling myths about justice and the other things you mention."[85] The game is indeed *for* Phaedrus. Immediately after Phaedrus expresses his admiration for the beautiful rhetoric of Socrates' speech on the soul, he turns to the political dangers of writing.[86] Phaedrus will not be making any journeys to the roof of the cosmos.

Has Socrates accordingly failed to apply his own account of philosophical rhetoric? Or is the underlying theme of the dialogue not the very discontinuity between vision and discourse that is playfully and seriously represented by Phaedrus? To raise an essential question that does not seem to have occurred to Derrida (and others), what would Socrates have said about the soul, and hence about writing, to an admirer of Isocrates? At the end of his second speech, Socrates explains apologetically to Eros that he has been forced to employ poetical expressions because of Phaedrus.[87] Whereas one could not expect a mathematical analysis of the soul, philosophical rhetoric accommodates itself to its immediate audience.

It is the failure to raise questions of this sort that renders the Derridean reading of the *Phaedrus,* for all its brilliance, an example of the "rustic wisdom" that Socrates attributes to the demythologizers of his day.[88] In this connection, what looks like subtlety on Derrida's part is in fact a misunderstanding. Derrida is right to say that Socrates will not bother myths with the scientific naiveté of rationalists. But he is wrong to add that Socrates will not bother *"with* them" (i.e., myths), "in order to free *oneself* for the relation with oneself and the pursuit of self-knowledge."[89] To the contrary, there is no other "relation with oneself" but the mythical, given the inaccessibility to human *logos* of the nature of the personal soul. The transformation of the world into a text, oddly enough, arises from the very neglect of myth that gives rise to the Enlightenment, and by a series of historical peripeties, to postmodern inversions of Enlightenment. The last stage is a consequence of the hyperbolical transformation of Nietzschean play into deconstructive industry: the soul is replaced by *Geist, Geist* by the unconscious, and the unconscious by *différance.*

The conceptualization of the world takes its most dramatic turn with Kant. The method of modern science is generalized into conditions for the possibility of an intellectual world. Plato's "likely story," based upon the mythological inference that the cosmos is good because it is intelligible, is thus replaced by mathematics, and the good is severed from intelligibility. In the next major reversal, the transcendental becomes language. So long as mathematics retains its paradigmatic influence, ontology is equated with semantics. But when mathematics is itself seen as a special dialect of language, semantics is replaced by grammar, or, in its meaningless but fashionable pseudonym, grammatology. Instead of things, we speak of referents; instead of referents, we speak of signifiers signifying themselves. The modern age begins in a dissatisfaction with the unstable and ambiguous relation between vision and discourse; it terminates in the assimilation of vision by discourse. In the postmodern age, seeing is writing. Writing is accordingly blind. The blind postmodern listens for the voice of Being; he hears nothing but the rustling of texts turning their own pages. As d'Alembert is replaced by Rameau's nephew, so Frege is deconstructed into Derrida.

# === 3 ===

## Hermeneutics as Politics

The Derridean deconstruction of "platonism" is the most recent episode in the quarrel between the ancients and the moderns. One may also understand it as the latest convulsion in the death throes of the Enlightenment. I do not mean by this to imply that the convulsion is sufficient in itself to establish the triumph of antiquity. Only moderns participate in a quarrel with antiquity. What remains to be seen is whether a resident of modernity can understand the terms of the quarrel with his ancestors in a way that is not distorted by the aforementioned convulsions. If we grant at the outset that human existence is nothing more than self-interpretation, or in other words that to be is to be interpreted, then understanding becomes, if not a convulsion, the dance of signifiers in the ballroom of our semantical imagination.

I have argued that Derrida's account of the *Phaedrus* goes radically wrong because he fails to appreciate the importance of the most obvious feature of Socrates' criticism of writing. Speech, according to Socrates, is superior to writing for political reasons. We can adjust our conversation to the nature of the interlocutor, in the way that the equity of the judge adjusts the written law to the individual case, whereas writing says the same thing to everyone. No doubt this is the surface of a deeper problem, but we cannot identify the problem unless we begin with the correct surface. As has been wisely said by a spokesman for an older hermeneutical tradition, "the problem inherent in the surface of things, and only in the surface of things, is the heart of things."[1] The surface in the case of the Platonic dialogue is the connection between hermeneutics and politics. Derrida might object that surfaces are a relic of the metaphysics of presence. The correct response to this is that surfaces cannot be deconstructed, since wherever we begin, they are always present *as* the beginning. The deconstruction of a surface accordingly brings us face to face with another surface, and all the more so if, as Derrida holds, there is no interior, that is, no distinction between inside and outside that is not itself the exteriorizing of the always absent trace.

From the very beginning, hermeneutics has been concerned with the communication between gods and mortals. It is no doubt true that at the deepest level, even in classical antiquity, this communication is private rather than public. For that very reason, however, private claims to divine revelation, as soon as they are made public, show themselves to be diverse and mutually inconsistent. The multiplication of publicity is not arithmetical but rhetorical. As a consequence, divine commands either found or dissolve communities. The interpretation of a divine command is necessarily a political act. This link between hermeneutics and politics can be broken only by anarchy or silence, in which case the recipients of divine revelations are transformed from citizens into hermits, wandering in their respective private deserts, and so at the mercy of the adjacent political authorities.

As we saw in the case of Kant, the rise of the historical consciousness, with its presumably keener hermeneutical eye, was accompanied by a lowering in the status of political philosophy. For Kant, to be sure, history is still fundamentally political. By the time of Nietzsche, politics has been transformed into an artistic creation, not to say a fantasy, of the radically transpolitical superman; nor is it by chance that the seventeenth-century hermeneutical depreciation of the imagination as subrational has been replaced by the exaltation of the hermeneutical imagination. The most powerful imagination incarnates itself as the will to power. Politics thus becomes indistinguishable from the private revelation of "the Roman Caesar with the soul of Christ."[2] The stage is set for the doctrine of human existence as the hermeneutics of individual resolution. Kant's moral person, Nietzsche's creative superman who is beyond good and evil, Heidegger's authentic individual whose choice of good and evil is rooted in historical destiny—we see here a steady decline in political self-consciousness, and hence too in the conscience, which becomes ontological rather than moral. The shift from the public to the private, from politics to existential ontology, are like stages in the psychoanalysis of the enlightened European bourgeois, who is liberated from his neuroses at the cost of his soul. Unfortunately, Caesar without the soul of Christ is also without the soul of Caesar.

According to Diotima, Eros binds divine and mortal into a discursive community. For the thoroughly enlightened Freud, Eros binds mortal and mortal into one; it is therefore apolitical.[3] Civilization demands libidinal ties of its own. It therefore interferes with sexuality, with the instincts and aggressivity, and consequently makes us miserable.[4] Freud summarizes his speculations on the conflict between civilization and the individual human being in terms of the excessive demands made upon the ego by the superego:

> it assumes that man's ego is psychologically capable of anything that is required of it, that his ego has unlimited mastery over his id. This is a mistake; and even in what are known as normal people the id cannot be controlled beyond certain limits. If more is demanded of a man, a revolt will be produced in him or a neurosis, or he will be made unhappy.[5]

So much for Enlightenment. However, we have not quite reverted to Rousseau, who advocated Spartan virtue in place of scientific progress as the source of human happiness. Rousseau's criticism of Enlightenment, and his political doctrine of happiness, are inseparable from a restriction on the "pleasure principle." This is the psychological root of Rousseau's rejection of luxury and of his famous observation that "ancient statesmen spoke incessantly of mores and virtue; ours speak of nothing but commerce and money."[6] For Freud, on the contrary, "what decides the purpose of life is simply the programme of the pleasure principle." But

> there is no possibility at all of its being carried through; all the regulations of the universe run counter to it. One feels inclined to say that the intention that man should be "happy" is not included in the plans of "Creation." What we call happiness in the strictest sense comes from the (preferably sudden) satisfaction of needs which have

been dammed up to a high degree, and it is from its nature only possible as an episodic phenomenon.[7]

In Freudian economics, the small change of the orgasm is the cash value of big business. This should be contrasted with an excerpt from the last great attempt to understand history as politics:

> For one calls him happy who finds himself to be harmonious with himself. One can also have happiness as one's standpoint in the contemplation of history; but history is not the basis for happiness. The periods of happiness are empty pages in the book of history. However, there is indeed satisfaction in world history; but this is not what is called happiness. For it is satisfaction of those purposes which stand above particular interests. Purposes having significance in world history must be maintained with energy through abstract will. The world-historical individuals who have pursued such purposes, have indeed satisfied themselves, but they have not wanted to be happy.[8]

By juxtaposing these passages from Freud and Hegel, we do not intend to reject happiness so much as to illustrate the debased notion of satisfaction that is the unintended legacy of the scientific Enlightenment. Freud's interpretation of the "purpose" of life as an unconsciously motivated and episodic phenomenon is the physiological version of Derrida's postmodern conception of life as the continuously self-differentiating "writing" of *différance*. In this context, freedom is discontinuous solipsism. Politics accordingly becomes at once an illusion and an instrument of domination: hence the ease with which so many postmoderns are able to make the connection between Freud and Marx. To reformulate an earlier conclusion: for Kant, history is the product of the dialectic of the passions. But for the postmodern, history has been *used up* by the dialectic of the passions. Whatever may be said about its ontological weaknesses, the philosophy of history that developed in the late eighteenth and early nineteenth centuries was intended to unify human existence in accord with the existentially moral and political teleology of the Enlightenment. This intention is intrinsic to Hegel's pivotal notion of the completion or fulfillment of history. As he put it in the lectures on the philosophy of history,

> what I have stated in a preliminary way and will say hereafter is not merely—not even with respect to our science [*Wissenschaft*]—to be

taken as a presupposition, but as an overview of totality [*des Ganzen*], as the result of contemplation engaged in by us—a result that is known to me, because totality is already known to me.[9]

In the last half of the twentieth century, "completion" or "fulfillment" has been replaced by the notion of "end," in the sense of the finishing off or dissolving of history. Posthistorical man is no longer man *or* historical but an unconscious episode of the discontinuity of time. Spontaneity has lost its ties to reason.

What is now called postmodernism is essentially a French invention, a transformation of various elements of German thought from Kant to Heidegger, in which the initially central position of politics in history is steadily dissolved by what is on the one hand a growing repudiation of the Enlightenment and on the other a carrying out of its program of universality. The separation of politics from history is accompanied by the continuous extension of the scientific study of social and political life on the one hand, and the replacement on the other of the political person or citizen by the "alienated" individual or victim of science. "Being," as it were, is subjected to two conflicting forces, reification and historicity. In this conflict, history is the stronger of the two forces; the *res* is historicized by its constituting concepts, which are no longer expressions of the transcendental ego but of a transient linguistic perspective. Accordingly, the resurrection of Hegel by twentieth-century French philosophers, who were themselves for the most part decisively influenced by Heidegger, did nothing to renew the status of politics in history. Instead, the Marxist doctrine of the withering away of the state, when combined with the influence of the so-called humanism of the writings of the early Marx, served to accentuate the already-powerful "existentialist" preference for pre- or postpolitical individualism.

The reinterpretation of the completeness of history as its end, with the correlative depoliticizing of politics, ostensibly still present in the form of the universal homogeneous state, was decisively prepared by the Hegel interpretation of a unique and eccentric Russian refugee named Alexander Kojève. Thanks largely but not exclusively to his lectures on Hegel at the Ecole des Hautes Etudes in Paris during the 1930s, Kojève influenced two generations of French intellectuals.[10] Among the auditors of his lectures were Maurice Merleau-Ponty, Raymond Aron, Jacques Lacan, Georges Bataille, Andre Breton, and Raymond Queneau. But this scarcely begins to indicate the degree of Kojève's influence in France, to say nothing of other countries. Kojève was a man of enormous intelligence, striking personality, and very wide learning. He came to the study of Hegel with competence in the history of art, Russian mysticism, and various languages and speculative philosophies of the Far East, in addition to European or Western philosophy. It is also relevant for what follows to note that, through the mediation of one of his students, Robert Marjolin, Kojève held a high post in the ministry of foreign economic affairs before and during the regime of General de Gaulle. His political influence in the government—through his membership in the ministry and in the French legation to GATT and to the United Nations, in which he functioned as a self-taught economist of world class—was perhaps second only to that of General de Gaulle. So Kojève told me; and his self-assessment was confirmed for me by Raymond Aron and André Philip, the latter the head of the French legation to GATT. According to Philip, whereas the other participating nations had a specialist for each article of the international treaty on tariffs, France had Kojève, who was a specialist on all the articles.

This brief résumé of Kojève's scholarly and political background is especially necessary in view of what will strike many readers as the bizarre nature of his most characteristic philosophicopolitical doctrines. Kojève is currently in low repute among professors of Hegelianism, who, partly through no fault of their own, have misunderstood his *Introduction to the Reading of Hegel* as an intended contribution to conventional academic scholarship. Despite his lectures at the Ecoles des Hautes Etudes, Kojève was not a professor. It is not so easy to say exactly what he was, although he preferred the term "god." For the time being I leave it at this. It was Kojève's intention to go as far as possible toward the overcoming of the separation between theory and practice and thus to bring about what he called the universal and homogeneous world-state. If a proper definition of a god is one who creates a world, then Kojève's intentions were divine.

To come back to our main theme, Kojève initiated the current emphasis upon conceptions like the end of history and the end of man qua Homo sapiens. On the surface, Kojève's ostensible Hegelianism, however eccentric, seemed to be an effort to complete the program of the Enlightenment. Accordingly, he defined the end of history as the complete satisfaction of characteristically human desire, namely, as the satisfaction of the desire for recognition (the ostensible Hegelian revision of Machiavelli's doctrine of the primacy of the love of glory). In more abstract terms, the end of history is the completion of essential human speech, as recorded in the categories of Hegel's dialecticospeculative logic and as enacted in the process of human history through the triumph of Napoleon at Jena in 1806 (to give here Kojève's "late" teaching). Subsequent history is to be understood not as genuine history or innovation but as the struggle of various sub-Hegelian sects to revolt against historical necessity. This struggle has already in principle been terminated by developments in the United States, Russia, and Japan, which are conspiring to render homogeneous, at least in its essence, what can no longer correctly be called "human existence." For having satisfied his desire and thereby terminated human history, Homo sapiens has reverted to animality or bestiality. Kojève made it plain what this means for the posthistorical individual. In the *German Ideology,* Marx prophesies that the posthistorical individual will hunt in the morning, fish in the afternoon, and in the evening, after dinner, engage in critical philosophy.[11] Kojève, who, like Socrates, was quite urban in his tastes, says nothing of hunting and fishing, but he entirely suppresses philosophy. This is because philosophy has been "completed" in the comprehensive historical discourse now culminating in Kojève's version of the withering away of the state, namely, the universal homogeneous state in which there is no longer anything to say. Having achieved wisdom, which is, as it were, "institutionalized" in the homogeneous discursive emptiness of global existence, human beings transform themselves into peaceful brutes who pass their time in art, sport, and eros. The reference to art should not confuse us; Kojève refers here to the unconscious constructions of birds, beavers, and other brutes. The only dualism in this conception of global brutality is that between the Americans (including the Russians, whom Kojève saw as European Americans) and the Japanese. Americans are "ugly" or incapable of any vestige of human behavior. Japanese are "beautiful" or, more accurately, aesthetic snobs, who thereby retain a certain human element (animals being incapable of snobbery), but only as empty formalism.[12]

It should go without saying that Kojève did not achieve his influence merely by means of these eccentric doctrines. They were backed up by thinking of a conceptual power and attention to detail that struck every competent witness as masterly. And furthermore, his "bizarre" conclusions were not entirely bizarre. That there is an element of truth in them is empirically implied by their influence: to a considerable extent, we owe to these conclusions the most pervasive intellectual fashions of the last thirty years. Philological sobriety is a very admirable quality, but it pales into historical insignificance in the face of philosophical madness, and by this last expression, I mean, of course, *genuinely* philosophical madness, not the idiosyncrasies of café intellectuals. The professor who spends twenty years in the library in an effort to understand three or four sentences of Hegel's *Science of Logic* is pleased by his hard-won ability to correct Kojève's "philological" errors. Nor will I deny that, in crucial cases, Kojève's interpretation of Hegel was philologically unsound. But the philologist is historically irrelevant; the winds of poststructuralism and deconstruction pass him by as he sits in his archives, not, however, without first disturbing the order of the pages of his manuscripts. This being so, in a deeper sense, Kojève is entitled to argue that "philological correctness" is a historical triviality, like the murder of millions of innocent persons in fulfillment of Hegel's observation that history is a slaughter-bench, a bench, in other words, upon which are prepared the feasts of the gods: the residents of the posthistorical utopia.

This is a very harsh and explicitly nonhuman argument. But if we are incapable of facing up to it, we shall neither refute it nor deflect it and shall thereby guarantee our own appearance beneath the executioner's axe. What we especially need to understand in the present inquiry is the extent to which Kojève's teaching, and hence his progeny, for all their talk of Hegelian dialectic and their unending hermeneutical mania (divine or otherwise), are representatives of the triumph of Oriental silence over Western discursivity. Certainly this much can be said: Kojève is for us a paradigm of the dialectical principle that every rational construction, whether mathematical or rhetorical, when carried through to its "logical" conclusion, contradicts itself. Those who insist upon purifying the ambiguous erotic conversations between gods and mortals into a universal and homogeneous discourse produce neither gods nor mortals but a hermeneutic of bestiality, and hence, neither discourse nor silence, but inarticulate noise. This is a process that will be expedited rather than stopped by the technological "Westernizing" of the African and Asian continents.

## II

In his commentary on Hegel's *Phenomenology*, Kojève makes the following striking assertion: "Rameau's nephew *universalized*—that is the *Aufklärung*."[13] The immediate sense of the assertion is that the "hero" of Diderot's novel is the expression of radical individualism, which, as universalized, is separated from the universality of knowledge. In Hegelian terminology, the separation of the universal from the particular is rooted in the certitude of absolute subjectivity or pure insight. To put the point in historical terms, the Cartesian *cogito* certifies itself and its cognitive work by intuition, the residual "platonism" of the *lumen naturale*. But intuition, even when associated with mathematics, is essentially private and silent. It cannot justify itself or distinguish itself from faith. The Enlightenment conception of knowledge as mathematics is thus marked by two vitiating defects. First, the mathematicizing of knowledge is the cause of a rejection of history and individuality. Action is thus conceived according to the paradigm of scientific discovery and technological construction: witness the mathematical sociology of Condorcet. The net result is a suppression of subjectivity. Second, this very universality, as a silent manifestation of faith, is not only incapable of providing a discursive or conceptual form to the historical experience of particularity but, as so incapable, allows particularity to run riot, or to multiply the ungrounded subjective element to infinity.

In sum, the historical individual is torn apart by the process of Enlightenment. Universal form contains an infinitely self-contradictory content, which in turn negates, instead of being synthesized by, that form. The direct political result is the French Revolution: the universal principle of freedom with the content of the Terror. Negativity is also the force of work or production however; out of Robespierre, it generates Napoleon. Hegel rejects the classical axiom that *ex nihilo nihil fit* because he rejects the intelligibility of the separation of Being and Nothing. We cannot enter here into the technical details of Hegel's logic. Suffice it to say that for him, Being and Nothing are abstract moments of the fundamental actuality of Becoming. To paraphrase this for the sake of clarity, Being and Nothing, or position and negation, determine and hence limit one another. The negative is accordingly always, as itself, the negative of something; hence, it is bringing something into being. The serious question remains, however, as to whether this process itself goes on to infinity, thereby negating each step and along with it the significance of the entire process, or whether it is cumulative and self-completing, thereby validating each finite step (which is also a negation) as an element of meaning within the intellectual totality.

According to Kojève's reading of the history of philosophy, there are two fundamental positions, of which the other doctrines are merely anticipations or variations. The choice is between Plato and Hegel.[14] On the Platonic account, wisdom is impossible because of the separation of the eternal from the temporal and the divine from the human. As a result, human discourse becomes *theology*. On the Hegelian account, one denies the separation of the eternal from the temporal, or identifies the two as the structure of the Concept, that is, the philosophical speech about totality or the whole. In this case, human history exemplifies the structure of intelligibility. But this in turn requires that history complete itself, or in other words that the structure of intelligibility reveal itself completely, not to intuition (or revelation) but to human discourse. As a consequence, not merely does man become wise, but he who is able to repeat the totality of this discourse becomes a god. There is then no hidden, separate, or transcendent God, no transcendent (or transcendental) principle of truth and goodness. The death of God is at the same time the death of man or, symbolically, the repudiation of personal immortality.[15] Man dies, to be reborn as a mortal god whose "deathlessness" consists in his wisdom or complete discursive account of totality.

But what is the *proof* of completeness? Kojève's reply is that a discursive account of totality must certify itself, and this is done when it is no longer possible to say anything new.[16] In other words, after the complete speech of wisdom, every attempt to enunciate a new principle, or to provide a new philosophy, results in the repetition of some finite part of the already completed "Hegelian" discourse. As such a finite repetition, it negates itself, that is, contradicts itself. For the development of the complete historical manifestation of intelligibility, and the explanation of this complete manifestation, proceeds by a series of finite negations.[17] The history of philosophy is accordingly a process in which one "position" turns into a more comprehensive doctrine by "negating" itself, that is, by showing an intrinsic limitation that is overcome, or seems to be overcome, by its successor. (It should be noted parenthetically that this process is not linear; there are many false resolutions at each stage.) Again, the discourse of explanation at each stage is of a just-completed historical epoch. There is no separation of truth from history. Those who believe themselves to be speaking of pure forms, God, or the transcendental absolute are in fact speaking about human action.[18] Since the owl of Minerva takes flight only at dusk, or since each philosophical doctrine is the discursive explanation of a just-completed epoch of world history, the comprehensive discourse must explain the comprehensive or final epoch of world history.[19] As comprehensive—that is, as the explanation of the historical epoch that explains all other epochs as their goal, perfection, or justification—the discourse of the sage is circular.[20] Circularity is thus a necessary mark of wisdom. One moves outside the circle only by contradicting oneself, hence by returning within it.

The question of whether history has indeed ended is therefore of crucial importance for Kojève. In discussing his responses to this question (there is more than one), it will be necessary to deal with the question of Kojève's relation to Hegel as well. Did Hegel in fact believe that history had been completed by the triumph of Napoleon at Jena in 1806? More comprehensively, is Kojève's interpretation of Hegel "sound" or is it an idiosyncratic construction from elements of Feuerbach, Marx, Nietzsche, and Heidegger? The decisive reply to these questions is that, as so posed, they are of almost no interest in the present inquiry. What we rather want to know is whether Kojève believed, or, given his own premises, was entitled to believe, that history had ended. We need to know this in order to deepen our understanding of the two main themes of this volume: the Enlightenment and postmodernism. Nevertheless, Hegel's meaning is certainly not irrelevant to our investigation. It is after all as an interpreter of Hegel that Kojève presents himself. In my opinion, the crucial point is this. Hegel was *required* by his own doctrine of the coincidence of human history and the Concept, as well as by the assertion that his teaching is the final and comprehensive *Wissenschaft* or completion of philosophy in wisdom, to believe in the completion of history. If history is not complete in principle, then Hegel's ostensible science is reduced to the level of merely another opinion in the history of philosophy. The Hegelian discourse is open to contradiction, or *Aufhebung,* so long as the future is "open."

As soon as we see this, the connection between postmodernism and the Enlightenment is clarified. The middle term is Hegel, or, more accurately, the dyad Hegel-Marx. Every dyad, in order to avoid lapsing into the bad infinity in which each element in turn asserts a transitory dominance, requires a third, synthesizing or stabilizing term. Kojève aspired to be that third term. Unfortunately, there is an instability within Kojève's own attitude to the end of history, which in my opinion leads his project to shipwreck. Let me state the consequence of this instability at the outset. It is not apparent whether history has been completed in Kojèvian wisdom or dissolved by the manifestly utopian, and therefore *Kantian,* nature of Kojève's project. As soon as we see that history cannot be completed, or, which comes to the same thing, that we can never *know* it to be completed (and hence that the Enlightenment is an abstract form in the process of being negated by its content), we are face to face with a fundamental choice. Either we lapse into silence, or else our discourse becomes the unending chatter of the posthistorical, posthumanist epoch in which *everyone* is dead. There are no more authors, divine or human, but only texts. Or rather, there is only *a* text, spinning itself out indefinitely. Postmodernism is *Rameau's Nephew* universalized.

In his posthumously published study of Kant, Kojève makes the following important assertion about what he calls (after Hans Vaihinger) the "as if" character of Kant's philosophy:

> In effect, experience shows . . . that Man may *live humanly* AS IF a statement which is false, not only in fact or for us[21] but also for itself, were true, on condition of *acting* in such a way as to transform the given world in such a way that the statement that *was* false before this transformation becomes true after it. In other words, the

> Kantian *As-if* has sense and value only as a *Project* of negating
> (=creative or revolutionary) efficacious action.[22]

For our purposes, we may validate Kojève's use of the expression "as
if" by reminding the reader of our discussion of Kant's historical
speculations as well as of the circular nature of his justification of
freedom.[23] Kojève goes on to say that "we" (Kojèvian Hegelians)
admit the empirical existence of that which is objectively irreal, which
we distinguish from the impossible by defining it as the real absence of
the possible. This is nothing other than the assertion of human freedom, but understood as rooted in the contingency of historical action.
For Kant, on the contrary, freedom is rooted in the noumenal; the
phenomenal world, to the extent that it is rational, and hence intelligible, is defined by necessity.[24] We must therefore live in this world
(which is in fact the only world) *as if* the freedom ostensibly accessible
in the noumenal world were also accessible here, or if it is not now, *as
if* it will be accessible in the infinitely distant future.

In order to move from the Kantian system (a halfway house between
Plato and Hegel) to the Hegelian system as explained by Kojève,

> it suffices to eliminate the notion of the thing-in-itself, to introduce
> the notion of teleology or of efficacious free action, to identify causal-
> ity with life . . . and to suppress finally the notion of the continuity of
> the development of the categories of objective reality and empirical
> existence. . . .[25]

But Kojève does not mean that this shift from Kant to Hegel is accomplished by an impersonal (or transcendental) historical necessity. *The
Kantian "as if" is a project of the human will, and so too is the
Kojèvian interpretation of Hegel.* It is true that Kojève conceives of
human history, the sole content of the discursive Concept, or of the
empirical existence of time, as human desire.[26] It is also true that, as
his paradigm of the master-slave dialectic is intended to show, human
desire, which is essentially the desire for recognition (or the desire to
command the other's desire),[27] gives rise to self-consciousness and
thence to discursive reason as the means of satisfying desire. Human
history is then, in Kojève's striking phrase, "the history of desired
desires."[28] Finally, it is true that the relation of each successive at-

tempt to attain satisfaction by an explanatory discourse has a definite logical relation to its antecedent (as for example the discourse of Plato was an attempt to synthesize the Parmenidean thesis and the Heraclitean antithesis). But the relation between the antecedent speech and its successor is not necessary or deductive. The shift from the antecedent to the successor is a negation or an act of human freedom.[29]

It is man, not God or a transcendental Concept, who is negative action.[30] But therefore man is free at each stage of history to terminate the process, whether by ceasing to speak or by resting content with some discursively imperfect version of (real or imagined) political security. In Kojève's technical terminology, the shift from theology to anthropology is necessary for the philosopher only.[31] And this, incidentally, is why Hegel's own discussions of religion cannot unambiguously be read as the atheistic assertions of Kojève's interpretation. Kojève calls this "an essential misunderstanding" that will endure as long as Hegelianism exists,[32] but he does not explain why. We may furnish the explanation: it is a free revolutionary act of effective negativity to give the ambiguous texts the "correct" reading, namely, the reading that renders Hegel's discourse coherent and the comprehensive expression of human satisfaction, that is, satisfaction in one's own complete (and therefore independent) wisdom. Hegel may have spoken ambiguously for prudential reasons, or perhaps to test the intelligence of his readers. In any case, it makes no difference *what* were the intentions of the historical Hegel. If necessary, we must understand Hegel better than he understood himself. Hermeneutics is politics.

Certain crucial inferences may be drawn from the preceding paragraphs. First, not all men are philosophers. There is a distinction between the few and the many, even in the posthistorical, universal, but not *homogeneous* world-state. Kojève asserts, contrary to his interpretation of Hegel's view, that man is not by nature a philosopher and, further, that not every man of action is a philosopher (which Hegel would not deny).[33] It is *not* the nature of human self-consciousness to extend itself until it acquires complete satisfaction. To the contrary, "one must make incessant efforts in order to enlarge more and more self-consciousness, which by nature tends to maintain fixed limits; and I believe that man might very well not make these efforts."[34] The best one could say is that this effort is made by some few men. And contrary to Hegel's frequent implication, these paradigmatic representations of humanity are not all philosophers. In fact, whereas history is understood after the fact by philosophers, it is produced by men of action, of whom the outstanding example is Napoleon.[35] Napoleon was certainly not a philosopher, nor was his empire a universal state of philosophers. Even if it is correct to say that the nonphilosopher participates in philosophy by virtue of residing within the final state, which is the comprehensive *objective* (as opposed to the discursive) manifestation of the concept, the distinction between philosopher and nonphilosopher, or, more sharply still, between wise and unwise, holds good.

At this point, we have to interject a more general observation, and will then proceed with our inferences. The natural distinction between philosophers and nonphilosophers leads to confusion in Kojève's various accounts of the universal homogeneous state. On the one hand, Kojève defines "satisfaction" as follows: to be unique in the world and nevertheless universally valuable.[36] Since Hegelian science is intended to replace religion in the postrevolutionary or posthistorical epoch,[37] it is among other things evident that the satisfaction previously derived by the nonphilosopher from religion must be furnished by entirely secular sources. We have already seen that philosophy is not one of these sources. In an exchange with his friend Leo Strauss on the relation between tyranny and wisdom, Kojève writes as though this were not quite true. The desire of the statesman (hence, we may infer, of Napoleon) for recognition, Kojève tells us, is infinite. He wishes to be recognized by everyone, and in the highest way. Hence he will strive to reduce "to the minimum the number of those who are capable of a servile obeisance only."

> In order to be "satisfied" by their authentic "recognition," he will tend to "liberate" the slaves, to "emancipate" women, to reduce the authority of families over their children by making the latter "adults" as rapidly as possible, by diminishing the number of criminals and of the "disequilibrated" of all sorts, by raising to the maximum the "cultural" level (which obviously depends on the economic level) of all social classes.[38]

On the other hand, in a letter to the same Leo Strauss, as the editor of their correspondence informs us,

> not flinching from Strauss' description of the final state as the state of Nietzsche's "last man," Kojève went on to describe its philosophers as administrators who educated the post-historical "Automatons." He was not here celebrating the joys of the Endstate, or "the realm of freedom;" instead, he was describing a process he saw being actualized in history. And he saw no way out.[39]

But we do not need to rely upon private correspondence in order to bring out the confusion (or contradiction). In the second edition of the *Introduction to the Reading of Hegel*, a now-famous footnote is added on pages 436–37, in which Kojève retracts his earlier statement that man will be made happy at the end of history by "art, love, play, etc. . . . ." Kojève tells us that he now realizes that, if man reverts to the stage of subhuman animality in the posthistorical epoch, then "art, love, play, etc. . . ." must also be given a purely subhuman interpretation. It is therefore wrong to say that man will be made "happy" by these activities. He will rather be merely *content*, since happiness requires self-consciousness, of which subhuman animals are incapable. This is in flat contradiction to the passage from the reply to Leo Strauss, to say nothing of many uncorrected statements in the body of Hegel commentary. In the new note, which expresses views dating from 1948, Kojève informs us that he now realizes "that the Hegelian-Marxist end of history was not still to come, but is already here." In other words, human self-consciousness, as represented *at least* by the philosopher, has now satisfied all of its desire for self-recognition by explaining the satisfied desires for self-recognition of the tyrant who rules the universal homogeneous world-state. I call special attention to the fact that, in the new note, *logos* and discursive wisdom have disappeared, or must have done so if history is indeed at an end and man has been replaced by the subhuman.

As we put together our picture of Kojèvian wisdom, we must bear in mind its two culminating stages, dating from before and after 1948. But in *both* periods, Kojève contradicts himself on the nature of the satisfaction that characterizes the end of history. The surface teaching is that philosophers and nonphilosophers alike will obtain satisfaction in the post-Napoleonic epoch, each in their characteristic fashion. The deeper and more pervasive teaching is that the pursuit of self-consciousness, wisdom, and happiness terminates in unconsciousness, silence, and sub-human contentment. Why is this? In the earlier (pre-1948) stage of his teaching, Kojève attributes the end of man to the complete satisfaction of his characteristic desire by the completion of wisdom as written down in the Hegelian text. In a curious anticipation of Derrida, Kojève says that the empirical existence of science is no longer the historical human being, "but a book of paper, that is to say, a natural entity."

> Certainly the book must be read and understood by men, in order to be a book, that is to say, something other than paper. But the man who reads it no longer creates anything and he no longer changes himself. He is no longer Time with the primacy of the future or history; in other words, he is no longer Man in the strong sense of the word.[40]

This man is the rational animal who has become, through the reading of the book, absolute Spirit, Spirit come-to-be or finished and perfect—"that is to say *dead*."

We can attempt to resolve this contradiction in our texts as follows. The satisfaction brought about for human beings by the efforts of the tyrant to achieve universal recognition lasts only for as long as the tyrant has not actually or entirely succeeded. In other words, as Kojève puts it in his pre-1948 teaching, the universal homogeneous state was present in germ together with the necessary and sufficient conditions for its expansion, according to Hegel, in 1806.[41] Kojève goes on to ask: can we deny that this germ and these conditions are present in our contemporary world? No one can prove that they are not, and hence that wisdom is impossible. We now understand clearly: the commentary on Hegel, with the exception of the post-1948 footnote, is a revolutionary project of Kojève's will, designed to keep history moving in its development toward completion. "Otherwise put, history might stop before attaining its truly impassable goal. One must therefore make efforts in order that it not be so."[42] All of this is stated with full candor in the 1946 article "Hegel, Marx et le Christianisme," from which I have already quoted. Here we read that history has not refuted Hegelianism. The most one could say is that history has not yet de-

cided between the interpretations of the left- and right-Hegelians.
Kojève then concludes:

> In our time, as in the time of Marx, the Hegelian philosophy is not
> a truth in the proper sense of the term. It is less the adequate discur-
> sive revelation of a reality than an idea or an ideal, that is to say a
> "project" which it is a question of realising, and thus to affirm, by
> action. Only what is remarkable is that it is precisely because it is not
> yet true that this philosophy is alone capable of *becoming* true one
> day. For it is alone in saying that truth is created in time thanks to
> error, and that there are no transcendent criteria. . . . And that is why
> history will never refute Hegelianism, but will rest content in choos-
> ing between its two opposite interpretations.
>
> One may therefore say that, for the moment, every interpretation
> of Hegel, if it is more than chatter, is nothing but a program of
> struggle and work (one of these programs calling itself *Marxism*).
> And that is to say that the work of an interpreter of Hegel has the
> signification of a work of political propaganda. Monsieur Niel is
> therefore right to say in closing that "Hegelianism presents some-
> thing other than a purely literary interest." For it may be that, in
> effect, the future of the world, and therefore the sense of the present
> and the significance of the past, depend in the last analysis on the
> manner in which one interprets today the Hegelian writings.[43]

No clearer statement can be found of the connection between
hermeneutics and politics. And this is the second inference from the
previous discussion. Kojève's reading of Hegel, addressed through an
elite audience to the "intellectuals" of his generation, was not intended
as a matter of literary interest (he neither instigated its publication nor
revised the transcripts of his lectures into a finished book). It was not a
contribution to philosophical scholarship but a revolutionary act, an
act of propaganda, and as he wrote in another context, "in a work of
propaganda, it is perfectly legitimate to employ certain artifices, while
at the same time reproaching one's adversaries for making use of
them."[44] To judge Kojève by the standards of the historical archive is
as senseless as to transform postmodernist political hermeneutics into
academic scholasticism.

We come now to a third inference. If history is not yet *fully* over, if it
may never do more than to choose, at some unspecified time, between
two opposing interpretations of its own destiny, if, finally, this destiny
is an as-yet-unfulfilled *project* of the human will, then Kojève is not

simply a Kantian who speculates on the hoped-for but infinitely distant culmination of history, to be brought about not by man but by Providence. Kojève, exactly like Plato, attempts to become a god, to create not merely the future but the comprehensive circle of time understood as the complete discourse that explains, and thereby creates, a human world. It goes without saying that such an ambition entirely transcends the imagination of orthodox Hegel scholars and will certainly strike them as mad. But that is the difference between academicians and philosophers. I must leave it to each reader to decide for himself whether it is better to be a "sound" Hegel scholar or a divine madman. However, there is a price to be paid for madness. In Kojève's case, he paid that price when he became convinced that history was indeed at an end and that it was after all Hegel rather than Kojève who had first understood and explained this.

Despite combining the gifts of the thinker with those of the statesman, Kojève was neither Hegel nor Napoleon. I mean by this that history had deprived him of the chance to fulfill his dream. After 1948, the most Kojève could claim for himself was the subordinate or daimonic task of bringing Hegel's wisdom up to date. What he had initially conceived as theological propaganda for himself, he now saw as in fact propaganda for Hegel. Even worse, if history was effectively over and the talking human animal had been suppressed in favor of the silent brute, what could Kojève make of his own discourse? According to Kojève himself, there is no philosophy in the posthistorical epoch. It must therefore be the case that history has not quite played itself out. To say nothing of others, Kojève was neither an American "animal" nor a Japanese "snob," the two types of posthistorical existence which his experience from 1948 to 1959 had convinced him were the contenders for the final and global determination of the "eternal present."[45] There is absolutely no doubt that he regarded himself as a master, an administrator of automata, and hence as a sage. Unfortunately, his appreciation of his own wisdom, or his self-recognition, must have been qualified after 1948 by his awareness that his error concerning the effective end of history necessarily compromised his understanding of history itself, as that understanding had been recorded by his disciples, and would continue to be recorded after his death.

In an interview that appeared in a French literary periodical shortly
before his death, Kojève spoke as follows:

> It is true that philosophical discourse, like history, is closed. That
> idea irritates. That is perhaps why the *sages*—those who succeed the
> philosophers and of whom Hegel is the first—are so rare, not to say
> nonexistent. It is true that you may not adhere to wisdom unless you
> are able to believe in your divinity. Well, people with a healthy *esprit*
> are very rare. To be divine: what does that mean? It might be Stoic
> wisdom or even play. Who plays? The gods: they have no need to
> react, and so they play. They are the do-nothing gods. . . . I am a do-
> nothing. . . . Yes, I am a do-nothing and I like to play . . . at this
> moment, for example.[46]

Kojève was wont to assign the roles of subordinate deities to his now-
famous disciples, for whom of course he was himself Zeus. For example, he told Merleau-Ponty, who was very handsome: "You will be
Apollo." After 1948, the identities of the Olympians inevitably
changed. Kojève continued to speak of himself as a god, but always, in
his final interview, playfully. "I tell my secretary that I am a god," he
once remarked to me, "but she laughs." Automata are not intended to
laugh. Nor could Kojève have forgotten his earlier teaching, namely,
that in the comic or bourgeois world, from which there is no escape to
an external deity, there is no satisfaction.[47]

The fundamental ambiguity in Kojève's teaching, which is in the
deepest sense an attempt to explain himself to himself, is that it could
not allow him to decide whether he was a *fainéant* god, a philosophical administrator of automata, or a potential Japanese snob. As I
believe he himself understood, his own discourse, with all its brilliance, came very close to silence. "Language is born of discontent.
Man speaks of the nature that kills him and makes him suffer. . . ."[48]
Is this not also true of a merely playful deity whose secretary laughs at
him? A seriously playful god, like Plato, would have said nothing, once
having created the text of the world. Kojève said either too much or
not enough. Had he remained silent, he could never have been refuted.[49] By continuing to speak after 1948, in other words, by continuing to philosophize, he refuted himself. It was necessary, however, for
him to speak, and not merely as a philosopher but as a human being.
This necessity, I believe, follows from the first step in Kojève's interpre-

tation of Hegel, which, as it stands, is an error. Human beings cannot become gods, but neither can they return to the subhuman level of bestiality, because self-consciousness or self-recognition cannot arise from the "struggle for recognition."[50] I cannot *recognize* my own desire, and hence myself, in the desire of another, unless I have already *cognized* it. The human being is human from the outset: we do not "become" human, nor do we cease to be human except by dying. On Hegelian—or at least Kojèvian—grounds, death is indeed death, and not a transition to some other existence.

# III

One cannot easily imagine Leo Strauss giving a newspaper interview in which he announces his divinity. Of course, possibilities arise in Paris that do not exist in Chicago. And there is a certain underlying analogy between the publications by Kojève and those by his friend and closest philosophical rival for the throne of Zeus. Leo Strauss was a German emigré to the United States and, for the major part of his career, a professor at the University of Chicago. Kojève was a Russian emigré to Paris and, despite his series of lectures at the *Ecole des Hautes Etudes* during the thirties, a civil servant, not an academician. In each case, the professional function was a not very successful mask of a certain eccentricity as well as of a separation from (even a transcendence of) their worldly titles. Nevertheless, it must be said that Kojève flaunted his eccentricity, whereas Strauss attempted, and to a surprising extent succeeded in the attempt, to conceal his eccentricity beneath the persona of a medieval rabbi. It is a sufficient comment on the difference between the Parisian intelligentsia and American university professors that Kojève was the most famous and the most admired thinker in France, whereas Strauss, although certainly notorious, was one of the most hated men in the English-speaking academic world. (I was about to strike out the word "hated" as too strong, but in fact it is correct.)

To be sure, a large part of Kojève's eminence stemmed from the greater attractiveness of what was taken as his "left-wing" teaching. Strauss, on the other hand, spoke for the detested "conservatives." In addition, and perhaps equally important, Kojève's expansive and flamboyant arrogance was not only admired by his Parisian audience but also muted by a kind of Slavic openness. Strauss, on the contrary, preached a message of spiritual aristocracy to a nation obsessed with egalitarianism, and the sweetness of his nature was seldom visible to any but his circle of students and close friends. Kojève's very boldness appealed to the contemporary spirit; Strauss counseled prudence and—apparently—a return to the past. Kojève was a philosopher whose originality could not be concealed by his claim to be a mere commentator on Hegel; Strauss was an extraordinary scholar who knew so much more than his colleagues that they regarded him as incompetent. But Kojève was one of those who understood Strauss's true worth, as well as the true nature of the Straussian enterprise, masked by the claim to be a commentator on Plato and the other Socratics, just as Kojève claimed to be a Hegelian.

We take our first step in understanding their long dialogue by comparing two passages from the interchange published under the title "Tyrannie et Sagesse." First, Kojève:

> When I confront the reflections inspired by the dialogue of Xenophon [the *Hiero*] and by the interpretation of Strauss with the lessons that may be derived from history, I have the impression that the relations between the philosopher and the tyrant have always been "reasonable" in the course of historical evolution. . . . The tyrant is entirely correct in not attempting to apply a *utopian* philosophical theory . . . because he lacks the time to fill the *theoretical* lacunae between utopia and reality. As for the philosopher, he too is correct when he refuses to push his theories to the point at which they rejoin the questions raised by current political affairs. If he were to do this, he would have no more time to occupy himself with philosophy, and would therefore have no more claim to give *politico-philosophical* advice to the tyrant. The philosopher is right to leave to a pleiade of intellectuals of all nuances . . . the job of bringing about a rapprochement at the theoretical level between his philosophical ideas and political reality. . . .[51]

In other words, the task of a god is to make a world that is safe for philosophy; the task of his worshippers (disciples) is to fill in the details.

The next passage is from Strauss's reply to Kojève's discussion-review of his commentary on Xenophon:

Plato would never have decided, even provisionally, in favor of the Spartan regime if the preoccupation of the philosopher for a good political order had been absolutely inseparable from the preoccupation that guided his political philosophy. In what then does political philosophy consist? In convincing the city that the philosophers are not atheists, that they do not profane all that the city regards as sacred, that they respect that which the city respects, that they are not subversive, and finally that they are not irresponsible adventurers but good citizens and even the best of the citizens. That is the defense of philosophy which was always and everywhere necessary, regardless of the political regime, because, as Montesquieu put it, "in all the countries of the world, people want morality" and "human beings, rogues in particulars, are, in the large, very honest: they love morality." . . . This defense of philosophy before the tribunal of the city was achieved by Plato with a resounding success (Plutarch, *Nicias*, ch. XXXIII), of which the effects have continued down through the ages up to our own time. . . .[52]

Both texts make entirely evident that political philosophy is the public appearance of philosophy, or, differently stated, that genuine philosophy cannot in the nature of things make a public appearance but must always present itself in an accommodated form. Kojève gives reasons based on the correct use of philosophical leisure, whereas Strauss announces a tension, even a contradiction, between the true interests of the philosopher and those of the city. As a son of the Enlightenment, decadent perhaps but still a son, Kojève holds out the prospect of a historical rapprochement between these two interests. Strauss, if not an outright opponent of the Enlightenment, gives us no reason to believe that the historical—and hence the political—resolution of the conflict between philosophy and politics will ever occur. But let us note here a point of crucial importance, which will gradually become more evident. The public advocacy of philosophical accommodation to the city is already a rejection of philosophical accommodation to the city. The initial impression that Kojève is historically up to date whereas Strauss is an anachronism must be modified by Strauss's peculiar candor. Strauss, too, is a son of the Enlightenment in this sense. That is his recognition of the contemporary circumstances.

I remind the reader that for Kojève, the distinction between philosophers and nonphilosophers continues to hold good in the posthistori-

cal epoch, at least until the disappearance of humanity in the proper
sense of the term. For him, then, exactly as for Strauss, political philosophy in the genuine sense is philosophical propaganda, albeit propaganda that may be given the salubrious name of philosophical rhetoric. It is true that Strauss restricts the use of the term "propaganda" to
apply to Machiavelli and his successors, or in other words to modernity understood as Enlightenment.[53] For Strauss, the crucial step in
Enlightenment is the struggle against revealed religion. Speaking of
Machiavelli and his great modern students, Strauss says:

> we no longer understand that in spite of great disagreements among
> those thinkers, they were united by the fact that they all fought one
> and the same power—the kingdom of darkness, as Hobbes called it;
> that fight was more important to them than any merely political
> issue.[54]

Strauss applies the term "propaganda" to the efforts of these thinkers
(who themselves were merely emulating Jesus and the early Christians)
in order to suggest that the attack lacks substance. Like Kojève, who
was obviously not lacking in the aforementioned understanding,
Strauss regarded religion as irrefutable, but not for Kojève's reason.
For Kojève, a speech is refuted when it contradicts itself (as for example, when it claims to explain everything but does not). As for most
moderns, possibility is for Kojève higher and more decisive than
actuality—until the end of history. And religion is a form of silence, or
attribution of genuine speech to an inaccessible deity who cannot be
contradicted. If one insists upon remaining silent, however, one becomes invisible or historically irrelevant.

Strauss makes the different point that mockery alone cannot refute
religion (and certainly not historical irrelevance), but neither can the
mere act of will to reject it on behalf of philosophy and science. Both
philosophy and religion rest upon an act of the will; their antagonism
is ultimately moral. This is because, in order to refute religion, "the
merely given world must be replaced by the world created by
man. . . ."[55] Man must become genuinely wise, and therefore omnipo-
tent: he must become genuinely divine. Needless to say, Strauss regarded this as impossible. Despite its moral motivation, the Enlightenment is a form of propaganda because it belittles its opponent and

exaggerates its own power, or is carried away by the charm of scientific and technical competence. At the same time, it is essentially vulgar, because it lowers the standards of morality or of spiritual refinement in the pursuit of popular success. It is not difficult to see that this critique was intended by Strauss to apply to Kojève as well. We must observe, however, that if philosophy is rooted in an act of will, then it cannot demonstrate its own truth. This holds good for Plato as well as for Machiavelli. To quote Strauss:

> Philosophy in the strict and classical sense is the investigation of the eternal order or of the cause or eternal causes of all things. I suppose therefore that there is an eternal and unchangeable order in which history takes place, and which is not in any way affected by history. . . . This hypothesis is not evident in itself. . . .[56]

This passage, and others like it in the Straussian canon, place him in a compromised position from which he is unable to extricate himself. The "classical" (or Straussian) hypothesis is *an act of will* and hence a moral matter. But the essence of the "modern" (Machiavellian or Kojèvian) hypothesis is the equally moral contention that the classical hypothesis is evil or has evil consequences. One cannot therefore confirm the classical hypothesis without refuting the modern hypothesis. But so long as one resists the Kojèvian inference that history is already at an end, this is in principle impossible, as was made explicit by Kant.

I therefore conclude that it is legitimate to call "classical" (or "Straussian") political philosophy "propaganda" with the intention not of insulting or belittling but rather of making explicit that it, too, is arguing from an indemonstrable moral perception, or claiming to know what it does not and cannot know. This claim is "conservative" in the sense that it takes the testimony of modern history to be sufficiently terrifying to justify the rejection of Enlightenment (or perhaps at a minimum, a return to the prudential Enlightenment of Bacon and Rousseau—but this is unclear). The modern claim is "radical" and indeed revolutionary, since it continues to believe in the possibility of the eventual triumph of Enlightenment, or at a minimum, that the struggle for Enlightenment is its own justification, whether or not it succeeds, just as freedom, or Kantian spontaneity, is its own justification.

Furthermore, it should not be forgotten that the "classical" doctrine is at war on *two* fronts. Perhaps even deeper for Strauss than the quarrel between the ancients and the moderns is that between Athens and Jerusalem.[57] Strauss identifies as coeval with philosophy the question *quid sit deus?*[58] But he never suggests that the philosopher, the archetypical citizen of Athens, is also a resident of Jerusalem. To the contrary, he never deviates from the view stated in the following words apropos Jehudah Halevi, but in such a way as to make clear that he is also speaking for himself: "Halevi knew all too well that a genuine philosopher can never become a genuine convert to Judaism or to any other revealed religion."[59] In a later formulation:

> According to the Bible, the beginning of wisdom is fear of the Lord; according to the Greek philosophers, the beginning of wisdom is wonder. We are thus compelled from the very beginning to make a choice, to take a stand.[60]

No competent student of Leo Strauss was ever in doubt as to his teacher's choice. When I once asked him if he seriously doubted that Descartes was a believer, he replied with passion: "philosophers are paid not to believe!" In his more playful moments, he would answer questions of that sort as follows: "Believe! Believe! As Lessing said, 'how I wonder what that word means!'" Strauss's own respect for and attention to the detailed statements on behalf of revealed religion were primarily intended as extensions of his own elusive propaganda for philosophy, or what he would have preferred to call his philosophical rhetoric. It was part of his attempt as a political philosopher to convince the city that philosophers are not atheists, "that they do not profane all that the city regards as sacred." At the same time, it does not follow that there was not for Strauss a real problem in choosing between Jerusalem and Athens. Neither does it follow that Strauss was an unmitigated "ancient" or resident of Athens. By publishing these observations, and indeed by devoting virtually his entire professional career to an exposé of the political rhetoric of philosophers, or the distinction between their esoteric and exoteric teachings, Strauss tacitly but unmistakably identified himself as a modern, and hence as a son, or stepson, of the Enlightenment. Strauss's critique of Kojève, and hence his defense of the classics, has to be understood as a defense of the conservative dimension of the Enlightenment. This fact also explains the occasionally noted similarity between his and Nietzsche's attack on modernity.[61] We will, of course, also have to understand the difference.

We must now turn to the crucial question: Why did Strauss devote so much effort to publicizing the existence of an esoteric teaching in the Western tradition? On the one hand, these efforts brought him and his disciples an almost unmitigated ridicule, not to say persecution, at least in the English-speaking academy. On the other hand, such publicity seems to violate the moral and prudential principles of the practice of esotericism itself. The first point is notorious and requires no documentation. The passage cited above on the nature of political philosophy is perhaps sufficient to confirm the second point, but to be certain, I will support it with other texts. For example, let us consider Strauss's description of the difference between the "early," or classical, and "later," or modern, esotericists. Those who came before the Enlightenment accepted as natural the distinction between the "wise" and the "vulgar." As a consequence, they denied the power of public education to efface this distinction, or to overcome the hatred of the majority for philosophy. Accordingly, they regarded concealment of genuinely philosophical views as necessary, "not only for the time being, but for all times."[62]

In the later seventeenth century, on the other hand, the view arose that suppression of free inquiry was a result of political immaturity, which could be removed by the progress of popular education:

> They concealed their views only far enough to protect themselves as well as possible from persecution; had they been more subtle than that, they would have defeated their purpose, which was to enlighten an ever-increasing number of people who were not potential philosophers. It is therefore comparatively easy to read between the lines of their books.[63]

One could reasonably suggest that, as a post-Enlightenment philosopher, Strauss lived in an epoch that, at least in the West, permitted virtually complete freedom of speech, with the possible exception of speech about esotericism. Even with the latter qualification, however, which was applied only in "liberal" circles, Strauss was permitted not only to publish his books but to achieve a position of considerable eminence in the academic world. The disbelief and ridicule that his views on esotericism engendered, and that were in any case intensified by his critique of social science, could therefore be taken as a consequence of the invalidity of the "early" or strong esotericist thesis. Disbelief concerning esotericism shows both that there is no need for it and that historical accuracy requires that we become familiar with the phenomenon.

In a rare passage that speaks to this point by raising the moral issue involved, Strauss evidently takes precisely this tack:

> Maimonides himself justified his transgression of the talmudic injunction against writing on the esoteric teaching of the Bible by the necessity of saving the law.

Maimonides is referring here to the disruption of the oral tradition because of the long diaspora.

> In the same way we may justify our disregard of Maimonides' entreaty not to explain the esoteric teaching of the *Guide* by appealing to the requirements of historic research. For both the history of Judaism and the history of medieval philosophy remain deplorably incomplete, as long as the secret teaching of Maimonides has not been brought to light. The force of this argument will become even stronger if we take into consideration that basic condition of historic research, namely, freedom of thought. Freedom of thought, too, seems to be incomplete as long as we recognize the validity of any prohibition to explain any teaching whatsoever. Freedom of thought being menaced in our time more than for several centuries, we have not only the right but even the duty to explain the teaching of Maimonides, in order to contribute to a better understanding of what freedom of thought means, i.e. what attitude it presupposes and what sacrifices it requires.[64]

If this statement were taken as a frank assertion of Strauss's own views, we would have to conclude that he accepted the contemporary liberal principle of unreserved freedom of speech and hence that he was, as it were, an Enlightenment philosopher. There are, however, difficulties in our drawing this conclusion from our passage. First, Maimonides did not advocate the publication of the secret teaching of the Bible. Instead, he stated that he would publish a *concealed* account of that teaching, as Strauss himself makes entirely clear. Maimonides reveals *that* there is a secret teaching, and he states the way in which he has himself concealed it. He does not reveal the secret teaching itself. The teaching is preserved from oblivion only for those few who are able to follow Maimonides' detailed account of his method of conceal-ment and who possess in addition the ability to "decipher" the hidden teaching. As Strauss puts it, Maimondes' "intention in writing the *Guide* was that the truths should flash up and then disappear again."[65]

Despite Strauss's extensive discussions in various places of Mai-monides' intentions and methods, he never did reveal "the secret *par excellence* of the *Guide*."[66] Strauss takes the reader partway through the silver filigree-work covering the golden interior of the *Guide;* he does not complete the journey into the interior itself.[67] A major criti-cism leveled against Strauss is precisely that he never tells us what is the secret teaching of the author he purports to be explaining, or else that the secret teaching is obvious and even platitudinous. Perhaps Strauss did not himself *know* the secret teaching; perhaps there was no secret teaching, but only a pretense. Or perhaps those who cannot find that teaching in Strauss's writings are themselves lacking in the requi-site subtlety. But if the last possibility is the right answer, then Strauss could hardly be practicing either the concealment or the revelation characteristic of the Enlightenment.

My own view on the matter is that Strauss's "revelation" of esoteric teachings, with respect to the "early" or pre-Enlightenment philoso-phers, *was itself exoteric*. In a real sense, it makes no difference whether Strauss did not know the original teaching or whether we cannot discern it. In order to understand Strauss himself, we need to start from his own practice of exotericism and the content of his political rhetoric. There would be no reason for him to suppress the partly hidden views of the Enlightenment thinkers, now that we live in an era of free thought (despite its being endangered from "outside"). These views were intended to be discerned, in order that the very society be created in which we now dwell. Conversely, if Strauss was not a son of the Enlightenment, it would be morally incumbent upon him to reveal their pernicious doctrines in order to criticize them. This criticism might take both an open and a hidden form. If, however, Strauss was an adherent of "early" esotericism, the situation changes.

In sum, whatever Strauss' private views, the key to his thought lies in his public, i.e. his published, views. The depths are contained in the surface. If the truths flash up, they must come to the surface.

Allow me to remind the reader at this point that we are not discussing a matter of "literary style" alone. The question of the exact nature of Strauss's political rhetoric takes us to the heart of his own deepest intentions. It alone allows us to approach, if not to determine, the inner content of his political philosophy. In his own words,

> in its highest form, communication is living together. The study of the literary question is an important part of the study of society. . . . The literary question properly understood is the question of the relation between society and philosophy.[68]

We cannot understand Strauss's attitude toward the Enlightenment, and hence his criticism of Kojève—or in more fundamental terms, what we can learn from him about the question of postmodernism, or our own future—unless we understand his rhetoric. Despite certain qualifications as to the impossibility of explaining parables by parables, Strauss in fact follows an analogy to Maimonides' own method: "the interpretation of the *Guide* cannot be given in ordinary language, but only in parabolic and enigmatic speech." This is true, not merely because, as Strauss tells us Maimonides asserts, "the explanation of secrets is . . . not only forbidden by law, but also impossible by nature."[69] It is true because Strauss's avoidance of parables and enigmas is itself a parable and an enigma.

To summarize, Strauss attempts to practice "early" esotericism in the language of the post-Enlightenment. Despite his clear recognition that one cannot simply return to the views or actions of the wise men of classical antiquity, Strauss shares their fundamental principle. Consider the following passage from a later essay devoted to the problem of esotericism. Strauss is discussing the criticism of an open-minded critic who has been influenced by the teaching of Alexandre Kojève, namely, Yvon Belaval:

> Belaval raises the further question whether every philosophy finds itself in conflict with politics or only dogmatic philosophies. I can only repeat that there is a necessary conflict between philosophy and

> politics if the element of society necessarily is opinion, i.e. assent to opinion. . . .[70]

As one could restate this, if Plato is correct, or more broadly, if the Socratic teaching about the permanent and necessary conflict between the city and philosophy is always true, then of course adherence to the Enlightenment is out of the question. Strauss's task then becomes that of "deconstructing" the Enlightenment while employing the language of the Enlightenment. Philosophy can *never* speak frankly in the public marketplace (or in the republic of letters), as is represented by Plato's absence from his own dialogues.

For the sake of variety, and in order to illustrate another side of Strauss's interests, we may document this point from his studies of Xenophon, the understanding of whom he regarded as an important preliminary to the understanding of Plato. Speaking of *Memorabilia* III, 8, Strauss says:

> It would not be wholly unreasonable to expect that the conversation with Charmides which immediately succeeded the conversation with Glaucon would in its turn be immediately succeeded by a conversation with Plato. But Xenophon knew better; he only points to the possibility of a conversation with Plato; the peak is missing; the ascent has come to an end.[71]

According to Strauss, the same principle is followed by Xenophon in his presentation of Socrates. Xenophon conceals those conversations in which Socrates discusses the most important "what is" questions, that is, questions about the natures of beings. Xenophon never explains Socrates' blissful activity.[72] He thus reveals by silence "the strictly private, partnerless character of Socrates' dancing."[73] And finally, Socrates' "whole wisdom can be shown without disguise only 'in fun'; so close is the connection between wisdom and laughter."[74]

The general outlines of the Straussian enigma are now clear. He is practicing something like Xenophontic or Maimonidean esotericism in the language of the post-Enlightenment scholar, at least until the very last period of his published works, in which the style of Al Farabi comes to the fore. It was often said of Strauss that he wrote like a Talmudist. But this is after all not quite right. Unlike the Talmudist,

Strauss gave the appearance, both personally and in print, of great frankness—not always, to be sure, but often enough to mislead. I do not mean that Strauss suppressed his conversations—or monologues— on the natures of the beings. I mean that his public defense of the classics, his notorious "conservatism," his quasi-Nietzschean critique of modernity, and his apparent revelations of secret teachings were the expression of a political program. Strauss, exactly like Kojève, prac- ticed the rhetoric of political propaganda. However, since his inten- tions were different from Kojève's, so too was his rhetoric. These differences are necessarily rooted in his conception of philosophy, to which we now turn.

We remind ourselves that Kojève regarded himself as a wise man, not to say a god. He claimed, whether on Hegel's behalf or, somewhat esoterically, under a Hegelian mask, to have carried out the challenge in Hegel's assertion that one cannot love wisdom unless one knows what one loves. Strauss's public account of philosophy, and thus of himself, was not quite the reverse of, but certainly in striking opposi- tion to, Kojève's claims. The difference in their performance is thus hardly surprising. Kojève gave detailed replies to the most important "what is" questions of philosophy. Strauss insisted that philosophy is not the answering but the raising of fundamental questions (which, for the most part, he identified only obliquely as equivalent to the partially concealed main themes of the Platonic dialogues). Whereas Kojève explicitly identified himself with Hegel, Strauss tacitly identified him- self with Socrates.

According to Strauss, "the 'experience of history' does not make doubtful the view that the fundamental problems . . . persist or retain their identity in all historical change." To grasp these problems as problems is to free oneself from historical limitations on the mind:

> No more is needed to legitimize philosophy in its original, Socratic sense: philosophy is knowledge that one does not know . . . or aware- ness of the fundamental problems and therewith, of the fundamental alternatives regarding their solution that are coeval with human thought.[75]

The same point is made in even stronger terms in the earlier reply to Kojève, from which I have already quoted. Strauss denies Kojève's claim that the alternative to intersubjective—that is, historical—confirmation of philosophical views is the particularity of the sect. In the original meaning of the term, philosophy is *zetetic,* or skeptical, "nothing other than real consciousness . . . of the fundamental and comprehensive problems." In thinking about these problems, it is impossible not to be attracted "toward one or the other of the rare typical solutions." In the absence of wisdom, the philosopher is transformed into a sectarian at the moment in which his subjective certitude concerning a solution equals or exceeds his subjective certitude of its problematicity.[76]

Strauss identified this view of philosophy with the representation in the Platonic dialogues of Socratic ignorance:

> Socrates, then, viewed man in the light of the mysterious character of the whole. He held therefore that we are more familiar with the situation of man as man than with the ultimate causes of that situation. We may also say he viewed man in the light of the unchangeable ideas, i.e. of the fundamental and permanent problems. For to articulate the situation of man means to articulate man's openness to the whole.[77]

The identification of the Socratic ideas as "problems" is obviously related to the assertion, cited earlier, that the eternal and unchangeable order, upon which philosophy in the strict and classical sense depends, is an assumption or supposition.[78] Socrates' awareness of the articulated whole is the presupposition of the perception of particular things.[79] Hence philosophy, the attempt to replace opinions about the whole by the knowledge of the whole—that is, knowledge of "the natures in their totality"[80]—is the attempt to acquire knowledge of its own suppositions, presuppositions, or awareness of "the mysterious character of the whole." In other words, it is prophecy or divine madness:

> For moderation is not a virtue of thought: Plato likens philosophy to madness, the very opposite of sobriety or moderation; thought must be not moderate but fearless, not to say shameless. But moderation is a virtue controlling the philosopher's speech.[81]

This passage, incidentally, explains with Socratic or Xenophontic brevity the difference between Strauss and Nietzsche. But it also enables us to grasp the crucial difference between Plato and Aristotle. Strauss says that, for the latter, "there is a natural harmony between the whole and the human mind. Man would not be capable of happiness if the whole of which he is a part were not friendly to him."[82] In other words, the whole is not for Aristotle a supposition; the rejection of the Socratic ideas is a rejection of the thesis that man may possess knowledge of the fundamental problems only, but not of the answers to these problems. Furthermore, it explains why Aristotle's writings contain far more "technical" discussions, analyses, and arguments than do the Platonic dialogues. Since Aristotle believed himself to be in harmony with the whole, he had confidence in his technical analyses of the parts of the whole. Aristotle is the father of professional philosophy in this sense. His twentieth-century descendants no longer speak of the whole, but in its place they furnish political rhetoric or ideology. Strauss did not resemble an "Aristotelian" philosopher; he presented very few "technical" arguments and no answers to "what is" questions. Whether or not he was capable of this sort of technical work, he tacitly offered the justification of Plato, and even of Xenophon.

Strauss's conception of the Platonic position is perhaps best captured if we combine the passages cited above with the following remark, intended as a summary of the *Theatetus-Sophist-Statesman* trilogy, but with special reference to the *Statesman:*

> For Plato, knowledge proper or striving for knowledge proper is philosophy. Philosophy is striving for knowledge of the whole, for contemplation of the whole. The whole consists of parts; knowledge of the whole is knowledge of all parts of the whole as parts of the whole. Philosophy is the highest human activity, and man is an excellent, perhaps the most excellent, part of the whole. The whole is not a whole without man, without man's being whole or complete. But man becomes whole not without his own effort. . . .[83]

This passage has many resonances for us. First, the Platonic conception of philosophy as knowledge of the whole is obviously rooted in a view of the unity of philosophy and science. It does not seem that we can return to this conception without jettisoning modern science. Strauss might reply that the classical conception of science is addressed to a different level of study of the parts of the whole than is modern science. But modern science presupposes the irrelevance and even erroneousness of a large part, not to say all, of this conception and its results. In addition, if we grant that classical science does address itself to a different level of study than does modern science, it would seem to be incumbent upon Strauss to produce some of the "what is" *answers* that are to be found, in however hypothetical a form, in the Platonic dialogues. Strauss would never have denied—indeed, he would have insisted—that there is a difference in rank between himself and Plato. Fair enough, but if this difference in rank is commensurate with the absence of all, or virtually all, technical discussion in Strauss's work, then how can we take seriously his claim to have understood Plato well enough to serve as our guide into the initial steps of the distinction between the exoteric and the esoteric teaching? Strauss comes dangerously close to implying that *all* technical discussions are exoteric—and this is unsatisfactory.

Furthermore, the passage cited above introduces the necessity of practical knowledge, hence its separation as well as its inseparability from theoretical knowledge. Strauss also says that "the whole human race, and not any part of it, is self-sufficient as a part of the whole, and not as the master or conqueror of the whole." If this was indeed Plato's view, it hardly replies to the claim of the founders of modernity that nature is *unfriendly,* and even *hostile,* to the human race. Was it Plato's ignorance of modern science, or his exoteric and ameliorative inclinations, that led him to view the human race as self-sufficient? The incompleteness of the whole is evidently extended on either hypothesis to the practical as well as to the theoretical domain. The initially hypothetical nature of philosophy, together with the ostensible impossibility of achieving answers to fundamental philosophical problems, guarantees the permanent incompleteness of philosophy. Even worse, it reduces our knowledge of the fundamental problems themselves to the level of opinion. As an act of the will, or a presupposition by which (as Socrates says in the *Philebus*) the philosopher exalts himself, philosophy, in the "strict" or "classical" sense, does not exist.

If Strauss understood as little as he claimed to understand of the Platonic dialogues, then he was not a philosopher as he himself defined the term. And such, incidentally, was his own view, although this is evidently unknown to his less competent disciples, who compound the absurdity by assuring us that they do not at all understand Strauss himself—as though this were a reason either for respecting Strauss or taking them seriously. All things considered, it seems to be entirely proper to contend that Strauss, like Plato, was in fact a Kantian. On Straussian grounds, we cannot be said to be living in a postphilosophical world, because there never was a philosophical world. If mathematicians dream that they are awake, "philosophers" are awake but befuddled with daydreams. It looks very much as though Strauss sanctions, or cannot defend himself against being taken to sanction, the view that *all* fundamental problems, and not just their possible fundamental solutions, are acts of the will. In this case, however, there are *no* philosophical problems, but only those problems by which we will ourselves to be bedeviled.

This is the difficulty of attempting to practice classical esotericism in the rhetoric of the late Enlightenment. The former requires a genuine concealment of philosophy, or at least the presentation of exoteric technical discussions of an apparently philosophical nature that will establish one's credentials, as it were, and enable one to engage in an effective exoteric teaching. The latter requires a still more technical, not to say systematic, exoteric teaching, as well as a lightly veiled esoteric argument for scientific Enlightenment, and hence for modern science in one or another of its philosophically justifiable forms. Strauss gives us none of these. Instead, we are offered prescientific arguments, or exhortations, for long-since rejected, not to say intrinsically absurd, doctrines like natural right and the philosophical significance of the rural gentleman. I will have more to say on this point below. Here it should be observed that those who will themselves to be postmodernists, let us say Derridean deconstructionists, have nothing to fear from the rhetorical bolts of Strauss and his less thoughtful disciples. They cannot be refuted by rationality, since there is no legitimate criterion by which to choose between reason and revelation—or therefore between reason and absurdism. In "deconstructing" the exoteric dogmatisms of the history of philosophy, Strauss would appear to have deconstructed himself as well.

Strauss's account of the phenomenon of esotericism, then, is in my opinion (and also in Kojève's) generally accurate—as the description of a historical phenomenon. Those who attack or even ridicule him on "philological" or "historical" grounds merely reveal their own obtuseness and incompetence. Often they show that they have not even grasped the nature of Strauss's thesis, as for example when they argue that a given philosopher did not practice esotericism because his publications are full of conventional assertions, "typical of the time in which he wrote." The serious question is not *whether* philosophers practiced esotericism—every thoughtful human being does so to one degree or another—but *why*. One last remark in this series of observations. I do not myself believe that Strauss's private views cannot be inferred from his publications. But if he in fact had a still more secret teaching that is indiscernible to mere mortals, this is irrelevant to us. Complete silence is completely invisible. Strauss, like Kojève, said either too much or not enough. I must rest my case on the evidence. On the one hand, Strauss had a political program for the preservation of philosophy in the "strict" or "classical" sense. On the other, he attempted to defend this program by the use of the rhetoric of Enlightenment (up to his last publications). To compound the problem, his conception of [the nature of] classical philosophy was inadequate because at bottom Nietzschean or modern, and therefore postmodern.


# IV

Leo Strauss cites the observation of Sir Thomas More that "Christ wept twice or thrice, but never find we that he laughed so much as once." Strauss goes on to say that Plato's or Xenophon's Socrates

> left us no example of weeping, but on the other side, he left us example of laughing. The relation of weeping and laughing is similar to that of tragedy and comedy. We may therefore say that the Socratic conversation and hence the Platonic dialogue is slightly more akin to comedy than to tragedy.[84]

One wonders why Strauss says "slightly." Although Socrates laughs "twice or thrice," he is invariably playful, and surely the playful is more akin to the comic than to the tragic, or rather, it is not akin to the tragic at all. Strauss's formulation of the point is actually derived, in my opinion, from his thesis that speech must be moderate. But if the dialogues are philosophical, even exoteric presentations of philosophy, the truth must flash out, and we may say, contrary to Strauss's implication, that it does flash out sufficiently to show us that philosophical speech, as a whole (and philosophy is always concerned with the whole), is immoderate or divinely mad. None of this has anything to do with the number of times that Socrates laughs aloud. But if we were to grant Strauss's assessment, the "noble reserve" and the "calm grandeur of the classics", for which, Strauss tells us, "a natural preference for Jane Austen rather than for Dostoievski" prepares us,[85] would in itself prevent us from anticipating that the classical philosopher will do much in the way of laughing or weeping.

Bearing in mind previous discussions, including that in chapter 2, it seems safer to say that the Platonic dialogues are like comedy depending upon the degree to which they make accessible the divine standpoint. Whereas laughter is more akin to playfulness than to serious labor, one need not laugh while playing. Kojève described himself as a playful god, not a laughing god. The Athenian Stranger, perhaps with a suppressed smile, contends that the divine is serious and the human is playful. He does not say that the gods do not laugh. Perhaps Kojève's failure to laugh while playing is a sign of the defective nature of his divinity, as I suggested in a previous section of this chapter. These are deep waters. Perhaps, however (and no more than "perhaps"), if we follow out this line of thought—one which is suggested by Strauss himself—we may reach the following result. The "noble reserve" and "calm grandeur" of the classics is tragic or comic depending upon whether philosophy is possible or not. If philosophy is *not* possible, except as a moral choice or act of the will, then the moderation and seriousness of the Platonic hero is not just laughable but absurd. In this case, there is no difference between the serious and the playful: everything is permitted.

Strauss (rightly) attributes to Nietzsche the view that the theoretical analysis of the relativity of all comprehensive views, if publicly disseminated, "would make human life itself impossible." He suggests that Nietzsche, "to avert the danger to life," could choose between a strict Platonic esotericism, or a denial of theory, and the assertion of the subservience of thought to fate. "If not Nietzsche himself, at any rate his successors adopted the second alternative."[86] As we have seen, Nietzsche's view of the fatality of theoretical analysis for life is more or less Strauss's view. Which of the alternatives he poses for Nietzsche did he himself choose?

In order to answer this question, we have to understand that Strauss's public persona as a conservative spokesman for classical natural right was intended by him as a salutary but exoteric doctrine. As I will show, it is hypothetical or manifestly based upon an act of the will. Strauss's frankness is sufficient to allow us to detect the rhetorical foundation of his political program. Within his powers, he wished to create a world fit for the habitation of philosophers and nonphilosophers alike. As a resident of the twentieth century, he had necessarily to adapt his rhetoric to his own time. This required an ingenious mixture of frankness as well as of devices suited to prepare (in Kojève's expression) "a pleiade" of disciples who would carry out the practical work. Those who regard such a project as "immoral," or who believe themselves to be technicians of scientific progress, have either abdicated their political responsibility or are simply unconscious agents of the world-constituting projects of others. One can also say on Strauss's behalf that technical ingenuity is the easiest and the least interesting part of philosophy. What is of utmost importance is the comprehensive intention. The two questions that have to be raised concerning Leo Strauss's teaching—questions whose validity he himself would have recognized—are whether his intentions were sound and his rhetoric suitable to the task. With respect to the second, Strauss faced a virtually insuperable difficulty. He could hardly make an impression on the twentieth-century intellectual by speaking entirely in the style of Xenophon or Maimonides, and he lacked the divine madness of Plato. His lack of technical genius was not a decisive defect with respect to the "purificatory" or exoteric component of his teaching. This lack could be compensated for by a judicious employment of political daring, of which the primary example was his publication of the harsh truths of esotericism. This satisfied the taste of the modern consciousness for novelty and also provided a basis on which to produce infantry troops consisting of those who would believe themselves to be gods merely by their proximity to the revelation of an unrevealed and justifying doctrine. Unfortunately, it also allowed the truth "to flash up" and thus to reveal the thoroughly modern presuppositions of Strauss's antiquarian rhetoric.

My thesis is that Strauss is himself almost a Nietzschean, but not quite: he comes closer to Kant in the roots of his thought. It should also be noted that his characterization of Nietzsche fits Heidegger more closely, but this is a minor point, and turns upon how we interpret the relationship between the will and fate, or what Nietzsche meant by *amor fati*. In my opinion, Nietzsche, like all great philosophers, engages in the divine prerogative of willing a world into being and hence of creating a way of life, not of submitting thought to this way. It is true that Nietzsche subordinates *theory* to life and that he identifies fate with the will to power. But this identification is itself carried out as an act of the will and on the basis of thought, according to which theory is subsumed as a species under the genus "art." Nietzsche wills the fatality of the triumph of the will to power, or the "artifice" (not quite a "theory" but nevertheless akin to one) that life is a creation of the strongest will.

From this standpoint, Nietzsche is himself a Kantian, namely, in the general but crucial sense that nature understood as the Greek *physis* is not accessible to us and hence that there is no independent standard for scientific "theories." All theory, including the theory of nature, is a construction: the value or sense of the theoretical entities comes from the will. The same must be said of Kojève, who, as a "Hegelian," is committed to the thesis that the classical doctrine of the closeness of nature is assimilated into, and reconstituted by, the conceptual structure of modern *Wissenschaft*.[87] For Kojève, the formula of modernity, "we know only what we make," is truly transformed into the slogan of popular Marxism: "man makes himself."

There is, incidentally, a fundamental difference between Plato and Nietzsche which would be accepted by Strauss. For Plato, the distinction between the constructive and the preconstructive senses of "theory" is also the basis for the distinction between nature as the standard of legitimate volition and nature as the product of the will to constructive knowledge. It is in this distinction that mathematics fulfills its role as the paradigm of "divine" theory (as opposed to human or poetic theory). In other words, esoteric as well as exoteric Platonism is grounded in the thesis that we have a satisfactory understanding of the natural articulation of life that is not the same as the assumption of the eternal order. To give a very simple but adequate example: nature provides us with the basis for learning from experience, or engaging in "calculation" (*logismos*) of a mathematical as well as a political kind.

But this type of natural reasonableness is not sufficient to grasp intellec-
tually the eternal order of the whole. At this point, divine madness is
required. Strauss calls this "an act of the will," which is in my opinion
not Platonic but Kantian. In any case, the distinction I have just drawn
seems to be what he has in mind when he says that philosophy depends
for its possibility on the single requirement "that the fundamental
problems always be the same."[88] These fundamental problems must
be "given" to human beings from the "foundation," namely, from
nature. But this is impossible if nature, like the eternal order of the
whole, is given to man by himself. I would state the point in slightly
different terms. It is not the eternal order which man discovers, but the
natural foundation for willing the eternal order to be.

Throughout his writings, Strauss repeats the distinction between the
philosophical and the prephilosophical, or what I contend are two
different senses of nature. Sometimes the point is given a political
formulation: political understanding thus becomes a necessary precondition for theoretical understanding. For example:

> Classical philosophy originally acquired the fundamental concepts of
> political philosophy by starting from political phenomena as they
> present themselves to "the natural consciousness," which is a pre-
> philosophic consciousness. These concepts can therefore be under-
> stood, and their validity can be checked, by direct reference to phe-
> nomena, as they are accessible to "the natural consciousness."[89]

This contention is supported by the rather dubious argument that

> Classical political philosophy is non-traditional, because it belongs
> to the fertile moment when all political traditions were shaken, and
> there was not yet in existence a tradition of political philosophy. In
> all later epochs, the philosophers' study of political things was medi-
> ated by a tradition of political philosophy which acted like a screen
> between the philosopher and political things, regardless of whether
> the individual philosopher cherished or rejected that tradition. From
> this it follows that the classical philosophers see the political things
> with a freshness and directness that have never been equalled.[90]

The argument is dubious because it does not meet the objection that
what classical political philosophers described with unequaled vivid-
ness was precisely their own political tradition. There is a much more
direct path to the desired conclusion of an enduring human nature,

although not one that is free from all "historicist" counterclaims. From time to time, Strauss himself follows this procedure. He needs to show that political motives, typical patterns of behavior, or, in sum, the "fundamental" political problems are the same in all times (known to us). If this can be done, then the Greeks as Greeks become irrelevant.

There is another way in which to bring out the dubiousness of Strauss's claims about classical political philosophy, a way which he himself seems to have discerned. In explicating the thesis of the unique accessibility of pretheoretical nature to "the natural consciousness," Strauss is necessarily claiming that not just philosophers but all intelligent Greeks had access to nature as the pretheoretical standard. But by his own admission, this was not the case:

> Since political controversies are concerned with "good things" and "just things," classical political philosophy was naturally guided by considerations of "goodness" and "justice." It started from the moral distinctions as they are made in everyday life, although it knew better than the dogmatic skeptic of our time the formidable theoretical objections to which they are exposed. . . .

The clear implication of this passage is that the moral distinctions of everyday life are known to all prior to theoretical reflection, which then raises severe questions with respect to these distinctions. But if these objections are not resolved, then the very hypothesis of a pretheoretical natural standard is not merely questioned but contradicted.

> In the sense in which these distinctions are politically relevant, they cannot be "demonstrated," they are far from being perfectly lucid, and they are exposed to grave theoretical doubts. Accordingly, classical political philosophy limited itself to addressing men who, because of their natural inclinations as well as their upbringing, took these distinctions for granted.[91]

This is all that we need to quote, although the entire page from which it is taken is instructive and should be carefully read. This is especially true of the citation from Aristotle's *Nicomachean Ethics,* which is itself circular in the same way as Strauss's argument. Only "good" men can become, or be habituated to be, good. There was in fact *no* pretheoretical agreement or knowledge *of a philosophically decisive kind,* available to the "natural consciousness." Instead, there was fundamental disagreement about the hierarchy of human ends, the relation between ends and means, and so on. If one is not excessively utopian, one may agree that *this* level of disagreement is by nature fundamental. It would then follow that this level does allow the fundamental political problems to "flash up" to the discerning eye. To say that the fundamental solutions are also made visible in this way is, however, to jettison the Platonic notion of divine madness. Strauss's own formulation of the "natural" situation allows us to infer only that the fundamental solutions were viewed differently by different persons. In other words, the classical political philosophers (assuming that they all agreed with one another) addressed themselves exclusively to those who agreed with them. It is unclear why Kojève is not justified in referring to this as the "spirit of the sect" (*esprit de chapelle*). Kojève's appeal to the standard of intersubjective certitude, as enacted by historical success, while itself problematic, is not refuted by Strauss's counterappeal to "friends."[92] After all, birds of a feather flock together. But birds are not ontologists of nature. This difficulty is in effect granted by Strauss in the context, when he concludes that sects are preferable to intersubjective certitude. This may be true, but it compromises the point about a naturally accessible standard.

One could even grant to Strauss that all men prefer virtue to vice, good to evil, justice to injustice, and the noble to the base. This is not philosophically decisive (although it is interesting) until we decide *what is* virtuous, good, just, and noble. Strauss knew perfectly well, however, that no serious "what is" questions are raised by the Socratic school about matters of this sort, because the answers are entirely relative to other and higher considerations. This is obvious from Socrates' distinction in the *Republic* between philosophical and demotic virtue, and it is obvious from the discussion of "right by nature" in book V, chapter 7 of Aristotle's *Nichomachean Ethics*. At the "esoteric" level of genuine or classical political philosophy, there is no serious theoretical defense against conventionalism, or for that matter, against historicism. Those who believe themselves to discern the truth, and who are able to do so, attempt to "persuade" the nonphilosophers by rhetoric and, where possible, by more direct means. They attempt to "habituate" the "many" in accordance with the insights of the "few."

However, the serious and radical quarrel between the ancients and the moderns is precisely about which elite cadre has the superior insights. One need not go so far as to say that a study of the traditions of the ancient Greeks is irrelevant to this quarrel. Obviously many modern thinkers regarded such a study as quite relevant to their ends, but the study in itself does not answer our question. It does not provide us with a natural criterion for making the choice between ancients and moderns. And Strauss's case is no stronger if we shift from the political to the theoretical, or to the contemplation of "the divine things." This is visible in passages in which Strauss provides an ostensibly natural justification for the doctrine of Ideas as kinds rather than as problems. In passages of this sort, Strauss speaks of nature as "a term of distinction" for splitting phenomena into the natural and the conventional. Ideas thus correspond to "ways which are always" as opposed to conventional ways.[93]

The apprehension of "ways which are always" constitutes prescientific knowledge, on which all scientific studies stand or fall.[94] In my opinion, there is something quite true in what Strauss says here (see chapter 4). Nevertheless, the general point in the passage just cited is vitiated by an equivocation on the term "knowledge." The sense in which we know that someone is a human being is not the same as the sense in which we know, or claim to know, scientific truths about human behavior. And knowledge of the first sort, however necessary, does not provide a standard for claims to knowledge of the second sort. Differently stated, social science does not depend for its value upon its ability to prove that a certain being is a human being. Strauss's main point is that *all* scientific knowledge depends upon accepting as knowledge the prescientific perception of natural kinds. These perceptions (which antedate the subtle fantasies of contemporary philosophers of modal logic) seem to underlie many of the discussions of the Ideas in the Platonic dialogues. If Strauss is right that we have a more or less direct or pretheoretical access to natural kinds— and I think that he is right—then he must be wrong both in calling the Ideas "fundamental problems" (unless he means that they are *also* problems) and in calling the doctrine of Ideas "very hard to understand," "utterly incredible," or "fantastic." What is "utterly incredible" is the attempt by modern philosophers to transform these natural kinds into ontological or semantical entities. But it does not follow from the soundness of the observation that our experience of nature is articulated into kinds or that this articulation is the precondition for scientific theory, that such an articulation provides us with genuinely fundamental philosophical knowledge. To take the example that Strauss himself insists upon most frequently, since philosophy cannot refute revelation, it may well be that the Ideas of natural kinds are not themselves natural at all, but contingent creations of God. Or they could be constituted by the transcendental ego.

Once we reject the contention that the way back to nature is by a return to the perceptions or doctrines of fifth- and fourth-century B.C. Greeks, it seems to me that Strauss's quest for the prescientific can be formulated more persuasively. We should first note, however, that this conception of a return to natural consciousness seems to have been influenced by Husserl. Whereas Husserl wished to "desediment" our concept of nature by returning to pre-Galilean science, his actual goal was the naive *Selbstverständlichkeit* of world-certitude. This is to be reached by laying bare the universal structure of the prescientific life-world, the world of the natural attitude or consciousness.[95] For Husserl, a genuine history of philosophy consists in the tracing of meaning structures to "primal self-evidence."[96] One could therefore say that Husserl wanted to remove the sediment of history, and with it the accumulated conceptual structures of modern science, from the originative "perception" of nature. But this perception is for him an idealistic "constitution" of nature by the transcendental ego. The Straussian desedimentation is intended to take us back to nature as a discovery by the individual philosopher qua historical human being, not by the transcendental ego. Strauss tries to avoid the historicist implications of his own position by claiming that historicity is a modern invention and that nature was directly accesible to the pre-Socratic Greeks. There is also a touch of Nietzsche and Heidegger in this claim.

That the ancient Greeks had no notion of historicity as an ontological dimension, however, is obviously irrelevant to the question of the truth or falsity of the contention that historicity is the essence of human existence. The contention may be false, but it is not refuted by the adoption of the standards of *some* residents of a distant historical period as paradigmatic or genuinely natural. On the other hand, one can certainly grant Strauss's point that a commitment to historicity is not the correct basis for determining the validity of the doctrine of historicity. If nature, or the prescientific, is accessible to human beings, then it must in principle be always accessible, even if it is covered over at certain times by the influence of "historicist" doctrines. But *is* it accessible in the way that Strauss states or implies, namely, as independent of our perspectives or opinions, even *as* we are viewing it perspectivally and necessarily with the assistance of opinions about it?

Strauss makes the reasonable claim that unless thinking is regulated by the everyday world of common sense, it soon becomes indistinguishable from the imagination. On his view, in other words, the exaltation of the imagination leads through the modern emphasis on mastery of nature to German Idealism, and from there to Nietzsche. His opponents make the equally reasonable reply that the everyday world of common sense is *already* a product of theoretical constitution (Husserl) or imaginative construction (Nietzsche). I myself would observe that common sense, on Strauss's own premise that thought is (divinely) mad, is incompetent to adjudicate a truly "fearless" (Strauss's term) philosophical thinking. Nevertheless, there is an indispensable element of truth in Strauss's claim, which reminds us of Bertrand Russell's assertion that philosophers must have a robust sense of reality. The claim is sound; the problem is that it is enacted in radically diverse ways. A philosophical theory can no more certify itself than can a scientific theory. Both are confirmed or invalidated with reference to something else. (I am here, of course, taking "theory" in the modern sense of a conceptual construction.) In mathematics, for example, a theory can be proved to be consistent only with respect to another theory. There are those who contend that the same procedure holds good in science, although this entails that the so-called natural world of prescientific experience is itself a product of scientific theories. This is in effect what Strauss means by "historicism": nature is a historical artifact, because theories are historical artifacts.

Later in this volume, I will argue that there is indeed a distinction between what the Socratics called "theory" and what modern thinkers mean by this term. But "theory" in the sense of the precondition for theoretical construction has nothing to do with Xenophon's opinions on the noble and the base. Stated with maximum simplicity, it is the capacity to "see" whether a theoretical construction makes sense, whether such a construction does what it purports to do, and whether its intentions are in harmony with our fundamental intentions or ends. These ends are in turn obviously founded in the life-world or the pretheoretical horizon of constructive activity. *But so are rival and contradictory ends.* To use Strauss's terminology, baseness is as much in conformity with nature as is nobility. The correct evaluation of nature is not "given" by nature in a direct, publicly certifiable manner, as Strauss himself has admitted. It is on my view not only possible but probable that, were we to enact a "city" rooted in Strauss's version of the "noble reserve" and the "calm grandeur" of the classical thinkers, the results would be restrictive and demeaning to the human spirit, and hence *base* rather than noble. And this is said with all due respect to Jane Austen.

After this necessary digression, let us return to Strauss's exoteric revelation of esotericism. The simplest way in which to summarize what has been said thus far is by repeating Strauss's judgment, attributed to Plato, that whereas thought must be fearless, speech must be moderate. In a slightly more subtle formulation, Strauss endorses Xenophon's failure to mention courage as a Socratic virtue. More explicitly, I take Strauss's error to be this: from the correct observation that there is always and of necessity a tension or indeed conflict between philosophy and the city, Strauss draws the false inference that it is always necessary for philosophers to accommodate to the city in the style of Plato, Cicero, Al Farabi, and Maimonides.[97] This inference is contradicted by Strauss's own procedures, as we have noticed at some length. Thus Strauss's apparent disregard of Socrates' advice in the *Phaedrus* to adjust one's speech to the audience is a part of his own exoteric accommodation to the circumstances of his time.

Strauss's exoteric speech may be described in a preliminary way as a compromise between the rhetoric of Xenophon and that of Nietzsche. In the writings of his mature period, there is a touch of Dostoievski in the style of Jane Austen. Strauss's last several books are much more inaccessible, closer to the late Henry James than to Jane Austen. I take this to reflect a diminution of power (Strauss was in poor health in the last decade of his life) rather than a substantial change of position. In any event, his reputation is based upon the work of his middle years, which represent him at the peak of his abilities. At all periods of his English publications, Strauss accommodated to the contemporary age in a way that seemed to violate our most characteristic prejudice. He regularly drew the inference from the moral distinctions as they are made in everyday life[98] to the thesis that an aristocracy of rural gentlemen is the political imitation of the rule of philosophers.

In *The City and Man,* Strauss associates the doctrine of rule by a landed aristocracy with Aristotle. However, in the chapter "Classic Natural Right" in *Natural Right and History,* Strauss's best-known work, he derives the same paradigm from Plato and Aristotle equally. Strauss takes the *Republic* to establish the conclusion "that the just city is not possible because of the philosophers' unwillingness to rule."[99] We must therefore turn to works like the *Laws* in order to determine Plato's "practical" political views. The arrangements of government as described in the *Laws* "are obviously meant to favor the wealthy; the regime is meant to be . . . a mean more oligarchic or aristocratic than a polity." And again: "only those can be citizens who have the leisure to devote themselves to the practice of citizen virtue."[100] In other words, "old money" is the condition for the leisure to devote oneself to virtue, and old money is rooted in the landed aristocracy. Whereas democracies favor the free development of all human types, including the best,

> Plato did not regard this consideration as decisive. For he was concerned not only with the possibility of philosophy, but likewise with a stable political order that would be congenial to moderate political courses; and such an order, he thought, depends on the predominance of old families.[101]

Only virtue guarantees the right use of freedom, and an education in virtue depends upon the leisure appropriate to habituation. From here, it is a short step to the preference for a rural aristocracy.

In the same passage, Strauss says that the ancients differed with us on the evaluation of democracy because of their different estimate of the virtues of technology. Very much in the style of Adorno and Horkheimer, Strauss notes that democracy requires unlimited technology, which in turn leads to dehumanization.[102] But the denunciation of the technological "reification" or "administration" of human life is today normally made in defense of freedom. One must wonder how the "ancients" thought virtue to be possible without freedom. It is difficult not to be suspicious of the thesis that people become virtuous by being "habituated" in the moral preferences of "gentlemen." By the same token, the aristocratic aestheticism of Horkheimer and Adorno is not an entirely persuasive basis for the rejection of technology. But more important here, once we take our bearings by the distinction between the philosopher and the nonphilosopher in the Straussian (and Kojèvian) sense, then all conceptions of virtue rest upon habituation or propaganda. The question is then: Which form of habituation is directed to the most noble conception of human life?

More important, the advocacy of the paradigm of the rule of gentlemen stems from philosophical, not merely political, conservatism. It rests upon the assumption that courage is not a genuine virtue, or that unrestricted thinking has dangerous consequences. If we grant that thinking must be fearless, it is difficult to see how it can be restricted to the apolitical leisure of a few private persons. It is not so easy to refute Kojève's thesis that once Socrates steps into the marketplace to conduct his conversations, the course of history is determined. By conversing in the presence of the politically active Athenian youths, even in the "exoteric" manner depicted in the dialogues, Socrates necessarily "politicizes" philosophy, or guarantees its spread via schools and sects, few of whose members will be capable or desirous of preserving Platonic esotericism. It therefore makes no difference *why* Socrates initiates these conversations. The political results must be "modern" rather than "classical."

The question then arises: Did Plato write moderately or fearlessly? In my opinion, Strauss tries to conceal the fearlessness of philosophical writing in general, and of the dialogues in particular, by generalizing the "local" thesis that the rural aristocracy is the best accessible regime for classical Greece, into the universal thesis of aristocratic conservatism. The best regime, he says, is "the object of the wish or prayer of all good men or of gentlemen . . . as that object is interpreted by gentlemen."[103] The best regime, although possible by nature, is "extremely improbable." We must therefore shift to the regime that is best under the circumstances, or reconcile "the requirement for wisdom with the requirement for consent."[104] The practical solution is to have a wise legislator "frame a code which the citizen body, duly persuaded, freely adopts." The classical view is that the code embodying wisdom must be entrusted to "the gentleman": "The gentleman is not identical with the wise man. He is the political reflection, or imitation, of the wise man."[105] Like the wise, the gentlemen look down upon the vulgar, or are experienced in the beautiful. Unlike the wise, "they have a noble contempt for precision" (hence technology) and "in order to live as gentlemen, they must be well off."

We are thus required by the texts to conclude that the following description of Aritotle's *Politics* is extended by Strauss to "the classics" in general, and specifically, to Plato:

> the life of the perfect gentleman points toward the philosophic way of life. . . . The gentleman is by nature able to be affected by philosophy; Aristotle's political science is an attempt to actualize this possibility.[106]

Strauss's exoteric doctrine amounts to this. The "conservative" or "prudential" teaching that is common to Plato and Aristotle is transformed into a generalized philosophical thesis according to which the gentleman, i.e. the rural aristocrat, is the practical imitation of, and points toward, the philosopher. I submit that this is impossible. It is philosophically mistaken, and it has bad political consequences for philosophy.

From a philosophical standpoint, the Straussian thesis violates the sharp Aristotelian distinction between theoretical and practical intelligence. However much gentlemen may look down upon the vulgar, they do not look up to philosophical theory, as Strauss perfectly well knew. To the contrary, perhaps the main purpose of Aristotle's political theory is to insulate politics from philosophical reflection. Why else invent practical intelligence and moral or political virtue? Furthermore, the Straussian thesis suppresses the Platonic teaching that philosophy is divine madness. It produces the impression that we can understand the philosophical content of the dialogues, or the dialogues as divine madness, by starting with the more accessible paradigm of the gentleman. Strauss certainly knew that this was false.[107] I must conclude that he did not seriously believe it. What we have here is his exoteric presentation of philosophy, designed to provide a protective political screen against the dangerous consequences of the necessary occasional statements that indicate the true nature of philosophy. It is part of the attempt to reconcile the rhetoric of Plato, Cicero, Al Farabi, and Maimonides to the exigencies of the postmodern era. In order to save philosophy, one must remind the potential philosopher of its fearless and divinely mad nature, but one must also guard against "maddening" the general populace, and in particular the "intellectuals," by encouraging them to believe that they are themselves divinely mad. The solution adopted by Strauss, in the light of the specific circumstances of mid–twentieth century America, was to effect a rapprochement with the "conservatives," who would be "habituated" to virtue by a special race of academic administrators, themselves acting under the impression that they are wise men.

We can make substantially the same point in another way. Strauss accepted Nietzsche's aristocratic criticism of modernity, and hence of Enlightenment. But he rejected Nietzsche's radical or rabble-rousing rhetoric. It is easy to appreciate Strauss's point when we note that Nietzsche's political effect was not on the aristocracy but on the rabble. We may also understand Strauss's reluctance to make too explicit his Nietzschean conception of philosophy as an act of the will. Nevertheless, there is a fundamental contradiction between Strauss's thoroughly modern, and hence Nietzschean, persistence in publicizing the dangerous esoteric doctrines of the philosophers and his ostensibly "classical" praise for the paradigm of the landed aristocracy. But entirely apart from the question whether Strauss was a sincere conservative, one has to question the political pertinence of his exoteric teaching. Are we seriously to believe that the way out of the postmodern crisis is by rehabilitating an American version of the eighteenth- or nineteenth-century English gentleman? And if we are, what has this gentleman in common with the contemporary populism that passes for conservatism?

It should never be forgotten that the publication by Plato of his dialogues, given the political circumstances of his day, was a revolutionary act of extreme fearlessness. This is true *despite* the various accommodations to those circumstances that Strauss pointed out throughout his career, with so much acuity and hermeneutical sensitivity, when he was not expounding his exoteric political views. By the same hermeneutical principles, one cannot select the proper public rhetoric without correctly understanding one's own time. And one cannot understand one's own time unless one engages in the fearless thinking recommended by Strauss himself. But fearless thinking has fearless consequences, and never more so than in times of extreme decadence. The late twentieth century is neither the fifth century B.C. nor the twelfth century A.D. It is not historicism to acknowledge this fact and take one's bearings by it; rather, to fail to understand this is to fall victim to historicism.

# V

Our extended consideration of the thought of Leo Strauss was intended, among other purposes, to inoculate us against the understandable tendency to dismiss Alexandre Kojève at first reading as a frivolous Parisian café philosopher. When we are talking about politics at a philosophical level, an excessive defense of moderation leads to an extremism that is closely related to the excessive defense of excess. Unfortunately, there is no coherent philosophical defense of moderation as moderation, or what might be called "good-natured and liberal muddling through." This is because philosophy is by nature immoderate. A rigorous and consistent defense of the Enlightenment, or the thesis that freedom is the highest good and scientific knowledge its most powerful instrument, leads *in principle* to what Kojève called the universal and homogeneous state. It leads to the suppression and indeed the exclusion of error and superstition. But whereas there are many forms of error and superstition, there is only one form of scientific truth—or so the Enlightenment claimed. The twentieth-century rebellion against *the* scientific truth—and the consequent popularity of doctrines of historicism and linguistic conventionalism, whether derived from Nietzsche or Wittgenstein—is thus a rebellion against the Enlightenment, and it comes dangerously close to being a rebellion against truth. Whatever was intended by the leaders of this rebellion, there can be no doubt that the thesis that art is worth more than the truth is the dominant principle of our time. We have protected ourselves against rationalism not by prudent moderation in its use but by a reckless embrace of recklessness, or the rejection of rationalism in favor of the imagination.

The popularity of hermeneutics in our own time is thus a mark of singular political as well as theoretical importance. It is a sign not of our greater understanding but of the fact that we have lost our way, that we understand nothing, except to the extent that we adopt rules and principles, which, however, must themselves be supported by an interpretation that hangs in the void. It is true that the void affords to a deity the opportunity to express the divine freedom of the creation of a world. But once created, a god's world is not deconstructed by the fecundity of pure negation. What we call freedom today is all too frequently the result of a failure to think through the corruption of finitude by history. This is why I have called postmodernism an extreme form of decadence. As so decadent, we lack the self-confidence of Kant, which has been dissipated after the last great effort by Hegel into positivism on the one hand and existential ontology on the other.

In my view, it is therefore correct to say that, beneath the veil of Kojève's playfulness, or indeed madness, there is as deep and comprehensive a reflection upon human nature as is to be found in Nietzsche, and certainly more profound than one finds in Heidegger. I do not mean by this that Kojève was superior to Nietzsche and Heidegger in all ways, or even that he was their equal as a thinker. The fact is that he was for all his frivolity more *sober* than either. He therefore forces us, if we take him with sufficient seriousness, to grasp the crucial fact that modern liberal democracies are the result of the *failure,* not the success, of the Enlightenment. It could therefore be argued that hermeneutics is the proper critical instrument of the liberal democracy. But we must also understand that this instrument has the fatal consequence of urging democracy toward anarchy. Contemporary pleasure in the announced death or end of philosophy, as we should have understood from the connection between that death and the deaths of God and humanity, is thus a trivial consequence of Kojève's announcement of the end of history. The universal homogeneous state turns into the era of Nietzsche's last men, exactly as does the postmodern era of unlimited deconstruction. To be posthuman is to be subhuman, not divine; to be beyond the subject-object distinction, and hence self-consciousness, is to be unconscious, not an Aristotelian god of thinking thinking itself.

The fragility of philosophy turns upon its middle position between hermeneutical relativism and universal dogma. To that extent I agree with Leo Strauss as against Kojève that a multiplicity of philosophical sects is preferable to a universal homogeneous state. But this is not enough to convince one of the merits of Straussian politics. Strauss was a great admirer of statesmen like Winston Churchill for their ability to act in a daring manner under circumstances of extreme danger, and on behalf of noble motives. But he did not fully appreciate the deep connection between theory and practice, or what one could call the application of Churchillian daring to the world-historical stage. The fact that philosophy holds to a middle position between relativism and universal dogma does not mean that philosophy must always be moderate in its public appearance. Contrary to Xenophon, courage is in fact a Socratic virtue. For this reason, and with all due reflection on the apparently paradoxical nature of what I am about to say, I conclude this segment of my study with the assertion that Plato was a "modern," not an "ancient."

# ═4═

# Theory and Interpretation

Every hermeneutical program is at the same time itself a political manifesto or the corollary of a political manifesto. In particular, this is true of the postmodern attack upon the Enlightenment. Needless to say, this attack has different faces. It is also true that not each version of the attack makes hermeneutics central to its own enterprise. But it is not by chance that hermeneutics has somehow become pivotal, a point of juncture, as it were, for schools as diverse as Frankfurt critical rationalism, late Wittgensteinian language analysis, poststructuralism, and deconstruction, to name only a few. The extraordinary multiplication of academic schools in our generation resembles nothing so much as the theological hypertrophy of the late Middle Ages. There is, however, this difference. Controversy over the essential features of the divine *parousia* has been replaced by confusion over the absence of divinity. One mark of the confusion is that political revolution has been concealed by the phenomenon of academic scholasticism. Especially in the United States, hermeneuts of the advance guard talk incessantly of presence and absence, epistemes and semiotics, difference and *différance,* even of phallocentrism and metaphysical domination, often in explicit conjunction with radical political projects, but in such a way as to leave us with the impression that politics is a subspecies of ontology.

   None of this is said in order to deny that there is a theoretical problem of major importance at the core of contemporary hermeneutical disputes. The problem concerns the very nature, and hence the possibility, of theory. My point is that even concentration upon a "purely theoretical" approach to hermeneutics is already a sign of the political phenomenon of *decadence*. Decadence arises from political despair, not from revolutionary fervor; in one version, this despair takes solace in elaborate methodologies and abstruse terminologies: a kind of epistemological (or postepistemological) aestheticism. In my opinion, the postmodern assault upon the Enlightenment is in general an example of decadence. The predominant view seems to be that, since the Enlightenment has failed, or even in certain cases since we are merely *bored* with it, and since Western philosophy, also known as "platonism," is simply a preliminary stage of that failure, all that remains for us is technical badinage. Objections to the reification of being have thus succeeded—in reifying being.

Is this a price that we need to pay? What if the disputes between conflicting hermeneutical schools are mere illusion? What if, all political questions to one side, there is no such thing as a theory of interpretation? Does it follow from this that we are no longer in a position to understand what we read? Or is it rather the case that hermeneutical theories make such understanding impossible? If this is right, then the destruction (and I mean *destruction*, not "deconstruction") of hermeneutical theories may return us to the older stage in which competent persons argued about the meaning of writings without interposing methodological filters between themselves and the texts. To anticipate, it is after all obvious that, despite all the mumbo jumbo of methods, canons, and antimethodological canons, we are still in the earlier position of presenting our interpretations of texts for the judgment of other interested readers. If there is such a thing as the interpretation of a text, as opposed to the writing of a new text by the ostensible reader, then it is obvious that there is a core meaning in the text that has been placed there by the author, who expected it to be intelligible to perceptive readers without the aid of elaborate hermeneutical tools. This leaves all the room that is necessary for unintended meanings. As our lengthy discussion of philosophical theology and the related problem of esotericism should have demonstrated, no text worth reading wears its meaning on its sleeve.

There are no canons by which one can usefully restrict legitimate from illegitimate readings. Nevertheless, this did not prevent generations of intelligent authors from communicating with intelligent readers. The reliance upon canons, apparently in opposition to the extreme relativism of the radical postmodernists, has the unfortunate consequence of trivializing the interpretation of works of genius. I see no reason to prefer conservative obtuseness to radical hypomania. Differently stated, the issue here is another version of our previous problem of the relation between prudence and madness. I would of course not deny that it is possible to write down on a sheet of paper prudential maxims to be followed by all competent readers. But competent readers do not require such a list, and its possession does not transform incompetence into competence. More seriously, it does not enable us to cross the bar from the commonsensical to the domain of divine madness. Instead, it empowers scholastic mediocrity to pose as the guardian of legitimate genius. For my part, I prefer hypomania to canonical stultification.

So much by way of preface; let us now turn to the task of deciding whether a theory of interpretation is possible on theoretical grounds.

## II

Decadence may be understood as an exacerbation of the nervous sensibility. Experience does not merely transpire; it accumulates. The result, as Nietzsche showed in such brilliant detail, is both intensification of perception and a concomitant deadening of the critical faculty. As the artist becomes more refined and penetrates to a deeper level of psychological analysis this increase in self-reflection leads also to a dissatisfaction with the traditional languages and forms of art. The ensuing creation of new forms becomes indistinguishable, not merely from a rejection of the old but from the dissolution of what is at first called "the traditional concept of form" and, eventually, of form itself. What looks initially like an extraordinary release of creative energy begins soon to deteriorate into what may be called experimental mannerism, or the unmistakable rictus of energy deflected into the attempt to find a lost bearing. Writing becomes initially more exquisite, and the increased subtlety of language stimulates a corresponding increase in the subtlety

of reading. By a gradual process of what looks like an increase in sophis-
tication but is in fact a narrowing of range and loss of creative impetus,
writing becomes more and more like reading: art deteriorates into criticism.[1] The scene is set for the advent of hermeneutics.

Reading is for us today no longer a pleasure or an illumination; it is
a problem. In my view, this is a natural consequence of the solipsism
that follows upon the ostensible progression beyond the subject-object
distinction. It is all very well to criticize the notion of the "object" as at
once a projection of the perspectival subject and a reification. The
repudiation of the subject, however, is also a repudiation of subjectivity in the salutary sense. Very far from liberating the deeper stratum of
creativity from the dilemmas of self-consciousness, the aforementioned repudiation brings with it an immediate intensification of those
dilemmas. It is not we who are assimilated into textuality; to the
contrary, the text is assimilated into us. The result is not a Gadamerian
*Horizontverschmelzung* but a disappearance of distinctions, hence,
not *différance* but identity. By a dialectical inversion, Heraclitean flux
is indistinguishable from Parmenidean monism. The identity or monad
is that of chaos.

As a mark of the reification that has resulted from the postsubjectivist
attack upon reification, we have only to note that technophilia, the
characteristic eros of the twentieth century, is widespread among our
academic hermeneuticists. Just as the "bourgeois" layman is unable to
perform any fundamental activity without the assistance of a technical
manual, so the "sophisticated" professor cannot read a page without
methods and antimethods. No one can say how we are to read our
manuals. The necessity of metahermeneutics has led to the paradoxical
proliferation of popular accounts or academic introductions to the esoteric documents of hermeneutics. Parasitic upon texts notorious for
their obscurity is a thicket of revised doctoral dissertations, praised or
blamed by reviewers in scholarly periodicals as they approach or recede
from the moronic criterion of "lucidity." I use the harsh term "moronic" because the standard of lucidity is derived from neopositivism
and thus from the very Enlightenment that the commented texts are
struggling to deconstruct. *Lucus a non lucendo:* the praise of absence is
itself praised as an emanation of presence.

If the entrance into the absolute is itself absolute, then so too must

be what Hegel and Wittgenstein in effect call the ladder to the absolute. One need not go to the absurd extreme of rejecting methodology
in its legitimate domain in order to observe that the obsession with
method is a sublimated form of the desire for the absolute. Descartes's
attempt to construct a universal method on the model of mathematics
was not a simple rejection but a *replacement* of metaphysics. In general, the Enlightenment attempts to replace what we may call the
metaphysical absolute by the absolute certainty of effective solutions
to practical problems. In our own century, the mathematical formalism of Hilbert is the outstanding example of the attempt to capture the
absolute in a methodological net. The problem I address is not so
much with method as with our attitude toward method. One cannot
perform the simplest acts of everyday life without method; but it does
not follow from this that everyday life requires the absolute grounding
of a metaphysics of methodology. The metaphysics of methodology is
the attempt to replace the judicious selection of methods by a comprehensive method of selection. In the case of hermeneutics, it is the
attempt to replace or to fortify the judgment of the reader with a
methodology for the selection of methods of reading.[2]

Decadence manifests itself as a loss of confidence in what Leo
Strauss called "the natural consciousness," presumably following
Husserl up to a point, who speaks of "the natural attitude." Unfortunately, Husserl's "natural attitude" is itself a methodological artifact,
whereas Strauss's "natural consciousness" is a historical perspective;
neither thinker escapes the nemesis from which he seeks to liberate
mankind. There is no privileged historical epoch and no technical
device for returning us to our senses. It is therefore wise to state at the
outset that the reader will be disappointed if he or she anticipates a
novel theoretical replacement for hermeneutical excess in these pages.
My procedure will be largely critical, because what is required here is a
"desedimentation" (in Husserl's phrase) but not a new construction.
Up to a point, one can offer a quasi-transcendental argument for the
necessary conditions of intelligibility. But these conditions are not
Kantian concepts or rules. It is precisely concepts and rules that need
to be understood and evaluated.

The remarks to follow, then, are neither a rejection of the need for
sound methods of reading nor a propaedeutic to a correct theory of

interpretation. Their purpose is to lend support to the thesis that a theory (in the modern sense of a conceptual construction) of interpretation is impossible. Again, this is very far from the charge that everything said or recommended by hermeneutical thinkers is worthless. As Nietzsche has also taught us, it is already a mark of decadence to be a resolute enemy of decadence. What one may hope to show is that the refined perceptions of a hermeneutical theoretician are valuable not because of but despite the incoherence of their theoretical substructures. There is no theoretical substructure to reading *or* to writing: there is only the infrastructure of the reader and the writer. Reading and writing are confirmations of Nietzsche's epigram that man is the unfinished animal. But this is precisely human nature, to be unfinished, and hence, to exist in and as the search for completion. If we replace human nature by an ontological theory, in the way that certain theologians replace the profound directness of religious acts and symbols with categories and ontological incense, we inevitably obliterate the sense of reading and writing. Being is not a text, nor does it provide us with the sense of a text. Unfortunately, however, neither do the canons of sound philology. Let us try to restate these generalities in greater detail.

# III

If there is no human nature that remains constant within historical change, and so de nes the perspectives of individual readers *as* perspectives upon a common humanity, then reading is impossible. Whether one's primary orientation is ontological or philological, interpretation depends upon the initial accessibility of the sense of the text as independent of clarification and deepening by the subsequent application of theories, methods, and canons. This point is at least implicitly recognized by those representatives of philological hermeneutics who formulate maxims recommending *subtilitas legendi* or *Verstehen*. And yet one cannot suppress a tear or a smile when reading these sincere invocations whose excellence cannot disguise their naiveté. We do not become subtle through the study of philology. To the contrary, only those who are subtle by nature will make an appropriate use of their philological training. And there are neither philological canons nor ontological definitions of subtlety.

I have suggested that hermeneutical theories are the consequence of two closely related processes of deterioration. The first is a progressive separation of our understanding of the obvious from an intensifying conviction that nature, and so human nature, is a historical myth that must be replaced by a scientific construction. Just as the intuitive comes to be stigmatized as the source of logical contradictions, so the obvious is relegated to the category of superstition. In fact, we continue to rely upon our intuitions and to take our bearings by the obvious. But in attempting to protect ourselves against the defects, real and imagined, of these beginnings, we obstruct their true nature by ever more complex methodologies. The second process of deterioration is a product of the refined sensibility of historical old age. Subtlety decays into ingenuity, and the speculative imagination, unrestrained by the standard of nature—or by "the given," which is now unmasked as an epistemological error—slips into the dream world of fantasy. It should never be forgotten that hyperbolical attacks on the metaphysics of presence are the "Continental" coordinate of "Anglo-Saxon" attacks on the notion of "the given."

One way in which to render more specific this process of double deterioration is by viewing it as the gradual disappearance of the distinction between theory and interpretation. The stages of this disappearance can be documented with considerable precision. At least since the time of Bacon and his two great successors, Descartes and Vico, but most dramatically since Kant, we find that the term "theory" is used in ways having little if anything to do with its etymology. The Greek word *theoria* designates a contemplative gazing upon divine phenomena, and by extension, a purely intellectual apprehension or vision of the natural order. At least until the time of Aristotle's tripartition of the sciences into the theoretical, practical, and productive, *theoria* is not restricted to the vision of pure forms but may also refer to the understanding of human nature, and especially of human deeds. For Aristotle, *episteme theoretike* is a discursive knowledge which is founded in sensuous and intellectual perception of natural beings as well as of the forms of species and genera. Nature, in the sense of the "essences" or "substances" of things, is neither produced nor modified (although it is "actualized") by the processes of cognition, whether intuitive or discursive.

Already in Plato, as well as in Aristotle, it is far from clear how the intellectual perception of the natural order is related to, and remains pure from modification by, what may fairly be called the constructive procedures of language, which are indispensable in the acquisition of scientific knowledge. In other words, the silence associated with the metaphor of vision is compatible with a passive reception of the natural order. But talking is already *making*, or what we call today concept construction. With Plato and Aristotle, we may describe this as the constructive activity of technical linguistic devices, by means of which we attempt to state what we have seen. There is, in other words, in speech as much as in writing, an *absence* of the purely visible, and *a substitution of a verbal construction for the absent being*.

It is for this reason that there can be no suppression of intellectual intuition in favor of discursive intelligence, contrary to some current interpretations of Aristotle. Discursivity is the necessary *supplement* to the intuitive perception of form. If the purely visible were entirely absent, then to know would be to construct discursively. To employ Derridean terms, substitution, supplementation, and surplus would at once become creation *ex nihilo*. It is therefore a fundamental error to regard the "supplementary" role assigned by classical theory to writing as in principle different from the same role assigned to speech. Supplementation is neither orientating nor superfluous. It stands to the direct perception of phenomena (formal as well as sensuous) as does art to nature. Art completes nature, but there must be a nature to complete if art is to be distinguished from fantasy. The ostensible rigor of discursive artifacts is thus compromised by the fact that judgment is also a discursive artifact. The modern axiom that we know only what we make carries with it the corollary that we make what we know. Knowledge is then poetry; to judge is thus to interpret.

One finds at the beginning of modern philosophy the intention of regulating discourse, or of preserving the distinction between theory and interpretation, by appeal to a natural standard of desire or passion. Whether this standard is conceived in physiological or voluntative terms, however, it is soon aborted by the steady triumph of the doctrine of historicity, or the view that even desire is a concealed discursive *interpretation,* a product of historical circumstances and perspectives. Nature is no longer completed but is rather produced by art. The historical perspective, also known as the linguistic horizon, thanks to the irony if not the cunning of history, thus in effect replaces the *parousia* of the discredited invisible essence of classical metaphysics.

It is important to emphasize that Aristotle's tripartition of the sciences into the theoretical, practical, and productive is not intended as an artificial conceptual schematism to bring order out of indeterminate beginnings. It corresponds to distinguishable but related aspects of nature. Thus theory is distinguished from the exercise of practical intelligence and is assigned a higher status in the order of excellence; but in a fundamental sense, theory is regulated by practice. From the standpoint of political life, it is up to the exercise of *phronesis* to determine who are the theoretical experts and what role they play in the public economy. Even the sage must tend to the needs of the body before he is free to cultivate the soul. Conversely, a soul that is politically cultivated is thereby qualified to establish those conditions that are essential prerequisites for the development of the sage. Perhaps the main point is this: whereas the man of *phronesis* may not always, or even often, be a man of *theoria,* there is a natural harmony between these faculties, independent of political distinctions, including those of distinct city-states as well as of historical periods.

The judgments of practical intelligence are directed toward the here and now, or toward particular, and hence at least partially contingent, events. But these judgments are not themselves radically contingent, because they are grounded in a perception of human nature that could be restated in theoretical terms. If the contingent is intelligible, that is, if it is amenable to judgment, then the basis of intelligibility or judgment cannot itself be contingent. It is true that the wise decision under present circumstances may be foolish under other circumstances, but the wisdom of the decision under present circumstances is not arbitrary. To judge is to understand, not to create *ex nihilo.* This point should be related to the previously cited Aristotelian maxim that art completes nature. One oversimplifies and misunderstands the Greeks by attributing to them the view that "life in accordance with nature" is validated by nature as an unvarying, perfect, and always benevolent standard. This oversimplification is impossible to sustain in the face of Greek myth and tragedy, which express vividly the profound discontinuities in human nature, as well as the senses in which the natural cosmos is hostile or indifferent to human life. Judgments in accordance with nature are those that *complete* nature. But the possibility of judgment, confirmed by success as well as by failure, means that there is a nature to complete. If this were not so, it would be meaningless to speak of man as the unfinished animal.

By way of a transition from classical to modern thought, we may say that, for the Greeks, the distinction between theory and interpretation is rooted in the distinction between seeing and making. Whereas we must state what we have seen, it is equally necessary to see what one is talking about. This is as true for the flights of divine madness as it is for the exercise of common sense. Common sense cannot negotiate the flight of divine madness, but it provides the ground from which divine madness ascends. The distinction between seeing and making, to continue, is not only incompatible with the modern project to master nature but indispensable to the rationality of the distinction between masters and slaves. If that distinction is discursive or "merely verbal," then it may be obliterated by an additional statement. What is a master from one historical or linguistic perspective is a slave from another. This state of affairs is guaranteed by the transformation of nature into a historical concept. The sense of power is erased by excessive garrulity; "analytical clarification" decays into infinite technical progress, and progress is indistinguishable from chaos.

The critical moments of the modern epoch are all visible in the mathematical, scientific, and philosophical writings of Descartes. Practice is first reunited with production, as in Plato, and then the distinction between theory and practice is dissolved. In order to transform human beings from natural slaves into masters of nature, one must reconstitute nature itself. Geometrical intuition, the Cartesian analogue to the Aristotelian intuition of essences, is an initial step in this process. The analysis of practical problems or physical bodies into geometrical schemata amounts to a "geometricizing" of the world. These schemata are then themselves replaced by equations consisting of ratios of the known and unknown magnitudes of the line segments in the figures. And the entire analysis proceeds in accordance with the intention of the investigator. Man's desire to solve problems and to achieve mastery regulates the method by which the natural world is prepared for what can without exaggeration be called "the will to power." Descartes's scientific writings thus confirm the traditional interpretation of the *Meditations,* according to which the *ego cogitans* is the direct ancestor of the Absolute Ego or principle of production of the empirical world. And the primary importance assigned to the intention of the investigator is reconfirmed by the *Passions of the Soul,* which requires citation. In article 142 of part 3, Descartes says: "I notice in us but one thing which might give us good reason to esteem ourselves, and that is the use of our free will. . . . it renders us in a way like God, by making us masters of ourselves. . . . " In article 143, Descartes defines *générosité* as the attribute by which we legitimately esteem ourselves, provided that we carry out all affairs that we deem best.

Moral virtue is the carrying out of "great things" (pt. 3, art. 156) through the exercise of *générosité* (which is something like Aristotle's "greatness of soul," but attached to the will). If we take this text in conjunction with the scientific writings as well as with the *Discourse on Method,* it is reasonable to perceive in Descartes the paradigm of the Enlightenment view of the identity of virtue and scientific knowledge. This amounts to an un-self-conscious identification of theory and interpretation, or the confidence in the self-evident truth of one overriding interpretation, namely, of the intrinsic or ultimate (and hence historical) virtuousness of the will to power. Descartes is the paradigmatic expression of the secularization of divine "authorial intention" in the creation of the book of the world. The book is legible not because it is indistinguishable from myself but because I have willed it into being.

The aforementioned self-confidence was attacked in complementary ways by Hume and Rousseau. If memory cannot be distinguished from imagination except by liveliness of sensation, and if causality and necessary connections are perceived as such because of habit or custom, then theories are not merely interpretations but *fantasies.* Hume's so-called empiricism would be better named "surrealism", and its role in the prehistory of Romanticism, existentialism, and contemporary historicist hermeneutics has not yet been properly appreciated. In Rousseau, the analogous development, a consequence of his denial of the identity between knowledge and virtue, is the subordination of reason to sensibility. Rousseau gives an ambiguous account of the implications of sensibility, an account in which traditional morality is compromised by an unmistakable penchant for the aesthetic fantasies of the solitary promenader. In principle, the net effect of the joint doctrines of Hume and Rousseau is not the natural-law teaching of the former or the classical republicanism of the latter but incipient nihilism. The world is an interpretation.

This sets the scene for Kant. Kant attempts to rescue scientific knowledge from the radical skepticism of Hume and to give a rational foundation to Rousseau's moral sensibility by his doctrine of the transcendental ego, according to which rational order is constituted by a set of logical conditions that are binding for all sentient creatures who employ sense perception together with conceptual thinking. According to Kant, we know only what we make, but the "made" world is not a historical artifact; with respect to its categorial determinations, it is a transcendentally constituted structure. In this specific and fundamental sense, it is, as it were, an *eternal essence,* not a contingent or perspectival consequence of an empirical interpretation. At the same time, it would be difficult if not impossible to say that the doctrine of the transcendental ego is "theoretical." Rather, theories are consequences of transcendental conditions. But the empirical content of a scientific theory is indeed contingent and historical. Whereas the conditions, and so the categorial structure of a theory, cannot be subject to interpretation, this in itself shapes, but is not the same as, knowledge of experience.

We do not need to explore the status of scientific laws and mathematical truths in Kant, because for our purposes what is of importance is that Kant's immediate successors regarded as unsatisfactory the dualism between the transcendental and the empirical. This dualism establishes a cognitively inaccessible domain of noumena which includes not merely things in themselves but also the human soul and God. The noumenal domain is thus the locus of the significance for human life of scientific theories. In an attempt to render this domain accessible to reason (*Vernunft*), the German Idealists transformed the transcendental ego from a set of logical conditions into a living absolute spirit, from which emanates (or is projected) the empirical world, but also the soul and, at least in the case of Schelling, God as well. In producing the world, the Absolute becomes accessible to human reason as the productive activity itself. This productive activity is inevitably historicized in the course of the nineteenth century and purified of its extrahuman character by Feuerbach, Marx, and Nietzsche. So, like Aristotle's "invisible essence" before it, Kant's transcendental ego is assimilated into the insubstantial blend of human or historical production. Mathematical reason is explained by dialecticospeculative logic, and this in turn is identified with the historical process. The next step is the dissolution of the ostensibly absolute nature of that process.

In the ensuing age of "theory construction," the understanding of a theory as a formal structure does not alter its artifactual status, since forms are taken to be, not "actualized," but literally created by human cognitive activity. The attack, whether Platonic or Kantian, against psychologism—led at first by Frege and Husserl, and then by Russell and the early Wittgenstein—has been effectively negated by historicist doctrines of linguistic activity. Not even Husserl's conception of transcendental subjectivity has proved immune to temporal and historical dissolution. As a result, the phenomenological *Wesensschau* has become a kind of optical illusion in which the discursive *Sinn* is the genuine, and genuinely historical, "essence" of visual appearances. Thanks in part to the influence of the later Wittgenstein but also to a variety of other factors, the same situation obtains in the mathematically or "analytically" oriented branches of the philosophy of science. Science as a linguistic process has triumphed over the pre-Darwinian, pre-Einsteinian sense of science as theoretical understanding of the immutable laws of nature. And thanks to alternative algebras, non-Euclidean geometries, the shipwreck of formalism, and the apparent infinity of possible axiom systems, exactly the same is true of mathematics. We now see that at the decisive level, theory has been transformed into interpretation. *Doxa* is the successor to *episteme*, and poetry has triumphed in its ancient quarrel with philosophy.

# IV

We are now in a position to assert the striking fact that as the scope of theory expands, the difference between theory and interpretation narrows. In general terms, the natural basis of theory, whether understood as the domain of *phronesis* or as the pretheoretical domain of common sense, is replaced by theoretical construction. Theories multiply, while at the same time they both confirm and invalidate themselves by producing their own presuppositions. To make the same point in more up-to-date terminology, the validity of each theory is relative to an indeterminate number of antecedent and coordinate "background" theories (just as a mathematical proof for the consistency of one branch of mathematics is relative to another mathematical theory). The cosmos of *theoria* is replaced by the multiple and multiply fractured worlds of competing or successive theories, with the result that unity is a question of interpretation. As we have now seen, the condescension expressed by many contemporary "rationalists" of a scientific or analytical bent toward the new popularity of hermeneutics is entirely unwarranted. It is a case of the pot calling the kettle black.

Our next step will be to illustrate briefly the self-vitiating consequences of the expansion and multiplication of theory, or its transformation into theory construction, by way of the example of hermeneutics. The science of hermeneutics originated as a philological attempt to fix the boundaries of the correct reading of Holy Scripture. Whereas the initial impetus was dogmatic, it was not long before the intrinsic relativism of philology, as well as the ostensible impartiality of science toward theological conflicts, produced both a multiplicity of philologically certified "correct" accounts of Scripture and a radically impious because quite "positivistic" scientific restatement of the hermeneutical problem. In Spinoza's *Tractatus Theologico-Politicus*, we see an influential example of the combination of these two tendencies. One could say that for Spinoza, there was a theoretical continuity between the attempt to read "the book of nature" and the attempt to read "the book of God." In principle, Spinoza had opened the horizon of a universal hermeneutic which is on the one hand scientific or which embodies the sound methodology of the adaptation of scientific reasoning to the needs of philology, but which on the other hand allows of a distinction between method and content. It would seem that a rigorous application of this method would lead to a repudiation of all claims to dogmatic certitude concerning Holy Writ. We see here the paradigm for the later definition of philological hermeneutics as a "regulative"

discipline which establishes canons, not laws, and which recommends
or guides us among the multiplicity of possible interpretations rather
than certifying one or the other as *the* correct interpretation. Differently stated, the regulative function of modern hermeneutics is a consequence of the *failure* of biblical hermeneutics.

In any case, the scientific sense of the theoretical function of hermeneutics was dropped in favor of the philological sense, when hermeneutics was extended by Schleiermacher and Boeckh to encompass first
the ancient humanistic texts and then more generally the domain of
the philological sciences. Thus Boeckh's major work on hermeneutics
bears the title *Enzykopädie und Methodenlehre der philologischen
Wissenschaften*. This shift from a natural-scientific to a philological
paradigm brings with it the decisive entrance of history, which had not
yet infected the experimental and mathematical sciences, into hermeneutics. The historical sciences cannot be mathematicized. In reading
the hermeneutical aphorisms of Schleiermacher dating between 1805
and 1809, in which he speaks of the infinite task of *Verstehen* as
*subtilitas legendi* (p. 31), and then emphasizes *Gefühl* rather than
methodical rules (p. 61), one thinks of Pascal's *esprit de finesse* and
Rousseau's *sensibilité*. The same theme leads in the 1819 manuscripts
to the linking of hermeneutics with rhetoric and dialectic (p. 80) and in
the 1829 manuscripts to the equation of *Verstehen* with *Auslegen* or
linguistic interpretation (p. 124).[3] It is scarcely necessary to insist
upon the importance of these notions for the development of the hermeneutical theories of Dilthey, Heidegger, and Gadamer. What we
rather need to notice is that Schleiermacher's maxims or "canons" are
quasi-mathematical in the sense that they are empty of content.[4] At
the same time, they are considerably weaker than mathematics, not to
say platitudinous, when considered as regulative maxims. It is useful
to be reminded of Plato's distinction between the measures of arithmetic and of the suitable, or of Pascal's distinction between the *esprit
géométrique* and the *esprit de finesse*. But is this the basis for a theory
of interpretation?

In his book on philological method, Boeckh emphasizes the historical as opposed to the purely conceptual nature of hermeneutics (pp.
18, 31), as well as its own "productive" or "constructive" function in
the reproduction of historical knowledge (pp. 14, 17).[5] In the natural

sciences, in other words, to conceive is to grasp things as they are. In the *Geisteswissenschaften*, thanks to the historical nature of *Geist*, to "grasp" is already to transform or to interpret. The scientific nature of the methodological aspects of philology are thus external to the historical or perspectival nature of the content or subject matter of philology. In an important passage, Boeckh defines the essence of *hermeneia* as "what the Romans call *elocutio*, that is, not understanding but making understandable" (p. 80). This last distinction embodies what we may call the "classical" conception of hermeneutics: one can make understandable only that which contains a potential sense. But the act of fulfilling this potency is entrusted to *elocutio*, not to mathematical reason. As in oratory or rhetoric, the selection of terms by the "eloquent" speaker is regulated both by his subjective capacities and by his assessment of the specific capacities of his audience. In order to be made understandable, the material must be "made" or reshaped, that is, interpreted. For Boeckh, the potency of sense inheres neither in the text nor in the interpreter alone but in their interaction. This is the philological basis for Gadamer's later doctrine of *Horizontverschmelzung* ("fusion of horizons").

Boeckh's distinction between understanding and making understandable is rooted in the same considerations that led Schleiermacher to associate hermeneutics with rhetoric and dialectic. The considerations issue in the enunciation of the hermeneutical circle: interpretation presupposes a knowledge that is derivable only from an understanding of the material to be interpreted (p. 84) The knowledge to which Boeckh refers is of course not an understanding of the detailed content of the text before having read it but a self-knowledge that allows us to understand the thoughts of other human beings. As we shall see, this point is given an ontological formulation by Heidegger. Heidegger apart, the philological conception of interpretation is plainly rooted in the thesis of a common human nature that remains stable within history. It is this common human nature, not of course uniform but qualified in endless ways, that is the content of our preunderstanding and that enables us to employ our philological tools in a manner that is not merely "valid" or "technically sound," but *subtle*.

At the same time, Boeckh's acceptance of the modern doctrine of the historicity of the human spirit contradicts his effort to ground under-

standing in self-knowledge. Boeckh echoes Schleiermacher's observation on the infinite nature of hermeneutical interpretation by citing the
orator Gorgias's *Peri Physeos*. The listener (or reader) never understands words in the same sense as the speaker. Boechk comments:
"Since therefore the alien individuality can never be completely understood, the task of hermeneutics can only be fulfilled through unending
*approximation*, that is, through a gradual approach that proceeds
point by point but is never completed" (p. 86). *Verstehen* rests finally
upon a natural capacity of tact (*der richtige Takt:* p. 87). Boeckh does
not notice that the infinity of the journey compromises the "correctness" of tact. There is in hermeneutics no equivalent to the limit of an
infinite series in mathematics. Boeckh also seems to confuse the "individuality" of the author's personality with the written sense of his text.

The shift from the paradigm of natural science to that of historical
philology is deepened by Dilthey and Nietzsche, who extend hermeneutics to the study of human history, and in Nietzsche's case still more
radically to the interpretation of the world as a series of historical
perspectives. Nietzsche, as it were, resolves, or attempts to resolve,
Boeckh's problem by transforming infinity into the closed circle of the
eternal return of the same. He fails to notice, incidentally, that in so
doing, he is adapting to his own purposes the central intuition of
Hegel. However, Nietzsche leaves the evidence of circularity or totality
to the vision of the individual interpreter. Dialecticospeculative logic is
thus replaced by aesthetic perspectivalism; the Absolute is rendered
logically incoherent in its new identity as the will to power. So too
Nietzsche celebrates Spinoza's *amor fati* as an anticipation of his own
teaching. But in substituting enthusiasm (in the literal sense) for the
deductive structure of fate, Nietzsche transforms pantheism into solipsism and fate into chance. There is no cosmological basis to support
the assertion that the world is a work of art and so that art is worth
more than the truth. The concept of being "worth more" depends
upon a hierarchy of values, as does Nietzsche's fundamental distinction between noble and base nihilism. But the self-assertion of value by
the "self", who is merely a phenomenal manifestation of the will to
power, amounts to the equation of interpretation with the fluxions of
chaos.

Heidegger atempts to rescue Nietzsche's main themes from chaos by incorporating them in an ontological structure that also rescues the hermeneutical circle of philology from inconclusiveness. He combines the radical individualism of Nietzsche's aesthetic perspectives and Kierkegaard's notion of genuineness in a transcendental structure that is at once Kantian and Hegelian. The finite world of man (*Dasein*) is organized by his categorial (existential) structure, which projects in advance the "formal" basis for individual interpretations of the content of the world. The "meaning" or "sense" of the world is "secreted" by man in a way that is intended to express the general structure as the individual decision or interpretation of the unique individual. But the structure is itself understood as temporal or historical, to be sure in the "ontological" senses of these terms. This is the Hegelian element in Heidegger's ontology. But the Hegelian element does not blend with the Kantian element of a transcendental structure of onto-logical categories (to borrow a Heideggerean hyphen). Having banished the Absolute to the transtemporal and transhistorical domain of what is in effect the *Jenseits* of classical Christian Neo-Platonism, Heidegger was never able to explain discursively (*Sein and Zeit* is a discursive or "academic" work of ontology) the ground of his existential categories. He was unable to progress beyond the level of Nietzsche.

In a word, Heidegger's early ontology is not a phenomenological description of the world but an *interpretation*. What are for the student of hermeneutics the crucial paragraphs 31 and 32 of *Sein und Zeit* thus inadvertently reveal the crucial shortcomings of the work as a whole. In these paragraphs, Heidegger explains how *Dasein* produces "in advance" the sense or meaning (*Sinn*) of all concrete interpretations of everyday life, itself the womb of all subsequent theorizing. It does this by means of the existential (i.e., ontological or categorial) faculties of *Verstehen* and *Auslegung* ("understanding" and "interpreting"), together with the "vision" or "transparency" (*Durchsicht*) that corresponds very approximately to a historicized *phronesis*. *Sinn* is thus for Heidegger itself an existential of *Dasein* and not a property of things (*Seienden*). This is the basis for the doctrine that the world is a text.[6] Accordingly, ontology is transformed into hermeneutics. But the relativism intrinsic to philology, the chaos that marks Nietzsche's will to power and Heidegger's inability to negotiate discursively the separation of the ontological from the ontic, are all fragments of traditional rationalism by comparison with postontological deconstruction, as Derrida himself insists. If the world is a text, then we who read it are nothing more than characters in its antiplot. It is no longer meaningful to speak of "understanding" or "interpreting," and the ostensible freedom from the domination of classical metaphysics becomes simply another version of *amor fati*.

In this context, to repeat, Heidegger is a traditional rationalist. But by in effect making the world a text and ontology into hermeneutics, Heidegger shows that he accepts the modern distinction between reason, as fundamentally mathematics, and poetry. The quasi-mathematical character of a discursively accessible categorial ontology, is dissolved by the poetic character of the unique perspectivism of what the Germans call *Decisionismus*. *I* give meaning to *my* world by choosing authentically. "Only *Dasein* can therefore be meaningful [*sinnvoll*] or meaningless [*sinnlos*]" (par. 32, p. 151).[7] Heidegger of course insists that the existential structure of *Dasein,* by which its decisions are regulated, gives stability and sense to the "authenticity" of the individual choice. These structures, however, are at best empty transcendental categories that make possible, not stability, but the human expression of the transience of its *lived* world. And at worst (as well as in fact), the structures are, as we have seen, themselves historical interpretations. Heidegger's analysis of ontological preunderstanding, or of the hermenutical circle, is thus not successful. He follows what amounts to Boeckh's standard philological thesis that all interpretation depends upon our having already understood (implicitly) what is to be interpreted. According to Heidegger, the circle is not vicious but the expression of the fact that *Dasein* provides from within its most general structure the categories and illumination upon which any interpretation rests (par. 32, pp. 152–53). In one sense, Heidegger goes beyond the philological position as well as the dualism of Kant by attempting to derive his categories from human existence rather than from scientific method or formal logic. However, this advance is negated by the analysis of "existence" as temporal *ekstasis*.

The Heideggerian "ecstasy" does not take human being "beyond" the contingency of the temporal process, but attempts to stabilize this process through its own pattern of change. The tenses—future, present, and past—replace Kant's table of categories. The hermeneutical circle is thus Nietzsche's eternal return, not with respect to the content of life, but with respect to the circularity of the temporal patterning of intentional activity. We can therefore see that the initial brilliance of Heidegger's technical mastery is in the end a *reductio ad absurdum*. Both the shaping categories and the shaped content of existence are derived from the temporalization process, which consequently erases that to which it gives birth, in the very act of genesis. Whereas *Dasein* secretes time, time secretes *Dasein*. This is a circle, but not a hermeneutical circle. In the last analysis, to interpret, or to give sense to the world, is to do nothing significant, nothing that signifies beyond its own expression. *The sign signifies nothing.* This is because Heidegger rejects both the classical doctrine of nature and the modern doctrine of the Absolute. There is neither an initial nor a concluding foundation to theory and so no basis for distinguishing between a theory and an interpretation.

After Heidegger, what? In the usual interpretation of logic, everything follows from a contradiction. When the agent of contradiction is a great and difficult thinker, the consequences of the contradiction obey a hermeneutical law of their own: philosophy is succeeded by professorial adaptation and commentary, which in turn gives rise in the following generation to the attempt to progress by taking up one or another of the premises that led to the self-contradiction in the late master's thought. However, whether because of the comprehensive force of Heidegger's thought or because in some sense Hegel was correct and history, or at least the history of philosophy, is completed, there has been no advance beyond Heidegger's *reductio ad absurdum*. We live in a generation of epigones. This is of course not to suggest that the epigones are all Heideggerians but to make the point that the master of hermeneutics in the late twentieth century is historicism, whether lightly concealed by appeals to philological responsibility or painted in the gaudy colors of structuralism and poststructuralist deconstruction. Linguistic horizons, deviant logics, the arbitrariness of axiom sets: all drink from the same waters as do the motley band of Marxist, Nietzschean, Freudian, Heideggerian, pragmatist, phenomenological, and even quasi-Kantian hermeneuticists of our academic community. Amidst the plethora of hermeneutical theories, what it means to be a theory is a matter of interpretation.

We may conclude this history of hermeneutics with the following remark. The initial purpose of hermeneutics was to explain the word of God. This purpose was eventually expanded into the attempt to regulate the process of explaining the word of man. In the nineteenth century we learned, first from Hegel and then more effectively from Nietzsche, that God is dead. In the twentieth century, Kojève and his students, like Foucault, have informed us that man is dead, thereby as it were opening the gates into the abyss of postanthropological deconstruction.[8] As the scope of hermeneutics has expanded, then, the two original sources of hermeneutical meaning, God and man, have vanished, taking with them the cosmos or world and leaving us with nothing but our own garrulity, which we choose to call the philosophy of language, linguistic philosophy, or one of their synonyms. If nothing is real, the real is nothing; there is no difference between the written lines of a text and the blank spaces between them.

# V

What is today called "hermeneutics" traces its proximate origins back to philology on the one hand and ontology on the other. It is, however, important to remember that the actual beginning of hermeneutics lies in the impasse that marks the attempt to establish biblical doctrine by the authority of the prophetic tradition, whether in the written word of God or by way of subsequent revelations. We should not be misled by the numerous contemporary references to pagan rhetoric, dialectic, and jurisprudence into supposing that, in the Greco-Roman world, there was a hermeneutical problem analogous to the one that perplexes the heirs to the Judeo-Christian tradition. Ambiguous statements attributed to the pagan gods were explained by the events of everyday life. Philosophers, although certainly aware that (in Heraclitus's words) "nature loves to hide," were convinced that she would also reveal herself to the ministrations of reason. Classical skepticism is the apparent exception that proves the rule. As Hegel pointed out, the ancient skeptics did not distrust reason but insisted upon man's ability to demonstrate by rational argumentation the impossibility of knowledge of the world. Even the Greek sophists, unlike their contemporary admirers, believed in human nature, as is obvious from the crucial example of the Protagorean principle that the good is the pleasant.

One need not accept Heidegger's oversimplification of the history of metaphysics as *Onto-theo-logik* in order to see that, as a characterization of post-Scriptural speculation, the term has merit. To summarize a complex process in a brief phrase, the failure of scriptural philology led to the bifurcation of hermeneutics into humanistic philology on the one hand and ontotheology on the other. It is true that in the course of time, ontotheology underwent an apparent ellipsis, transforming itself into ontology, with theology relegated largely to the role of denominational substitutes for ontology. But one may detect even within ontology the concealed presence of the hidden God (a phrase that is only apparently pleonastic). At the risk of pressing the metaphor too far, let us make the suggestion that history becomes the surrogate within modern ontology for the hidden God. By another strange irony of history, when Heidegger cites Hölderlin to the effect that "the gods have flown away from this parlous epoch," he is speaking neither as a pagan nor a Christian, but as a Jew. Heidegger's "Hebraic" tendencies could be further documented by a detailed study of his preference for listening to seeing and to the coordinate substitution of the voice of an invisible Being for the *parousia* of eternal form.

The Jews are the chosen people; with them, history in the proper sense begins. History, or the story of the Jews, is the quest for the hidden God, or at least for the Messiah. For those of little faith, history is thus virtually indistinguishable from nihilism. As to the Christian, the arrival of the day of judgment, or the fulfillment within eternity of his temporally conditioned faith, is postponed indefinitely by the (to him) barely comprehensible tenacity of the Jews. The historical people prefer the hope of the future to the blessing of presence. This obstinacy condemns the Christian to a continuation of historical existence, and the cleft opened within eternity by history casts a shadow of ambiguity over Holy Writ. *Theoria* is postponed indefinitely, to be represented for the time being (a curiously resonant idiom) by interpretation. In the absence of God and nature, the world is fractured into a multiplicity of "worldviews," a misleading expression in which the echo of vision is in fact a camouflaged reference to discourse. The divine *logos* becomes human language. The sign is detached from its referent; between them, in place of the hidden God, stands the concept, artifact of historicity.

So much for the theological substructure of the present division (not of course absolute) between philological and ontological hermeneutics. It is this substructure, as articulated by the developments summarized in the preceding two sections of this chapter, that explains the historicism common to both schools of thought. The fundamental difference between these two schools corresponds to the difference between history and historicity. Philological hermeneutics takes its bearings by the text as an "objective" artifact, the product of an intentional consciousness whose meaning can be deciphered with the assistance of the techniques and methods of the *Geisteswissenschaften*. The regulative function of hermeneutics is thus the humanistic counterpart to the scientific experiment as explained by Karl Popper. In both cases, hypotheses are refutable but may never be confirmed by the application of sound methodology. In both cases, the genuinely scientific or secure component is the method together with its negative results. The true or positive meaning of the content remains within the domain of belief, or *doxa,* rather than of knowledge, or *episteme.* Needless to say, the contingency of our grasp of the content affects the techniques of the method, which is subject to progressive revision as technical knowledge grows. But it is precisely *technical* knowledge that grows, external to the enduringly doxic status of the content of the hermeneutical experiment.

The legitimacy of *techne* in scientific methodology is certified by practical results, even in those cases in which our understanding of the "theoretical" situation is uncertain or a matter of interpretation. A good example is the success of physicists in employing wave or matrix mechanics to derive successful explanations of natural phenomena from the theoretically disputable or ambiguous phenomena of quantum physics. But the practical results of a philological interpretation of a humanistic text certify nothing other than the power of that interpretation. The practical results are produced by the interpretation. If the measure of validity in interpretation is the power to persuade, then philological hermeneutics is a testimonial not to objective methods but to the will to power. In fact, even as a methodologist, the philological hermeneuticist turns to history in the attempt to distinguish legitimate from illegitimate interpretations. As a result, his interpretations illustrate with depressing frequency the fundamental defect of history as the standard of legitimacy. The thesis that every text must be understood within the context of its historical period—and so that the intentions and results of the author are a function of his historical perspective (political, social, economic, psychological, scientific, and so on), that even the senses of words undergo change through historical transformation, that there is no enduring stratum of human nature, and consequently no problem, let alone solution, apart from a given historical formulation—leads inexorably to the conclusion that *there is no meaning of the text to be grasped by the reader who belongs to a different historical perspective.*

In a way much more extravagant, and hence more paradoxical, than obtains within quantum physics, the hermeneutical attempt to understand a text by the techniques of historical philology interferes with the meaning of that text. On the one hand, the philologist speaks of objectivity; on the other, he renders objectivity in principle impossible. The common assumption that everything must be understood historically leads to the consequence that nothing can be understood, not even the validity of one's methods, let alone their significance. Or else it leads to the consequence that all understanding is self-understanding. To interpret a text is in fact to produce one's own text. This is why orthodox philology, saturated as it is by historicist assumptions, is not in a strong position to resist the onslaught of postmodern deconstructive criticism. Our historicity leads us, as it would seem, to produce differing interpretations of the same text at different periods of our life; the "sameness" of the text disappears, and identity gives way to difference. On this point, I cannot find any real difference between the two "orthodox" hermeneutical schools represented by H. G. Gadamer and Emilio Betti.

Betti's Kantian orientation strikes me as an empty formalist gesture that does not conceal his failure to think through the consequences of his substantive historicism. Gadamer is entirely superior to Betti in the quality of his interpretations. Furthermore, there is considerable merit in his critique of the attempt to establish methods of interpretation and in his recommendation of classical *prudentia* or *subtilitas legendi*. Yet after devoting more than half of *Wahrheit und Methode* to what is certainly intended as an objective or sound exposition of the thought of the founders of hermeneutics, Gadamer, without any visible recognition of the contradiction, cancels the validity of his own expositions by promulgating a doctrine according to which objective interpretation is impossible. Instead, Gadamer holds that an interpretation is a *Horizontverschmelzung*, a fusion of one's own historical perspective with that of the author being interpreted (pp. 357–59).[9] The inner historicity of experience (p. 329) guarantees the uniqueness of each standpoint or perspective. When Gadamer formulates the Heideggerian thesis that "Being that can be understood is language" (p. 450), he implicitly equates the understandability of Being with its production by the speaker. To read, and so to understand, is to create works of art.

Gadamer is surely no less aware than Betti of the need for philological competence. He is undoubtedly correct to hold that there are no canons that serve as an equivalent to *subtilitas legendi* or that philology does not engender *prudentia*. He is surely mistaken, however, and, despite his greater subtlety, in the same way as the philologists, when he attempts to apply classical *phronesis* to a modern historicist view of human nature. At his best, namely, in presenting his textual analyses, Gadamer demonstrates that the gift of understanding is indeed superior to method, and even, thanks to his own *phronesis* or *prudentia*, to an internally incoherent theoretical foundation. When Gadamer is illuminating about Plato, Dilthey, or Heidegger, it is because the doctrine of *Horizontverschmelzung* is erroneous, just as its philological equivalent, the relativity of historical perspectives, is erroneous. Both fall short of the ontological complexity of history, which is intelligible despite its multiplicity of perspectives. Ontology to one side, the student of Heidegger and the descendant of Boeckh share a common and vitiating historicism. But Gadamer rises above this in the best of his readings, and this is a sign that Boeckh was in fact right to invoke *der richtige Takt*. Ontology and philology are both helpless in the face of the work of genius. It is as absurd to reduce an extraordinary production to "the prevailing views," "established tropes," and "customary procedures of genres" of philology as it is to dissolve it in our own effort to appropriate it. In both cases we are left grasping at air.

The philologist is correct in his assertion that a lack of sound methods leads to the obliteration of the distinction between subtlety and madness. But even if he understands that subtlety is prior to, or independent of, and must itself regulate, all philological methods, he has no way qua philologist to distinguish between subtlety and mediocrity. Since there are no canons for the exercise of subtlety, the philologist is in practice all too often driven to the desperate expedient of equating subtlety with the exercise of sound methodology. The usual result is to define subtlety in terms of historical consensus, that is to say, in terms of the doctrines that characterize the school to which the individual philologist belongs. For there is no such thing as a philosophically neutral philology, except in the sense of the establishment of linguistic procedures to be employed by someone who is not neutral, whether for good or for bad, in the exposition and the evaluation of texts. To repeat, this consensus is itself a kind of *Horizontverschmelzung,* or fusion of two historical constructions. The given community of scholars, whether Marxist, Freudian, positivist, or Heideggerian, "fuses" with the historical community of the text. But the text is itself bypassed and invisible. Homer, Vergil, Descartes, Goethe all are situated within "the context of their time." But this is to place them within the precise dimension from which their genius was employed to detach them. The discontinuity between genius and mediocrity is covered over with a porous mesh of self-dissolving historical platitudes. And the result is to encourage, indeed, to justify, the "madness" of postontological hermeneutics. If truth is a platitude, or if there is no truth but only art, then why should there not be extraordinary art? Why should we be bored to death by historical soundness, if soundness is itself without objective value? *Only disconnect:* thus one might restate E. M. Forster's famous maxim. The tragedy of philological hermeneutics is its often honorable lack of awareness that it is the secret cause of deconstruction.

Deconstruction stands to ontological hermeneutics as does negative to positive theology. As Derrida himself insists, deconstruction necessarily occurs within metaphysical thinking. The fact is, however, that Derrida and his disciples take their bearings neither by metaphysics nor by postmetaphysics. We cannot begin with what has not yet been written, which in any case, once it appears, must itself undergo deconstruction. Instead, we begin with a religious longing for the "not yet," the *deus absconditus* understood as the "never." Derridean hermeneutics is in a way like the Kantian critique, in the sense that it hovers "above" rather than within or outside metaphysics and states the conditions for the possibility of deconstruction. It is religious to the extent that the "beyond" is a *Jenseits,* but at a more immediate level, the discursive articulation of the desirability of deconstruction is an expression of the fashionable post-Hegelian inversion of the ideology of the Enlightenment. The modern celebration of freedom (which, as Fichte asserted, is higher than Being), given a Marxist tincture as well as an anarchic nostalgia, is detached from the sobering spread of illumination and linked to the maddening plunge into darkness.

Despite the "Hebraic" ancestry of Derrida's thought, an ancestry that is already plain in Heidegger, there is no question here of orthodoxy. Like the assimilated Reformed Jew, Derrida is thoroughly "up to date." It is therefore misleading to speak of Derrida's textual exegeses as Talmudic, as I pointed out in an earlier chapter. The esoteric wisdom of the Talmud is a prudentially disguised version of a positive teaching, whereas Derridean deconstruction is the intemperate revelation of what Hegel called the terrible labor of negativity, except of course that for Derrida there is no negation of the negation, no *Aufhebung.* Nevertheless, there is an introductory or predeconstructive justification that serves as a positive doctrine, which is parasitic upon ontology.

We may therefore disregard, from our standpoint, the distinction between construction and deconstruction, and refer to ontological hermeneutics as the principal contemporary alternative to philological hermeneutics. In so doing, we do not imply that every ontological doctrine is itself a theory of interpretation. Some theories of interpretation that look vaguely like ontologies are neither that nor legitimate forms of interpretation. To take the outstanding example, all talk of "phenomenological hermeneutics" that attempts to derive its justification from Husserl rather than Heidegger is surely incoherent. Once we discard academic jargon, what, for example, does it mean to speak of "a phenomenological reading of *The Wings of the Dove*"? Husserlian phenomenology is a descriptive method, not an ontological doctrine, and certainly not an interpretation. An exact description of *The Wings of the Dove* would be at best an error-free reproduction of the text of the novel and at worst a restatement of the text in Husserlian terminology. To give one more example of a Kantian as well as a Husserlian flavor, what light is cast upon the novel in question when we are correctly informed about the structure of the transcendental ego of which not only Henry James, but every failed novelist, is an exemplification?

A hermeneutical ontology is one that treats the text, whether a philosophical essay, a work of art, or a dream, as a sign, not of its own sense, but of some comprehensive theory of human existence, even of Being. An example is Freud's doctrine of the interpretation of dreams. The analyst does not treat the dream as a conscious product of human intentionality, in which the author constructs, for an end known to himself, both the explicit and concealed elements as parts of an integral whole. Instead, the analyst "deconstructs" the dream as dreamed in accordance with a general dictionary of signs, in order to arrive at the decoded message from its actual author, the unconscious (an ancestor of Derridean *différance*). The message is taken to be an expression in local or contingent terms of the Freudian ontology of the soul. If we exaggerate slightly and regard the explicit or presented meaning of the dream as an interpretation of experience in its own right, we may say that one theory is interpreted within another, presumably more general theory. This is in principle the scientific procedure that is formalized in the axiomatic method. The "consistency" of the dream is thus demonstrated within the "logic" of the theory of the interpretation of dreams. For reasons that do not require spelling out, few if any would quarrel with the attempt to provide an explanation of dreams from the waking domain of theory. But this is because it is intuitively persuasive to us that the sense of the dream is at best unclear in its own terms, that dreams are insubstantial. The application of ontological hermeneutics to humanistic texts, however, is itself an unconscious affirmation of the Shakespearean metaphor: "we are such stuff as dreams are made on, and our little lives are rounded with a sleep."

Ontological hermeneutics treats the text as indirect evidence of a general doctrine of Being, or in other words, as data to be transformed, and hence replaced by a theoretical artifact. The deeper affiliation between the apparently distinct schools of ontological and philological hermeneutics is evident from the fact that in both cases, one perspective is replaced by, or fused into, another. But there are two preliminary questions that need to be answered. First: Can we actually see a "perspective" in its own terms, as it is seen, or seen through, by its genuine residents, *before* we assimilate it into our own theory? Second: Is the value of conflicting perspectives itself perspectival, or can we interchange perspectives for the better? If the answers to these two questions are negative, then hermeneutics, or theorizing in general, becomes pointless pseudointerpretation, that is to say, dreaming.

It is worth noting that perspectival hermeneutics has its logical counterpart, and in a way its source, in the Kantian thesis that discursive thinking is judgmental, not propositional. Without misrepresenting Kant, we may say that every judgment is an "interpretation" in the following sense. To say that *S* is *P* is not to perform an analysis upon a preexisting structure but to constitute or synthesize that structure by subsuming one item under a determinate category. In Kant, of course, these subsumptions or interpretations are transcendental, and in no sense either subjective or historically contingent. They become so, however, when the transcendental ego is either historicized or suppressed outright. The categorial structure of judgment is then transformed into a linguistic horizon. Recourse to logic or mathematics changes nothing, since even formal languages are expressions, through their axioms or presuppositions, of a contingent linguistic act of the will.

Ontological hermeneutics is similar to contemporary mathematical theory in two senses. First, one theory (the local theory of the text as intentional artifact) is interpreted within another, presumably more general or fundamental theory. Second, the ontological theory is itself a system of judgments rather than of propositions, because what the ontologist means by "theory" is precisely "interpretation." That this point holds true of contemporary axiomatic mathematics is plain from the Löwenheim-Skolem theorems, the general purport of which is that an axiom set cannot uniquely specify a system of mathematical objects. In other words, axiomatics cannot fulfil the precise purpose for which it was devised. The question of which system of objects is intended thus becomes a matter of the judgment, intuition, or common sense of the model theoretician, in other words, of judgment modified by conventional agreement.[10] Axioms are thus interpretations in the double sense that one set must be validated by the authority of another

set and that the model-theoretic function of the axiom set is not categorical: the theorist must exercise *der richtige Takt*.

Given this hermeneutical similarity between ontology and mathematics, it is useful to consider the one case in contemporary thought
where there seems to be a precise distinction between a theory and an
interpretation, namely, in the study of the foundations of mathematics. We have already suggested that the distinction here too is ambiguous if not spurious. But an example will also illustrate the practical
disadvantages of using a general theory in which to interpret less
general theories, of which one subspecies is the humanistic text. The
abstract or formal nature of the analogy between ontological and
mathematical hermeneutics permits us to employ this example without
running the risk of blurring the numerous specific differences between
the two enterprises.

There is a wide range of specific mathematical theories, for example,
of geometrical form, algebraic equations, real numbers, and so on.
There is also a specific theory, set theory, which may be called "general" in the sense that it purports to be a theory of all mathematics.
The peculiar status of set theory arises from the apparent fact that any
mathematical object can be defined as a set. (The hermeneutical analogue here with respect to texts would be to define any text as equivalent to a theoretical entity within a general ontology.) It therefore
seems to be possible to interpret (in a sense about to be explained) all
parts of mathematics within set theory. What one does is to add the
special axioms of the branch of mathematics at issue to the axioms of
set theory. Let us suppose that we do this with the axioms of geometry.
The variables in the axioms of set theory can be interpreted as designat-
ing geometrical objects, and the predicates or relations of these axioms
can be defined as geometrical predicates or relations. We can now do
two things. First, we are in a position to prove metatheorems about the
theory of geometry. For example, if we can prove within set theory
that the special axioms of geometry are tautologies of set theory, we
have proved that if set theory is consistent, so is geometry. Second, we
can prove additional theorems in geometry by proving their logically
equivalent theorems in set theory.

There are obvious advantages that accrue from the interpretation of
some other mathematical theory within set theory. It is not so obvious

that analogous advantages accrue from the interpretation of, say, a novel or a philosophical treatise within a general theory of interpretation of texts as texts. For example, it might very well be a rule of that part of our theory dealing with interpretations that a legitimate interpretation must be consistent. There seem to be two ways in which one could show consistency. The first way is formal. We would then have to agree upon a method by which to formalize the interpretation (and presumably the text as well). In so doing, however, we would have shifted from general hermeneutics to mathematics. Even assuming success here, the specific interpretation would be assimilated to a general form of interpretation. This might be interesting in its own right, but it would add nothing to the specific interpretation, which was achieved, and could only be achieved, by nonmathematical means. We note further that the theory of interpretation, at least with respect to the rule of consistency, would itself be interpreted within set theory and first-order predicate logic.

We can safely agree that the hypothetical procedure just sketched would be of technical interest to mathematical but not to humanistic hermeneutics. The second way of showing consistency, appropriate to informal or humanistic texts, is by explaining the text in some natural language and leaving it to the audience to see, by their own act of reading, that the interpretation is comprehensive and coherent. In other words, using "hermeneutics" now in its narrow sense, if we formalize, then we are no longer doing hermeneutics but concerning ourselves with a new theoretical artifact: a formal abstraction. But if we do not formalize, *we are merely stating our interpretation.* If we and our audience accept the rule of consistency in hermeneutics, there are no further rules by which to show that we have achieved it. There is, incidentally, a serious difficulty attached to the employment of the rule of consistency in humanistic hermeneutics. Ironical texts like *Gargantua and Pantagruel,* dialectical texts like Plato's dialogues, and witty texts like Molière's plays are examples of texts that present a consistent teaching or message as concealed by a surface that is inconsistent or absurd when taken literally. No rules can teach us how to interpret esoteric texts, or how to penetrate the masks which, as Nietzsche assures us, are loved by whatever is profound. And what, in any case, does "consistency" mean in the case of works of art?

To come back to the general example, there are also disadvantages that accrue from the interpretation of a mathematical theory within set theory. Analogies to these disadvantages are plainly visible within a general theory of ontological or humanistic interpretation. To continue with the case of geometry, we gain no insight into what is significant or profound in geometry by translating it into set theory. These distinctions normally arise from geometrical intuition, which cannot function if it is deprived of its proper objects. Contemporary formalizations of Euclidean geometry thus typically assume from the outset what would be for Euclid and his contemporaries wrong if not dubious: the logical equivalence of geometry and algebra. Even granting that geometry can be algebraicized with no logical problems, we leave the domain of the intuition or direct reflection upon objects of unique types for the domain of equivalences. But reflection upon equivalences will not reveal to the geometrician problems worth exploring, as reflection upon geometrical objects can do. It will not protect the geometrician from the mechanical labor of proving trivial theorems. The creative imagination of the geometer, in order to be directed to its proper task, must do geometry, not set theory. Finally, the translation into set theory disguises the ontological differences between geometrical and algebraic objects.

There is a parallel to all of this in ontological hermeneutics. The generalized restatement of a definite text, in order to be of value in its own right, must be based upon a proper understanding of the text itself. If we read a poem as an example of an ontological theory of being, then we are not paying attention to the poem as poem. Furthermore, we are deprived of our poetic intuition, which is replaced by ontological speculation, just as geometrical intuition in the previous example is replaced by algebra or logical analysis. This is not an objection to a general theory of poetry. But such a theory is valid if and only if it understands what poems are, and there is no apparent way in which to arrive at such an understanding except by the close study of actual poems.

The point made above about equivalence needs to be expanded. The statements of set theory are statements about sets and not about geometrical objects. Even though a statement about sets may be shown to be logically equivalent to a statement about a geometrical object, the former statement depends upon the latter statement (or upon the independent existence of geometry). A logical equivalence is a relation. The shift from geometry to set theory in our example is representative of the deeply held modern conviction that mathematics—and, finally, all rational knowledge—consists in the relations of intrinsically unknowable things rather than in the natures of things. But the interpretation of a humanistic text is based upon the assumption that the text is intelligible in itself, not as a member of a logical equivalence to something else, say to a theoretical element in a general ontology. If we are genuinely interpreters of the text itself, then we cannot in that guise be fundamental ontologists. Furthermore, an ontology of (say) artworks is not itself a set of relations or of logical equivalences, but once more a specific account in some natural language of the artworks as artworks. A completely general ontology is validated by its success in casting light upon entities of all kinds, including works of art or humanistic texts. But these must first be understood in some sense that is prior to the general ontology. Otherwise, we can never say that the general ontology succeeds in explaining or in applying to such particular art works.

If it is true that set theory is a general interpretation of mathematics, it is not true that set theory does something analogous to what a general theory of humanist interpretation is supposed to do. Set theory does not tell us what it means to be a mathematical object. It tells us only that mathematical objects may be represented by sets. It would be meaningless to claim that mathematical objects are "ultimately" sets. Second, set theory does not tell us what it means to be a mathematical theory. It tells us things about the formal structures of theories, but it can do this if and only if we know that what we are studying is in fact a mathematical theory. Third, set theory is useless in the task of giving an informal interpretation of a mathematical theory or of mathematics in general, as for example of the philosophical, artistic, or even political significance of mathematics.

As it turns out, however, a general theory of interpretation also does not do what such a theory is supposed to do. First, it does not tell us what it is to be a text of *this* kind but rather (ostensibly) what it means to be a text of any kind. However, it is fair to suggest that properties holding good for texts of all kinds will also hold good of things other than texts, and perhaps of everything. It does not, incidentally, follow that everything is a text. Second, a general theory of interpretation does not tell us what it means to be a theory but (at best) only what it means to be an interpretation, that is, provided we accept certain presuppositions or historical perspectives. Third, if a general theory of interpretation offers a general distinction between legitimate and illegitimate interpretations, such a distinction will be both too general and too clumsy to distinguish between relevant and irrelevant, or profound and trivial, interpretations.

Our mathematical example casts light upon two general contentions of this chapter. The first is that, even at the most abstract level, contemporary attempts to distinguish between theories and interpretations are failures, mainly because these thinkers reject both the pretheoretical talent of natural reason (sometimes called *phronesis*) and the domain upon which the talent may be exercised, or finally the "absolute" termination and fulfillment of the historical process of interpretation. The second is that, even within mathematics, one pays a price for the shift from one theory into another, a price that in the case of ontological hermeneutics is not accompanied by any balancing advantages. In sum, a theory of interpretation is impossible upon the premises of contemporary theoreticians of interpretation. What remains is philology or madness, each in unconscious pursuit of *phronesis*.

# =5=

## Conversation or Tragedy

In his essay "On the Study of Greek Poetry," Friedrich Schlegel, one of the most neglected of nineteenth-century thinkers, has this to say about modern poetry:

> It makes no claims at all to objectivity, which however is the first condition of pure and unconditioned aesthetic worth, and its ideal is the interesting, i.e. subjective aesthetic force.

A few pages later, we find the following passage on modern aesthetics:

> Blunt or false feelings, confused or wrong judgments, defective or common intuitions, will not only generate a multitude of separately incorrect concepts and principles, but also fundamentally wrong directions of investigation, totally inverted fundamental laws. Hence the dual character of modern theory, which is the undeniable result of its whole history. It is namely in part a true impression of modern taste, the abstract concept of inverted praxis, the rule of barbarism; in part the useful constant striving for a universal science.[1]

I know of no better concise statement on the contradiction intrinsic to the modern development of hermeneutics. This contradiction is the engine that drives the Enlightenment on its inexorable journey into postmodern decadence.

One does not need to take the side of the ancients in order to recognise that modernity is not so much a body of doctrines as a style of existence. This style exemplifies the conviction that freedom is higher than Being and, further, that Being is the mere negation of freedom.[2] If every determination is a negation, to be is the same as not to be, in accord with Hegel's *Science of Logic*. A scientific account of totality that is at the same time the expression of human freedom requires the assimilation of Nothingness into Being and of Being into the subjectivity of conceptualization. The world becomes my concept, and the "positive" moments of the concept are at once productions of a hypostatized negative activity. In simpler language, beings deconstruct themselves as they are constructed by the process of genesis that is ostensibly the same as the process of self-consciousness. Accordingly, science is knowledge of the *ground* of positive structure, namely, of the *nihil* from which beings come and into which they return. To be is at bottom to be nothing. But if logic or scientific law is a product of nothing, it cannot express the conceptual articulation of what produces, and so hides behind or within, phantasms of rationality. The production process of phantasms is not the same as reality unmasked. Kant's noumenal domain is thus equivalent to silence. This is the theoretical counterpart of the uneasiness that is the dark side of the will to freedom. In John Locke's words, "the chief, if not the only spur to human industry and action is *uneasiness*." This is what Hegel means by "the peculiar restlessness and dissipation of our modern consciousness."[3]

The attribution of priority to freedom, in short, leads to the assimilation of Being by Nothingness and of happiness by uneasiness. The constant striving for a universal science succumbs inevitably to constant striving. As our ability to take refuge against uneasiness in the search for universal science diminishes, our obsession with the exceptional particular increases: the true gives way to the interesting. Science is unmasked as rhetoric. In the terminology of the previous chapter, theory decays into interpretation. Accordingly, the impetus toward political universalism, rooted in the expurgation of error and ignorance by truth, dissipates into the empty universalism of "fairness" or "seeing the other person's point of view." If each viewpoint defines a world, then the earlier aristocratic desire of the philosopher to become a god reappears—by way of a "negation of the negation" that lowers but does not raise to a higher level—in democratic form: we are all gods. Or, as the point would have to be made in the posttheological epoch, we are all interesting. To be sure, the prejudices of the philosophers are replaced by those of the academicians, yet we can take comfort in Hegel's observation that history is a slaughter-bench, an observation that remains true even when the true is replaced by the interesting.

In order to understand the political heritage of the Enlightenment, one must be able to derive from the will to freedom both the tendency toward universal tyranny and the decay of the universal into a manifold of discontinuous particulars. Stalin and Mao, like Napoleon before them, are the political incarnation of mathematical reason; Western liberalism corresponds to the early nineteenth-century rediscovery of the axiom that *ex nihilo nihil fit*. If there can be no compromise with error and superstition, then the appeal to the republic of letters is at best a rhetorical device by which one requests the tolerance of the existing authorities toward their own destruction. Conversely, if a hundred flowers are indeed to bloom, they cannot do so in the form of the seventeenth-century geometrical garden but require the chaotic freedom of a field of wildflowers and weeds. Domination and chaos are the inseparable twins of Enlightenment. It is essential to understand that they are not the extreme points of conflicting tendencies but that they rather function jointly within the sinews of "progressive" political action.

To illustrate my point: one may attempt to defend a "pragmatist" conception of liberalism in the manner of Richard Rorty, who, in a recent discussion with Jean-François Lyotard, says: "for us, 'rational' means simply 'persuasive' and 'irrational' means 'evoking force'."[4] On this critical point, Lyotard's reply goes deeper:

> to persuade is not to convince. Persuasion is a rhetorical operation, and the Greeks knew that this operation utilises trickery [*la ruse*], mental violence. I therefore pose the question: may the duty to be free be an object of persuasion?

And again, after speaking of the murder of an amiable and legitimate French king by the revolutionists of 1792, Lyotard goes on to say:

> We [French] cannot forget that this crime is horrible. This is to say that when we try to think about politics, we know that the question of legitimacy may be posed at each instant. We know this by our

history, for we have nevertheless changed our constitution some ten times since this crime, and this is not by chance. The question of legitimacy is always pertinent, à propos no matter how small a political fact, and this is not the case in the United States. The same is true for literature. The difficulty that the Americans, and also the English and Germans, have in understanding that which we call *écriture* is linked to this memory of crime. When we speak of *écriture*, the accent is placed on that which is necessarily criminal in *écriture*, something which is forgotten the instant that one begins to speak about literature in purely academic terms.[5]

Let us put to one side the question of Gallic hubris in attributing to writing in general the inherited properties of French *écriture*. Lyotard's statement is important for us in two distinguishable but related senses. First, it reminds us in a polite but firm manner that too much of the Anglo-Saxon celebration of postmodernism reduces politics to the question of who will be the next president of the Modern Language Association. Having said this, I should add that more than one Frenchman who speaks of domination and the crime of écriture has been prepared to accept extravagant lecture fees from his American cousins as well as the adulation of Anglophone disciples in the war against the metaphysics of presence. I leave it an open question whether this is a nobler tactic in the revolution of liberation than Maoist terrorism. Certainly it is more convenient for both parties to this bourgeois affair. Second, Lyotard's remark on the crime of *écriture*, if we connect it to the Derridean sense of "writing," reminds us of Heidegger's essay "The Saying of Anaximander." Anaximander explains the continuous destruction of generated things as their "making recompense" (διδόναι γὰρ αὐτὰ δίκην) to each other for their unrighteousness (ἀδικία) through the ordering of time. Heidegger connects this to his thesis that Being conceals itself through the uncovering of the world of beings. "Each epoch of world-history is an epoch of error," namely, the mistaking of the temporal appearance of beings for Being.[6] According to Heidegger, ἀδικία means to be "out of the groove." The "groove" is "presence" or tarrying between coming forward and passing away. Generated beings are "out of the groove" because, although they are transient, they attempt to "stand fast in their tarrying in the sense of what is simply permanent."[7] In other words, they pretend *to be*. Justice is therefore deconstruction.

I want to put this last point in a general way, without restricting it to the particular case of Derrida. French postmodernism can be understood in the light of Heidegger's interpretation of Anaximander, with the crucial difference that *Sein* is replaced by *Nichts*. Accordingly, Heidegger's "poetic thinking" is more or less silently rejected as a romantic relic of the onto-theo-logical epoch and is replaced by Nietzsche's paradigm of the artist-warrior, or the recognition that to create is necessarily to destroy. To be is to be guilty of the crime of preventing something new from coming into being: "Nous sommes tous des assassins." Hence the pathos of Lyotard's characterization of the difference between himself and Rorty: "he is conversational; I am tragic."[8] I accept this as a fair statement of the alternative response to the identification of freedom and spontaneity. On the one hand, the product of spontaneity is pointless; on the other, it is guilty of the crime of the destruction of its antecedent and the suppression of its successor.

The uneasiness that accompanies the modern sense of freedom leads at the beginning of the Enlightenment to relatively conservative doctrines. I do not believe that we can understand this conservatism as merely an exoteric accommodation to political authority. To the contrary, it expresses very well the inner harmony between traditional and enlightened authoritarianism. Both are rooted in a perception of the dangers of transience: "tragedy" is the correct political equivalent to Heidegger's ontological "error." The tragic note already sounds in the agreement by political philosophers of the seventeenth and eighteenth centuries on the limitations of human nature. The continuous emphasis on power from Bacon onward is mitigated by a perception of the dangers intrinsic to the concomitant unleashing of the passions. And yet, the moderns must build upon the passions, because intellectual power requires the will to activate it, and the will is moved by passion or desire, not by clear and distinct ideas.

In classical political philosophy, passion or desire must be habituated by the intellect.[9] Plato does not distinguish the will as a separate part of the soul, and the status of willing is quite unclear in Aristotle.[10] The situation changes radically at the beginning of modern philosophy. For Descartes, the free will is the one thing that gives us good reason to esteem ourselves and "makes us in a certain sense

similar to God."[11] Descartes goes on to define the pivotal passion of
*générosité* as the highest legitimate self-estimation, stemming from a
"firm and constant resolution" to use one's free will "to undertake
and execute all those things that one will judge to be the best."[12] It
would be easy enough to say that the central role of the will is a legacy
of Christianity. In a sense, this is true, but one cannot fail to notice that
the modern philosophers employ this Christian legacy for the revolutionary purpose of making man the master and possessor of nature. If
we are sufficiently versed in philosophical theology, we may already
sense the reverberations of Feuerbach in the Cartesian doctrine of
*générosité*. From this standpoint, there can be no doubt that the modern age is a secularization of Christianity. Jesus Christ, or God become
man, is the prefiguration of man become God.

According to Leo Strauss, classical philosophy, no less than modern,
is an act of the will. Nevertheless, there is a difference between the
ancients and the moderns with respect to the relation between the will
and the intellect. As Socrates puts it, the classical philosopher wills
that the intellect be god. One could almost say that, from Descartes
forward, the intellect resolves that the will be god. Somewhat more
accurately, the intellect is an instrument of the will to freedom, and
this accounts for the emphasis upon power in modern philosophy.
Despite the exaltation of mathematical and experimental science as the
mediate source of power, modern philosophy *demotes* the intellect by
making it instrumental to the will. In so doing, it necessarily *promotes*
what from the classical standpoint is the lower part of the soul. Modern man wills to be free because he cannot accept restraints upon his
passions or desires. In the metaphorical language of (genuine)
Platonism, he rejects the Ideas as restraints upon Eros. Wonder, or awe
in the presence of the divine, is replaced by curiosity, or the desire to
know "what makes the divine tick." At a deeper level, the desire to be
a god is intensified by modern anticipations of the infinite power of
science. But at the same time, there is a clear perception of the danger
attendant upon launching this revolution. The Cartesian "firm and
constant resolution" is a characteristic of the best or most powerful
individual souls. But in order to do what they believe to be the best,
these souls must also unleash the passions of the great multitude of
unphilosophical human beings. The political consequences are vola-

tile. The masters require servants, but they must beware lest the servants become masters.

The seeds of Romanticism are therefore already visible in the eighteenth-century celebrations of Enlightenment. As d'Alembert admits in the *Preliminary Discourse*, "the nature of man, of which the study is so necessary, is an impenetrable mystery to man himself, when it is clarified by reason alone."[13] Hegel's attempt to resolve the mystery by the dialectic of master and servant, in which the Christian is transformed into God by the conceptual assimilation of the "mystery" of Christ, is too rational to resist the "uneasiness" of the modern consciousness. Precisely if the founders of modernity are correct, and ignorance is superstition, the unleashing of passion and desire guarantees the triumph, not the conquest, of superstition. For passion and desire cannot tolerate *any* restrictions, least of all those of the intellect. The rationalist version of the will to power, developed in the seventeenth century, becomes the nonrational (if not irrational) will to power of the nineteenth century.

Very far then from constituting a linear progression, modern history advances through an exchange of disguises of its originating condition. The future of Enlightenment is Romanticism disguised as postmodernism. No doubt the future of postmodernism is yet another disguise of Enlightenment. But the task of the philosopher, by common agreement of ancients and moderns, is not merely, or perhaps not at all, to predict the future. It is rather to create the present by an act of will. From this standpoint, one may both appreciate the enlightening component of contemporary deconstruction while at the same time urging that it has not gone far enough. If there is a lesson to be learned from Nietzsche, perhaps it is that, in times of disordered "digestion" (his own term), we require a purge of strong rhetoric. My own "deconstructions" of some contemporary doctrines have been undertaken not as part of a return to the past but in the service of *philosophia perennis*.

# II

Philosophy, understood as theology, is impossible unless Nietzsche is right to have Zarathustra call man the unfinished animal. In the Platonic dialogues, this unfinished nature is called Eros. One frequently encounters in the twentieth century, especially among the postmodernists, a critique of Platonic Eros as a rejection of the body. It is not understood that what Plato means by recommending the transformation of sexual energy into the desire for wisdom is not radically different from what Nietzsche calls "chastity." When Zarathustra condemns the despisers of the body, he says that "the body is a great intelligence [*Vernunft*], a multiplicity with one sense, a war and a peace, a herd and a herdsman." But this has to be read in conjunction with the praise of chastity:

> Is it not better to fall into the hands of a murderer then into the dreams of a lustful woman?
> And look at these men, if you will: their eyes speak—they know nothing better on earth than to lie with a woman.
> There is filth at the bottom of their souls, and woe if their filth still has something of spirit in it![14]

This is of course not to deny that there is a difference between Plato and Nietzsche. The difference is not about chastity (understood as the purity of the soul) but about the limitations on Eros. I should like to express this as a difference in the assessment of mathematics. Platonic Eros obeys an unmistakably mathematical principle, according to which madness, or excessive courage, is regulated by the fitting, or by prudential as opposed to numerical measure. This explains the regular (and regulative) presence of mathematical rhetoric in the Platonic dialogues, in contrast to the virtually complete absence of a genuinely mathematical methodology. In Plato, the mathematics of fate is that of Eudoxian proportions. In Nietzsche, fate has nothing to do with mathematics, although it is not entirely distinct from the related sobriety of philology.[15] Nietzschean fatality is the limitation of death or finitude. Number and proportion are accordingly for him transient projections of the will to power, which is, ironically, limited by its own circularity—an irony that Nietzsche presumably overlooked.

Human existence is for Nietzsche a circular exchange of philological interpretations, not of a text, but of the will to power. But by accepting (again, without acknowledgment) the seventeenth-century doctrine of the primacy of power, Nietzsche relinquished the possibility of distinguishing between noble and base interpretations. By a further irony, he was unable to free himself of the "scientific objectivity" of nineteenth-century philology, an objectivity he denounced because of its destructive effect upon life. The distinction between noble and base nihilism is therefore disconnected from Nietzsche's central insight. The invocation to noble nihilism becomes something less than a noble lie: let us call it a gesture whose nobility is compromised by the emptiness of its symbolism. Nietzsche accordingly is *powerless* to prevent the interpretation of power as success.

The consequences of this powerlessness for postmodernism may be illustrated by a brief discussion of one of the most influential and highly praised philosophical books of the past decade, Richard Rorty's *Philosophy and the Mirror of Nature*. As a pragmatist, Rorty would presumably not describe himself in the "tragic" resonances of European Nietzscheanism. At the same time, one could do worse than to call him a cheerful nihilist. At a social level, I find in his book an American optimism of the "can do" variety, yet diluted by a wide and un-American erudition in the recent European philosophical and literary tradition. Cheek by jowl with Dewey, Quine, Kuhn, and Davidson, one finds Heidegger, Gadamer, Habermas, and Derrida. The result is that Rorty's pragmatism, or its political equivalent, liberalism, seems to have been deconstructed into an informed academic conversation, marked, to be sure, by good humor rather than by professorial acerbity (except with respect to the failures of traditional philosophers from Plato to Kant), but nevertheless managing to provide a Mandarin version of the will to power in his distinction between those who are "interesting" and those who are not. Whether intentionally or not, Rorty therefore exemplifies the Anglophone progeny of Nietzsche. Power has become fashion.

Rorty accepts the view of the Enlightenment as an anticipation of contemporary liberalism. He accordingly affirms "the (entirely justified) notion that the preservation of the values of the Enlightenment is our best hope."[16] Nevertheless, Rorty repudiates both the scientific Enlightenment of d'Alembert and the moral Enlightenment of Kant. The conception of scientific truth is replaced by a blend of Wittgenstein's language games and Thomas Kuhn's doctrine of paradigm shifts.[17] The categorical imperative disappears in the rubble of

Rorty's destructive analysis of the transcendental ego, which is replaced by linguistic intersubjectivity and physiological psychology.[18]
Rules are accordingly weakened from concepts of pure reason to
"rules of the game" (my expression). The republic of letters, when
seen through Rorty's microscope, resembles neither an aristocratic
geometrical garden nor a casual field of weeds and wildflowers, but
the void. The mirror of nature smashed (and the status of the microscope concealed by Rorty's polemics against Platonism), we may now
rest content that there is nothing "out there," or in other words that
there is no "*real,* indissoluble philosophical problem *somewhere* in
the neighborhood."[19]

Rorty has written a polemical book, and he therefore invites a polemical reply. We do well to resist this invitation, or at least to approach as
nearly as possible on this point the chastity to which Zarathustra (no
mean polemicist) exhorts us. A little chastity is a dangerous thing, but a
moderate amount is an Aristotelian (if not a Zarathustran) virtue. We
must therefore observe, however moderately, that by the tenets of his
own doctrine, Rorty could have no evidence and no "arguments" in the
current Anglo-Saxon sense with which to persuade us that there is
nothing "out there." Rorty's conversation is guilty of the crime signaled
by Lyotard and is therefore tragic. He reiterates objections to "outworn
vocabularies and attitudes," and employs historical caricatures in order
"to show that the problem of reason cannot be stated without a return
to epistemological views which no one really wishes to resurrect."[20] It
must be emphasized here that Rorty is not in a position to defend the
accuracy of his historical readings but only to contend that they are
interesting. It is therefore not polemics on our part but rather playing by
the rules of the game to reply that these readings bore us. For by "no
one," Rorty clearly refers to those of his tastes. It is true that Rorty begs
the question, but I take it that logic is not an admissible standard here.
We have to rest content with boredom.

For Rorty, there are no problems, since there is no reality, but only
"new and more interesting sentences."[21] We see here the American
version, descended from analytical philosophy, of Derridean textuality
and *écriture.* The crime of illegitimacy is now the failure to be a
member of a fashionable conversational circle. As is necessarily the
case for all those who tacitly equate Being with language, there is for

Rorty no irreducible difference between human beings and "inkwells or atoms." Parisian postmodernists replace ontology with liberation. Rorty evidently equates liberation with etiquette: "to think of Wittgenstein and Heidegger as having views about how things are is not to be wrong about how things are, exactly; it is just poor taste."[22] In slightly different terms, Rorty, like John Dewey, is not a political but a social thinker: "assertions are justified by society rather than by the character of the inner representations they express."[23] Rorty also maintains that the role of the hermeneutical philosopher (and he apparently considers himself to be such) is "to perform the social function which Dewey called 'breaking the crust of convention.' "[24] This function is clearly connected to, if not identical with, what Rorty represents as the "edifying" or "reactive" nature of his own teaching.

I do not believe that Rorty succeeds in explaining (or even in seriously addressing the question of) how philosophy can be both edifying and reactive. In his account, the task of hermeneutics, whether of written or spoken sentences, resembles an endless series of high-level academic conferences, or the exemplification rather than the destruction of bourgeois civilization:

> the point of edifying philosophy is to keep the conversation going rather than to find objective truth. Such truth, in the view I am advocating, is the normal result of normal discourse. Edifying philosophy is not only abnormal but reactive, having sense only as a protest against attempts to close off conversation by proposals for universal commensuration through the hypostatisation of some privileged set of descriptions.[25]

There is something in this passage that is noble and well said, and I respect Rorty for it. But destructive reaction is not creation, and it is hard to see how it can be edifying—necessary, perhaps, but not edifying. One might agree with Rorty when he says that "great edifying philosophers destroy for the sake of their own generation," unlike the great systematic philosophers and scientists who build for eternity,[26] if he had added that creation must follow destruction and wondered whether it is possible to create for one's generation only.

Hegel warns us that philosophy must guard against the temptation to be edifying. Rorty has followed Hegel's advice too well. For without creation, reactive edification is indistinguishable from what Nietzsche calls "slave morality." In the *Genealogy of Morals,* Nietzsche associates the "reactive" with hatred, envy, the desire for vengeance, and so with ressentiment and the slave morality.[27] The active type is marked by the desire for mastery. Needless to say, Rorty is not obligated to use his terms in the sense given to them by Nietzsche. But his use of terms leaves him open to the aforementioned Nietzschean accusation.

Rorty, like those who are edified by his book, gives a liberal interpretation to the will to power. In a way that reminds one of Kojève's Japanese flirtation, there is a muted appeal to the aesthetic sensibility as a justification of linguistic good taste: conversation, to be sure, takes the place of the tea ceremony. I do not accuse Rorty of ressentiment, yet one occasionally wonders whether there is not a note of disappointment underneath his frequent derogatory references to the "errors," "mistakes," "confusions," and "blunders" of the great thinkers of the past. This stylistic flaw is an unfortunate residue of Rorty's previous incarnation as a specialist in analytical philosophy. One wonders whether the denial of scientific objectivity is a sign of psychic damage by scientific objectivity. However this may be, Rorty accepts the continental rhetoric of the end of metaphysics, as we see from a previously cited exchange with Lyotard. He also holds that "it is from France that the most original contemporary philosophical thought comes to us," although he is disquieted by its antiutopian character and cannot understand how "French thinkers are so ready to say things like 'May 68 refutes the doctrine of parliamentary liberalism.' "[28]

We have already seen Lyotard's reply to Rorty's liberalism (a liberalism with which, let it be recorded, I am in deep sympathy). It could also be said that Rorty inconsistently fails to react to what the advanced French thinkers find politically interesting. Rorty would presumably reject my own way of explaining this failure, namely, as a virtue of Yankee common sense. If this is so, it is because of the more general thesis that "common sense" is a vulgarization of the metaphysics of presence (or the glassy essence, in Rorty's own terminology). Rorty rejects not only the mirror of nature and the glassy essence but a "natural 'moral genus' that is inherent in our biological species." Very well. But this leaves unclear the basis upon which Rorty makes the following additional statement:

that which the pragmatist seeks are strongly cosmopolitical narrations [*récits*], but which are not narrations of emancipation. He believes that there was never anything to emancipate, and that human
nature has never been in chains. To the contrary, humanity has
succeeded in creating a nature little by little, by way of very large and
very rich "mélanges of opposed values." Recently, it seems even that
humanity has succeeded in producing a particularly good nature—
that from which has resulted the institutions of the liberal west.
Pragmatism abandons the revolutionary rhetoric of emancipation
and of denunciation (shared by Voltaire, Julien Benda, and Edward
Said) for a reformist rhetoric extolling more tolerance and less suffer-
ing. If it has an idea (in the Kantian sense) in mind, it is that of
tolerance rather than of emancipation.[29]

What is Kantian about this statement is not the "idea" of tolerance
but the term "cosmopolitical." We see here Rorty's view, already
expressed in *Philosophy and the Mirror of Nature*, that liberalism is
the continuation of the Enlightenment. In fact, however, Kant was a
political conservative. He was not thereby intolerant: the equation of
intolerance with conservatism is a liberal prejudice. Pragmatist liberalism is in any case a dubious concept; the pragmatist ought to act
liberally or conservatively depending upon what "works." But let us
grant the designation. Pragmatist liberalism is a consequence of the
destruction of the foundations of Kantian doctrine, a destruction, as I
have argued, that stems from the Achilles' heel of spontaneity. Without such foundations, Rorty's pleas for tolerance must strike the ears
of the postmodern revolutionary as the posturing of an American
Colonel Blimp. I deplore this, but I also deplore the fact that, by
equating human nature with historicogeographical values, the only
sense in which Rorty could be said to be "reacting" to the narratives of
his French fellow conversationalists is by making himself a candidate
for the guillotine.[30]

# III

In a lecture dating from 1976, Michel Foucault seems to take us back to
the productive vision of the seventeenth-century founders of modernity:

> Schematically, we can formulate the traditional question of political
> philosophy in the following terms: how is the discourse of truth, or
> quite simply, philosophy as that discourse which *par excellence* is
> concerned with truth, able to fix limits to the rights of power? . . .
> My problem is rather this: what rules of right are implemented by the
> relations of power in the production of discourses of truth?[31]

In another text from 1976, Foucault refers to his support for "an
insurgency of subjugated knowledges" in opposition to the "tyranny
of globalising discourse,[32] and again, to "the kind of theoretical coronation of the whole which I am so keen to avoid."[33] We may be
permitted to see here a contemporary reenactment, under the disguise
of historical liberation, of the modern revolution against the ancients.
Foucault is, despite a certain modesty with respect to his own "frag-
mentary, repetitive and discontinuous" work, whose character is that
of "febrile indolence,"[34] a partisan of post-Nietzschean frankness on
the subject of power. Discourses of truth are produced by power.
More specifically, any society is permeated by relations of power,
which are themselves established by, and function as, the production
of discourses of truth. "We are subjected to the production of truth
through power and we cannot exercise power except through the
production of truth."[35]

In a 1977 interview, Foucault rebukes those for whom power is
merely repressive:

> What makes power hold good, what makes it accepted, is simply the
> fact that it doesn't only weigh on us as a force that says no, but that it
> traverses and produces things, it induces pleasure, forms knowledge,
> produces discourse. It needs to be considered as a productive net-
> work which runs through the whole social body, much more than as
> a negative instance whose function is repression.[36]

It follows that the reciprocal relation of truth and power is a mark of
*every* regime, capitalist or socialist (although Foucault leaves open the
case of communist China):

> The essential political problem for the intellectual is not to criticise
> the ideological contents supposedly linked to science, or to ensure
> that his own scientific practice is accompanied by a correct ideology,
> but that of ascertaining the possibility of constituting a new politics
> of truth.[37]

Finally:

> the political question, to sum up, is not error, illusion, alienated
> consciousness or ideology; it is truth itself. Hence the importance of
> Nietzsche.[38]

Let us sum up. Power, as articulated within the repressive structure
of a political society, produces truth. At the same time, we *exercise*
power by the production of truth. *Truth is a political product,* presumably of the will to power. Foucault thus reduces philosophical theology to power politics. On this point, he is entirely superior to Rorty in
clarity and depth (as is to be expected of a "student" of Kojève). But
Foucault also appears, throughout the collection of interviews and
lectures from which I have quoted, as a *revolutionary,* a seeker after "a
new politics of truth." Why? On this point, unfortunately, Foucault
relativizes Kojève to mutually inconsistent poles of discourse: on the
one hand, the objective student of power; on the other, a man of the
left who vacillates between anarchism and Maoism.

What is Foucault's theoretical foundation for the rejection of bourgeois society? Why should we reject the "tyranny of globalising discourse" or "the theoretical coronation of the whole" on behalf of the
liberation of "subjugated knowledges"? Does not the use of terms like
"tyranny" and "coronation" on the one hand and "subjugated" on
the other beg the question by invoking the pathos of the sentimental
left, a pathos to which Foucault, as the sober, even ruthless analyst of
power, has no right? One could even suspect that this pathos is
Foucault's exoteric teaching, that he has a hidden agenda of domination lurking under the rhetoric of liberation. But there is a further
difficulty here: the universal role assigned to power as a kind of anony-
mous principle of production does not provide a basis for a hidden *or*
a public agenda. By adopting as his own what amounts to the will to
power, Foucault admits in advance that there is no truth, but only
art—that is to say, production. It turns out that politics is justified as
poetry, and only as poetry. Perhaps the only element of rhetorical
accommodation that goes uncontradicted is the edifying use of "discourse," no doubt adopted to lull his academic readers into thinking
that "reeducation" means hermeneutics rather than murder. Nevertheless, murder is in this context a kind of poetic production, and *de*

*gustibus non disputandum est.* Here is the esoteric link between Foucault and Rorty. The Parisian revolutionary, like the American reactive edifyer, does not wish to be bored. He has his tastes; certain things
"interest" him. And he will conceal this private agenda beneath fashionable left-wing rhetoric. However sharp his political contours in
contrast with his American admirers, Foucault proves to be flaccid and
verbose in comparison with his Maoist interlocutors.[39] The disinter-
ested or scientific study of power contradicts the passionate commitment of the left; the intention to liberate subjugated knowledges contradicts both scientific objectivity and the subjugating impulse of
power politics.

Foucault's rebellion against "globalising discourse" and "the
whole" is at bottom an essentially bourgeois phenomenon of decadence. I suggest that the statements collected under the title *Power/
Knowledge* be read in conjunction with the today largely forgotten
novel by J. K. Huysmans, *Against the Grain.* When the late modern
bourgeois intellectual surrenders to the historical fatigue described so
vividly by Nietzsche, he turns to the "liberation" of subjugated
pleasures—whether in the form of "knowledges," "abnormal discourse," or, as in the case of des Esseintes, Huysmans's hero, random
mixtures of colors, sounds, and smells. A radical political program
such as Maoism (and anarchism is excluded here) is *always* a
"globalising discourse," and hence it is necessarily *enlightening,* in
the sense of Robespierre, rather than "liberating" in the sense of
Foucault. In order to enlighten the masses, it is necessary to replace
superstition by truth, and hence to universalize the masses. This is
undoubtedly the reason why Victor, the Maoist interlocutor, brings
to a close the discussion with Foucault as follows: "I think we are in
agreement about the interpretation of actual practices. But perhaps
we have not really got to the bottom of our philosophical differences. . . ."[40] On the fundamental point, I am afraid that it is Victor
who is the better philosopher. But then, Foucault is a postphilosophical and posthumanist connoisseur of subjugated discourses, not a
philosopher at all. Nevertheless, we should take very seriously
Foucault's "practical" acceptance of Maoism, even if Foucault did
not. To those with a genuine perception of the modern era, it gives a
valuable sign of the "dialectical" process by which Romanticism,

having been sterilized by decadence, is transformed into the next disguise of Enlightenment.

As I compose these lines, I am aware that many of my readers will dismiss me as a spokesman for the political right. But this is a conditioned reflex of the bourgeois, middle-class intellectual. I take my stand with Victor, and hence with the exoteric rhetoric of Foucault, in insisting upon the Enlightenment thesis of the reciprocal relation between power and knowledge. When one listens to the "edifying discourse" and postontological *niaiseries* of the academic disciples of Derrida, Foucault, and the Maoists with a posthuman face, one wonders whether a certain "reeducation" or indeed "liberation" of "the enemies of the people" and hence of "the masses" is not in order. I should like to think of Foucault that the alliance with Maoism in a late period of his life, however finally ineffectual, was a sign of his growing awareness of the intimate connection between hermeneutics (or for that matter "genealogy") and politics. He must have wanted to repudiate statements like this one, dating from 1964 and cited by a recent valuable study:

> the death of interpretation is to believe that there are signs, signs which have a primary, original, real existence. . . . The life of interpretation, on the contrary, is to believe that there are only interpretations.[41]

This statement is an expression of the edifying school of liberationist hermeneutics. It also closely connects Foucault with the notion, apparently rejected by him in his Maoist period, that truth, or belief in an objective reality, is the metaphysical version of violence and domination. As Foucault moved closer to (without reaching) Victor, he seems to have understood that truth is by its nature repressive—of falsehood, ignorance, and superstition. Unfortunately, this understanding was compromised by an inexpugnable taste for "discontinuity," which no doubt resulted in the shift to the post-Maoist, or "ethical," stage, a stage of an ethics of individualism, not of political or social groups. The decadent author of *Les Mots et les choses* was not able to take the decisive step toward the global tyranny of Enlightenment.

We may be grateful for Foucault's honor that this indecisiveness finally produced a separation between him and Maoism. And yet, it also underlines the inadequacies intrinsic to his political awareness. In the years preceding his death, Foucault, by means of what two recent French writers have called an "equivocity on the notion of subject," turned back to the subject in the sense of "the form of the subjugated individual," and hence, as it might seem, to humanism, even to the Enlightenment "discourse of the rights of man."[42] At the same time, Foucault rejected, just as he had during his earlier periods, the "subject" in the sense of modern subjectivity. In the light of this equivocation, he could praise the Greeks for developing an ethics without subjects and advocate a return to the Greeks in a way strangely reminiscent of Leo Strauss, not in order to repeat their ethics but rather to facilitate the bypassing of modernity in the production of a postmodern ethics of individual choice.[43] The French scholars conclude, no doubt rightly, that "Foucault *new look*" was an illusion and that he remained faithful throughout to his denunciation within modernity of "the tyranny of identity, of the normative, or of the universal with respect to the individual in his difference."[44]

What is the "difference" between Foucault's accommodation to Maoism and his final turn to the rights of man? Only this, in my opinion: two different discursive modalities in the continuous and impossible effort to avoid boredom. An ethics of individual choice remains an attack on the bourgeoisie and hence on the mathematical universalism of the Enlightenment. Perhaps Foucault discerned, toward the end of his life, that the essence of Maoism and of bourgeois conformity is the same. Foucault was always an advocate of spontaneity, but never of Kant's conservative restrictions on its consequences. Thus too Foucault could never truly acquiesce in Rortyean liberalism, despite its rhetoric of tolerance, since, as Lyotard explains, persuasion is also violence and suppression. But the tragedy is that *nothing is left* except the random eccentricities underlying the "ontological" pretentiousness of *différance*.

Those who are obsessed by language come finally to the conviction that there is nothing but interpretation. In order to understand the political implications of this conviction, we must put to one side the predeconstructionist fixation on philology and exact scholarship. In fact, if there is nothing but interpretation, these fixations fall away of their own accord: we have been liberated. There is nothing "out there" but ghosts of uninteresting truths; truth is superstition.

"True" enough—at the theoretical level. But we Maoists understand a deeper theory, one that springs from the identity of theory and practice in the will to power. At this deep level, ten thousand feet *below* good and evil, a level by its nature esoteric, we understand that edifying hermeneutics is the fifth column of the army of future Enlightenment. Edifying hermeneutics is the exoteric doctrine of the will to power, an instrument of the cunning of reason, a stage in the dialectical self-destruction of bourgeois civilization. In political terms, edifying hermeneutics (and perhaps even unedifying hermeneutics) is an expression of middle-class fear of the violent and repressive nature of truth. We close with the prophetic words of a French Maoist of a bygone generation, Georges Sorel:

> A social policy founded on middle-class cowardice, which consists in always surrendering before the threat of violence, cannot fail to engender the idea that the middle class is condemned to death, and that its disappearance is only a matter of time.[45]

# Notes

## Introduction

1. Matei Calinescu, *Faces of Modernity* (Bloomington: University of Indiana Press, 1977), p. 164.
2. "Psychoanalysis and the Polis," in *The Politics of Interpretation*, ed. W. J. T. Mitchell (Chicago: University of Chicago Press, 1983), p. 83.
3. See Pamela Major-Poetzl, *Michel Foucault's Archaeology of Western Culture* (Chapel Hill: University of North Carolina Press, 1983), p. 42: Foucault's political theory "approaches not only anarchy but nihilism."
4. See Allan Megill, *Prophets of Extremity* (Berkeley: University of California Press, 1985), p. 233. Megill notes that, after 1970, Foucault refers to his work as "genealogy" rather than as "archaeology," and in a Nietzschean sense: "Foucault's turn to radical activism is closely tied up with his discovery of the rhetorical possibilities offered by the thought of Nietzsche."
5. *Les Mots et les choses* (Paris: Gallimard, 1966), pp. 342–45.
6. *Ibid*, pp. 327ff., 333, 396.
7. *De la grammatologie* (Paris: Les Editions de Minuit, 1967), p. 16; J. F. Lacan, *The Four Fundamental Concepts of Psychoanalysis*, tr. Alan Sheridan (New York: W. W. Norton, 1978), p. 198: "A signifier is that which represents a subject. For whom?—not for another subject, but for another signifier."
8. *Nietzsche and Philosophy*, tr. Hugh Tomlinson (New York: Columbia University Press, 1983), p. 9.
9. *Ibid*, p. 22.
10. *Ibid*, p. 190.
11. *Ibid*, p. 48.
12. *Ibid*, pp. 54, 2.

13. *Ibid*, p. 56.
14. This inference is drawn by Vincent Descombes in *Modern French Philosophy* (Cambridge: Cambridge University Press, 1980), p. 165.
15. *Science of Logic*, tr. Arnold Miller (London: Allen and Unwin, 1969), p. 67.
16. *Ibid*, p. 70.
17. Quoted in Major-Poetzl, *op. cit.*, p. 35.
18. *Negative Dialectics*, tr. E. B. Ashton (New York: Continuum, 1983), pp. 5–6.
19. *Ibid*, p. 56.
20. *Dialectic of Enlightenment*, tr. John Cumming (New York: Seabury Press, 1972), p. 6.
21. *Ibid*, p. 24.
22. *Ibid*, p. 18.
23. Cf. *Negative Dialectics*, p. 11.
24. *Realism and Reason* (Cambridge: Cambridge University Press, 1983), p. xiii.
25. *Ibid*, pp. xvii–xviii.
26. *Die philosophische Diskurs der Moderne* (Frankfurt: Suhrkamp, 1985), p. 342.
27. *Ibid*, p. 344.
28. *Ibid*, p. 346.
29. *Ibid*, pp. 366–67.
30. *Ibid*, p. 395.
31. *Ibid*, pp. 397, 399.
32. *Ibid*, p. 349.
33. *Knowledge and Human Interest*, tr. Jeremy J. Shapiro (London: Heinemann, 1972), pp. 312, 314.
34. *Ibid*, pp. 314–15.
35. The theoretical weakness of Apel's version of the doctrine is immediately evident from his contention that social history mediates between scientific and intersubjective or hermeneutical experience. "Social" contains all the defects of Habermas's "inter."

# Chapter 1

1. *Pensées*, in *Oeuvres complètes*, ed. Jacques Chevalier (Paris: Bibliothèque de la Pléiade, 1954), no. 91, p. 1113. For inquietude during the Enlightenment, cf. Jean Deprun, *La Philosophie de l'inquiétude en France au dix-huitième siècle* (Paris: J. Vrin, 1979).
2. *Pensées*, no. 168, page 1132. Cf. Leo Strauss's characterization of John Locke's doctrine of human life as "the joyless quest for joy" in *Natural Right and History* (Chicago: University of Chicago Press, 1953), p. 250.
3. See the important article by Emil Fackenheim, "Kant's Concept of History," *Kant-Studien* 48, no. 3 (1956–57): 381–98, esp. 396. Fackenheim's general approach is developed in considerable detail by Y. Yovel in *Kant and the*

*Philosophy of History* (Princeton: Princeton University Press, 1979). This is the best work on the subject, and I have learned much from it. As my intentions are not philological, I restrict myself here to an indication of the main points on which I differ from Yovel. He sees Kant's view of history as primarily moral (pp. ix, 30, 47, 116, 174, 197), although he is aware of the fundamental difficulties in such a view. I believe that Kant's conception of history is in its main thrust neither natural nor moral. Yovel is led to identify two independent systems, natural history (culture) and moral history (p. 278), and also a history of reason which is necessary but (on Kantian grounds) impossible (p. 286). I see one dimension of history, ontologically independent, not rational, moral, or political but the neutral *Aufhebung* of the three. Yovel believes that Kant possesses a metaphilosophical theory which accounts to a significant extent for the rise of rationality in rational terms (p. 212). This is closely connected to Yovel's failure to see the irrational consequences of the spontaneity of reason and the primacy of the will over the understanding (pp. 15; 19; 39; 99; 131; 150, note 12). Finally, there is no mention in Yovel's book of the last consequence of Kant's rejection of orthodox religion: the deification of man (the highest instance of which, the deification of Kant, is mentioned by Yovel on page 247, note 31, as an absurd consequence of Kant's unmodified view, and is thus rejected by Yovel).

4. *Discours préliminaire de l'Encyclopédie,* in *Oeuvres de d'Alembert,* vol. 1, pt. 1 (Geneva: Slatkine Reprints, 1967), p. 17.

5. *Essai sur les élémens de philosophie,* in *Oeuvres,* vol. 1, pt. 1, p. 122.

6. *Ibid.,* p. 125.

7. Cf. Kant's remark about human life as a *Possenspiel* in *Über den Gemeinspruch: Das mag in der Theorie richtig sein, taugt aber nicht für Praxis,* in *Kleinere Schriften zur Geschichtsphilosophie, Ethik, und Politik* (Hamburg: Felix Meiner Verlag, 1959), p. 108.

8. For Bacon's view on the relation between science and politics, see his utopia, *New Atlantis,* in *Works,* ed. Spedding, Ellis, and Heath (Boston: Brown, 1861), 5: 411: the Father of the House of Salomon says, "And this we do also: we have consultations, which of the inventions and experiences which we have discovered shall be published, and which not: and take all an oath of secrecy, for the concealing of those which we think fit to keep secret: though some of those we do reveal sometimes to the state, and some not." Cf. Rousseau, *Discours sur les sciences et les arts,* in *Oeuvres complètes* (Paris: Bibliothèque de la Pléiade, 1964), p. 29. For the aesthetic sensibility, see *Confessions* (Paris: Garnier, 1952), 1: 218ff., 2:179; *Les Reveries du promeneur solitaire* (Paris: Garnier, 1949), pp. 1, 5–6, 18, 68, 83; *Emile* (Paris: Garnier, n.d.), p. 238. See also my *Nihilism* (New Haven: Yale University Press, 1968), pp. 77–78.

9. *Le Problème de la vérité dans la philosophie de Nietzsche* (Paris: Editions du Seuil, 1969), p. 304.

10. There is a good analysis of political or "external" freedom in Kant in W. A. Galston, *Kant and the Problem of History* (Chicago: University of Chicago Press, 1975), pp. 197ff.

11. *Kritik der reinen Vernunft* (Hamburg: Felix Meiner Verlag), B74–75, B93 (hereafter cited as *KrV*).

12. *KrV*, B430, B561, B573ff.; *Kritik der praktischen Vernunft* (Hamburg: Felix Meiner Verlag, 1952), pp. 57, 115, 117 (hereafter cited as *KpV*). In what is perhaps the most obscure section of the *KrV*, Kant also speaks of a spontaneity of *Selbstbewusstsein* that "die Vorstellung *Ich denke* hervorbringt" (B312). As Kant says later in the same work, I am conscious of the spontaneous function of *Verstand* within myself, but I have no intuitive, nonsensuous perception of myself as *Ding an sich* that is the seat of this spontaneous function. For our purposes, we can ignore this peculiar reference to spontaneity (which is of course crucial to a complete understanding of Kant's technical doctrine). For further discussion of these and related points, see G. Prauss, *Kant über Freiheit als Autonomie* (Frankfurt: V. Klostermann, 1983), and B. Ortwein, *Kants problematische Freiheitslehre* (Bonn: Bouvier, 1983).

13. KrV, B561.

14. Cf. Ortwein, *op. cit.*, pp. 15–16.

15. *KpV*, pp. 3–4.

16. *KrV*, B766–97.

17. "Zwar denke ich Vieles mit der allerklarsten Überzeugung, was ich niemals den Mut haben werde zu sagen, niemals aber werde ich etwas sagen, was ich nicht denke." Cited by K. Löwith in *Von Hegel zu Nietzsche* (Stuttgart: W. Kohlhammer, 1953), p. 104.

18. *KrV*, B776. Yovel (*op. cit.*) is especially good in showing the exoteric status of Kant's analysis of orthodox Christianity (pp. 93, 109, 116, 214ff).

19. *Beantwortung der Frage: Was ist Aufklärung?*, in *Kants Werke*, Akademie Textausgabe (Berlin: Walter de Gruyter, 1968), 8: 35.

20. This thesis is developed in the essay *Idee zu einer allgemeinen Geschichte in weltbürgerlicher Absicht*, which I cite from *Kants Werke*, 8. Yovel (*op. cit.*), following Eric Weil, speaks of "the cunning of nature" (pp. 8f., 31 *et passim*). I think it is better to speak of the cunning of history, to which is assigned the (impossible) task of reconciling the conflicting claims of reason, morality, and politics.

21. *Op. cit.*, pp. 395–96.

22. *Kritik der Urteilskraft* (Hamburg: Felix Meiner Verlag, 1954), p. 301 (hereafter cited as *KdU*). Fackenheim, *op. cit.*, p. 396.

23. *KrV*, B777.

24. *Ibid.*, B777–78.

25. *Ibid.*, B778.

26. *Was ist Aufklärung?*, p. 37.

27. *Ibid.*, p. 29.
28. *Zum ewigen Frieden: Ein philosophischer Entwurf, in Kleinere Schriften*, p. 164.
29. *Was ist Aufklärung?*, p. 38.
30. *Ibid.*, p. 39.
31. *Ibid.*, pp. 35—36.
32. *KrV*, B766—67.
33. *Ibid.*, B767.
34. *Ibid.*
35. *Ibid.*, B199—200.
36. *Ibid.*, Bxxxv.
37. *Ibid.*, B767—68.
38. *Ibid.*, B769—770.
39. *KpV*, p. 4.
40. *Krv*, B772—73.
41. *Ibid.*, B774.
42. *KpV*, p. 128.
43. *Ibid.*, p. 132.
44. *KdU*, pp. 261, 279—80.
45. *Ibid.*, pp. 298—300.
46. *Ibid.*, p. 301.
47. *Discours sur les sciences et les arts*, p. 6.
48. *KdU*, p. 312.
49. *Ibid.*, pp. 300, 313.
50. *KpV*, pp. 140—41.
51. *Ibid.*, p. 141.
52. *Ibid.*, pp. 92, 100—01.
53. *Über den Gemeinspruch*, pp. 87—88.
54. *Zum ewigen Frieden*, p. 160.
55. *Ibid.*, p. 161.
56. *Ibid.*, p. 151.
57. *Idee zu einer allgemeinen Geschichte*, pp. 21—26.
58. Cf. *Mutmasslicher Anfang der Menschengeschichte, in Kleinere Schriften*, p. 56.
59. *Über den Gemeinspruch*, p. 108. Cf. *Mutmasslicher Anfang*, p. 56.
60. *Idee zu einer allgemeinen Geschichte*, p. 30.
61. *KdU*, p. 322. Cf. *KpV*, pp. 144f., 164—67.
62. *KpV*, p. 164.
63. *Ibid.*, p. 4.
64. *Philebus* 28C.
65. *Über den Gemeinspruch*, pp. 78—79.
66. *KpV*, p. 87.
67. *Von einem neuerdings erhobenen vornehmen Ton in der Philosophie, in Kants*

*Werke*, 8:393. Kant adds: "Die Philosophie des Aristoteles ist dagegen Arbeit." This helps us to understand the impulse of modern and "rationalist" scholarship to transform Plato into Aristotle. Modernity is a time of *Arbeit*, not of aristocratic play.

68. Cf. my previously cited *Nihilism*.
69. *Statesman* 310C–311C.
70. *L'Archaeologie du savoir* (Paris: Gallimard, 1969), pp. 21, 172.
71. *Menschliches, allzu Menschliches*, in *Werke*, ed. K. Schlechta, (Munich: Carl Hanser, 1954), 1: 966, par. 221.
72. *The Legitimacy of the Modern Age*, tr. R. M. Wallace (Cambridge: MIT Press, 1983), p. 99.
73. *Ibid.*, p. 55.
74. *Ibid.*, p. 75.
75. *Ibid.*, p. 126.

# Chapter 2

1. *De la grammatologie* (Paris: Les Editions de Minuit, 1967), p. 95.
2. Cf. "Violence and Metaphysics: an Essay on Emmanuel Levinas," in *Writing and Difference*, tr. A. Bass (Chicago: University of Chicago Press, 1978), pp. 79–153.
3. *Ibid.*, pp. 102–03.
4. "Freud and the Scene of Writing," in *Writing and Difference*, p. 203.
5. *Epistolae* B, 314c1–3.
6. "La pharmacie de Platon," in *La Dissémination* (Paris: Editions du Sueil, 1972), pp. 85–86. English trans.: B. Johnson, trans., *Dissemination* (Chicago: University of Chicago Press, 1981), p. 76. I have used Johnson's translation, occasionally modified, in this essay.
7. *Statesman* 290d6ff.
8. "Pharmacie," p. 86 (Johnson, p. 76). For the equation of platonism and metaphysics, see also French text, p. 172.
9. Cf. Nietzsche's reference to Kant in *Jenseits von Gut und Böse* as "der grosse Chinese von Königsberg," *Werke*, 2:675, par. 210.
10. "Pharmacie," p. 86 (Johnson, p. 77).
11. *Stromata* I, 10, 2: Ἐν γοῦν τοῖς Νόμοις ὁ ἐξ Ἑβραίων φιλόσοφος Πλάτων. . . .
12. For further references, see J. Mansfeld, *Die Offenbarung des Parmenides und die menschliche Welt* (Assen: Van Gorcum, 1964), p. 6.
13. *Olympians* V. 25–27; cf. *Pythians* VIII. 95ff. and *Nemeans* VI. 1ff.
14. For extensive documentation, including references to Plato, see Jean Pepin, *Idées grecques sur l'homme et sur dieu* (Paris: Société d'Edition "Les Belles Lettres," 1971).
15. *Nicomachean Ethics* X. 7, 1177b2, 1177b26–31.

16. Cf. *Republic* X. 589e4 and Shorey's note to that passage in his edition in the Loeb Library; see also *Phaedrus* 248c3ff.
17. *Metaphysics* A. 2. 982a6ff.
18. *Ibid.* 982b30, 983a2ff.
19. *Laws* VII. 803b3ff.
20. Cf. "Pharmacie," pp. 96, 111ff (Johnson, pp. 85, 95ff.), for Derrida's view on the constraints placed upon Plato in his authorial intentions by external structures (of language).
21. For philosophical pederasty, see *Symposium* 211b5 and *Phaedrus* 249a2, 252e2ff, 256a5ff.
22. "Pharmacie," p. 177 (Johnson, p. 153).
23. Derrida says instead that "Plato thus plays at taking play seriously," "Pharmacie," p. 181 (Johnson, pp. 157). This is not at all the same thing, but rather the atheistic imitation of the "theological" original.
24. "Pharmacie," pp. 171f. (Johnson, pp. 148f.).
25. *Ibid.,* p. 165 (Johnson, p. 143).
26. *Ibid.,* p. 178 (Johnson, p. 154).
27. *Ibid.,* pp. 125ff. (Johnson, pp. 110ff., 147ff.); see Johnson, pp. 129ff., for Derrida's view on writing as the exterior and speech as the interior. Cf. "Pharmacie," p 118 (Johnson, p. 104).
28. See note 3.
29. "Pharmacie," p. 172 (Johnson, p. 149).
30. *Ibid.,* pp. 118, 147–49 (Johnson, pp. 104, 129–30): note the denial that it makes sense to ask whether Plato consciously manipulates the chain of significations that Derrida is exhuming. "In a word, we do not believe that there exists, in all rigor, a Platonic text, closed upon itself, complete with its inside and its outside." It is permissible to link words that are present in a text to words that are absent from it, "given the *system* of the language. . . ." See p. 182 (Johnson, p. 158), on the contradiction between Plato's criticism of writing and the fact that he wrote so much.
31. *Ibid.,* p. 146 (Johnson, p. 127).
32. *Ibid.,* p. 144 (Johnson, p. 126).
33. *Ibid.,* p. 159 (Johnson, p. 139).
34. *Ibid.,* pp. 118–22 (Johnson, pp. 104–07).
35. *Ibid.,* p. 118 (Johnson, p. 104).
36. *De la grammatologie,* p. 60.
37. *Ibid.,* p. 31.
38. "Pharmacie," p. 127 (Johnson, p. 111).
39. *Theaetetus* 189d7ff.; *Sophist* 263d10–e6.
40. See note 26.
41. "Pharmacie," p. 192 (Johnson, p. 166).
42. *Ibid.,* p. 193 (Johnson, p. 167).
43. *Ibid.,* p. 75 (Johnson, p. 67).

44. *Ibid.*, p. 181 (Johnson, p. 157).
45. *Ibid.*, p. 182 (Johnson, p. 158).
46. *Ibid.*, p. 182 (Johnson, p. 158).
47. *Ibid.*, p. 176 (Johnson, p. 152).
48. *Phaedrus* 265c1, 8–9. Socrates also says that his treatment of *logos* in this dialogue is playful (278b7).
49. Eros is said to be a god at *Phaedrus* 242d9.
50. I limit myself to citing *Phaedrus* 235d1, 242c1ff., 274c1 for the connection between hearing and myth.
51. Consider 249d6ff.; in order to rectify the *logos* of τὸ ὄν, Theaetetus must "look more closely" (Σκόπει δὴ σαφέστερον) at what he says, i.e., at the fact that he grants directly the presence (not "existence") of the μέγιστα γένη.
52. *Phaedrus* 274c1, 244a5ff.
53. *Ibid.*, 244a7–8; madness comes to us θείᾳ δόσει; see *Symposium* 203c6ff. for the changing nature of Eros.
54. *Phaedrus* 254a3ff.
55. *Symposium* 210e3–5.
56. Derrida is certainly mistaken in his asertion that "à la différence de la peinture, l'écriture ne crée même pas un phantasme" ("Pharmacie," p. 159 [Johnson, p. 138]). Cf. *Sophist* 232a1ff; *Phaedrus* 264b3ff, 270b4ff, 271c10ff.
57. "Pharmacie," pp. 120–22, 133ff. (Johnson, pp. 106–07, 117ff.).
58. *Phaedrus* 278d3.
59. *Republic* VI, 510b4ff. (note the distinction between the mathematician's use of *dianoia* at 510d5–11a1 and the dialectician's use of *logos*, in the sense of proceeding exclusively with Ideas, at 511b3ff.); *Phaedrus* 265e1ff. (the dialectician, like the butcher, carves at the natural joints), 266b3ff. (Socrates is a lover of division and collection), 270d1ff. (we must distinguish whether something is monoeidetic or polyeidetic, and determine its power); *Sophist* 218d2 and 235c4 (diaeresis is a kind of hunting), 253b8ff. (dialectic, the science of free men, is the "spelling out" of formal structures); *Philebus* 15a1ff. (diaeresis is eidetic numbering). For a more detailed study, see my *Plato's Sophist* (New Haven: Yale University Press, 1983).
60. "Pharmacie," pp. 120, 192ff. (Johnson, pp. 106, 166ff.).
61. *Ibid.*, p. 177 (Johnson, p. 154).
62. *Ibid.*, p. 192 (Johnson, p. 166). The balance of the paragraph makes the same point again with a bow to the topic of the parricide.
63. *Epistolae* B, 314c1–3; cf. "Pharmacie," p. 177 (Johnson, p. 154), where Derrida rightly says that Socrates will never be a father because his seed is sterile.
64. "Pharmacie," p. 189 (Johnson, pp. 163–64).
65. *Ibid.*, p. 118 (Johnson, p. 103).
66. *Ibid*, pp. 168, 177, 179 (Johnson, pp. 145, 153, 154f.).
67. See note 63.

68. *Symposium* 211b5; cf. *Phaedrus* 249a2 (philosophical pederasty).
69. "Pharmacie," p. 83 (Johnson, p. 74).
70. *Ibid.*, p. 165 (Johnson, p. 143).
71. *Phaedrus* 229b7–9 (young girls), 234d5 (*synebakcheusa*), 238d1 (*nympholeptos*).
72. *Ibid.*, 229b4ff.
73. 230b1; cf. *Theaetetus* 152c8, 154d3.
74. *Menexenus* 235e3ff., *Theaetetus* 149a4ff.
75. *Gorgias* 485b7–e2; *Symposium* 216d2ff., 219a5ff., 221a8ff.
76. Cf. *Phaedrus* 244a8f, 245a3, 253a6.
77. Cf. my study *Plato's Symposium* (New Haven: Yale University Press, 1968).
78. *Phaedrus* 278b7ff., 278e4, 279a2ff.
79. *Ibid.*, 258d1–5.
80. The shift to noble writing occurs at 258d7, then back to writing and speaking (which are inseparable throughout) at 259e1. Psychagogy is introduced at 261a8; Phaedrus states his ignorance of it at 261b5.
81. 262c8 (paradigm); 264c2ff. (writing as alive).
82. "Pharmacie," p. 83 (Johnson, p. 74).
83. *Phaedrus* 270b4–9; cf. 270d9–e4.
84. *Ibid.*, 276c3–10.
85. *Ibid.*, 276e1–3.
86. *Ibid.*, 257c1ff.
87. *Ibid.*, 257a3–6.
88. *Ibid.*, 229e2ff.
89. "Pharmacie," p. 76 (Johnson, pp. 67–68).

## Chapter 3

1. Leo Strauss, *Thoughts on Machiavelli* (Glencoe, Ill.: The Free Press, 1958), p. 13 (hereafter cited as *TM*).
2. Nietzsche, *Aus dem Nachlass der Achtzigerjahre*, in *Werke*, 3:422.
3. *Civilization and Its Discontents*, tr. J. Strachey (New York: W. W. Norton, 1961), p. 55.
4. *Ibid.*, pp. 33, 55f., 62.
5. *Ibid.*, p. 90.
6. *Discours sur les sciences et les arts*, p. 19.
7. *Civilization and Its Discontents*, p. 23.
8. Hegel, *Die Vernunft in der Geschichte* (Hamburg: Felix Meiner Verlag, 1955), pp. 92–93.
9. *Ibid.*, p. 30.
10. Vincent Descombes, *Modern French Philosophy* (Cambridge: Cambridge University Press, 1983), pp. 9–47.
11. *Die deutsche Ideologie* (Berlin: Dietz Verlag, 1960), p. 30.

12. *Introduction à la lecture de Hegel,* 2nd ed. (Paris: Gallimard, 1976), pp. 435ff. (note 1): "tous les Japonais sans exception sont actuellement en état de vivre en fonction de valeurs totalement *formalisées,* c'est-à-dire completement vidées de tout contenu 'humain' au sens d'"historique' " (p. 437).

13. *Ibid.,* p. 135.

14. *Ibid.,* pp. 283ff.

15. *Ibid.,* pp. 75, 384f., 394, 540 (the final source of all Hegel's thought is the acceptance of death and finitude).

16. For a systematic presentation of this claim, see *Essai d'une histoire raisonnée de la philosophie païenne* (Paris: Gallimard, 1968), pp. 11–185.

17. *Introduction,* pp. 73, 93.

18. *Ibid.,* pp. 331, 371, 420.

19. *Ibid.,* pp. 272, 276, 287ff.

20. *Ibid.,* pp. 287, 304, 393.

21. I.e., for Kojève.

22. *Kant* (Paris; Gallimard, 1973), p. 99. Cf. p. 101.

23. For Kojève's statement of this circularity, see *Kant,* p. 58.

24. *Ibid.,* pp. 98–99.

25. *Ibid.,* pp. 198–99.

26. *Introduction,* p. 376.

27. *Ibid.,* p. 12.

28. *Ibid.,* p. 13.

29. See note 17.

30. *Introduction,* p. 167.

31. *Ibid.,* p. 294.

32. "Hegel, Marx et le Christianisme," *Critique* 3–4 (1946): 340.

33. *Introduction,* pp. 398–402.

34. *Ibid.,* p. 398.

35. *Ibid.,* pp. 404–05.

36. *Ibid.,* p. 146.

37. *Ibid.,* p. 197.

38. "Tyrannie et Sagesse," in *De la tyrannie* (Paris: Gallimard, 1954), p. 232 (hereafter cited as "TS").

39. "Natural Right and the End of History. Leo Strauss and Alexandre Kojève," by Michael Roth. Typescript (kindly supplied by the author), p. 19. The cited letter is dated Sept. 19, 1950. See also Roth's article "A Problem of Recognition: Alexandre Kojève and the End of History," *History and Theory* 24, Vo. 3 (1985): 293–306. This is the same year in which Kojève's discussion of Strauss's *On Tyranny* first appeared in *Critique.*

40. *Introduction,* p. 394.

41. *Ibid.,* p. 290.

42. *Ibid.,* p. 404.

43. "Hegel, Marx et le Christianisme," pp. 365–66.

44. "Christianisme et Communisme," *Critique* 3–4 (1946): 311. Roth, "Natural Right," p. 24, n. 19, quotes a letter from Kojève to Tran Duc Thao (Oct. 7, 1948), in which he explicitly calls his interpretation of Hegel an "oeuvre de propaganda destiné a frapper les esprits."

45. *Introduction*, pp. 436–37.

46. *La Quinzaine Littéraire*, no. 53 (1–15 July, 1968), p. 19.

47. *Introduction*, p. 254.

48. *Ibid.*, p. 117.

49. *Ibid.*, p. 286.

50. *Ibid.*, pp. 11–14.

51. "TS," p. 278.

52. *Ibid.*, pp. 332–33.

53. *What Is Political Philosophy?* (Glencoe, Ill.: The Free Press, 1959), pp. 45–46 (hereafter cited as WPPH); *TM*, p. 173. For the role of Hobbes in this process, see *Natural Right and History* (Chicago: University of Chicago Press, 1953), pp. 198f. (hereafter cited as *NRH*).

54. *TM*, p. 231.

55. *Spinoza's Critique of Religion* (New York: Schocken Books, 1965), p. 29 (hereafter cited as *SCR*).

56. "TS," p. 343. Cf. *NRH*, pp. 75–76, and Richard Kennington, "Strauss's Natural Right and History," *Review of Metaphysics* 35, no. 1 (Sept. 1981): 69. The *NRH* passage partly conceals Strauss's view by embedding it in a commentary on Max Weber.

57. See *Jerusalem and Athens* (The City College Papers, no. 6; New York: City College, 1967) (hereafter cited as *JA*).

58. *The City and Man* (Chicago: Rand McNally, 1964), p. 241 (hereafter cited as *CM*).

59. *Persecution and the Art of Writing* (Glencoe, Ill.: The Free Press, 1952), pp. 104f. (hereafter cited as *PAW*).

60. *JA*, p. 5.

61. Victor Gourevitch, "Philosophy and Politics I–II," *Review of Metaphysics* 22, nos. 1–2 (Sept.–Dec. 1968), p. 306, n. 156. This is a valuable study containing many sound insights.

62. *PAW*, pp. 34–35.

63. *Ibid.*, pp. 33–34.

64. *Ibid.*, p. 56.

65. *Ibid.*, p. 66.

66. Introductory Essay to *The Guide of the Perplexed*, trans. with introduction and notes by S. Pines (Chicago: University of Chicago Press, 1963), p. xvii.

67. *The Guide of the Perplexed*, part I, p. 12.

68. *CM*, p. 52.

69. *PAW*, p. 57.

70. *WPPH*, p. 229.

71. *Xenophon's Socrates* (Ithaca: Cornell University Press, 1972), p. 74 (hereafter cited as *XS*). Cf. "TS," p. 296.

72. *XS*, pp. 8, 29f., 116f. Consider esp. pp. 124 and 148.

73. *Ibid.*, p. 148.

74. *Ibid.*, p. 170.

75. *NRH*, p. 32.

76. "TS," pp. 316–17.

77. *WPPH*, pp. 38–39. Cf. Gourevitch, *op. cit.*, p. 300. Strauss comments on the ideas as separated forms in *CM*, pp. 119–120, but he makes it clear that, as conventionally understood, the doctrine "is very hard to understand; to begin with, it is utterly incredible, not to say that it appears to be fantastic." Nothing Strauss says makes the doctrine easier to understand or less fantastic.

78. "TS," p. 319.

79. *NRH*, p. 125.

80. *WPPH*, p. 11.

81. *Ibid.*, p. 32. Cf. *XS*, p. 31: "As for justice, the whole *Memorabilia* is devoted to it; courage is not counted among Socrates' virtues."

82. *CM*, p. 41.

83. "Plato," in *History of Political Philosophy* (Chicago: Rand McNally, 1963), p.. 51 (hereafter cited as "Plato").

84. *CM*, p. 61. Cf. *XS*, pp. 140, 159.

85. "TS," p. 296.

86. *NRH*, p. 26.

87. *Phänomenologie des Geistes* (Hamburg: Felix Meiner Verlag, 1952), p. 30.

88. *NRH*, p. 35. If the ideas are the fundamental problems, then the ideas must always be the same, contrary to Kennington, *op. cit.*, p. 67, although Kennington may be right in saying that philosophy for Strauss does not require these problems to be "separated" from natural things.

89. *WPPH*, p. 75.

90. *Ibid.*, p. 27.

91. *Ibid.*, p. 85.

92. "TS," pp. 246–47, 251, and Strauss's reply, p. 314. Strauss's claim that whereas we run the risk of sectarianism, we avoid it by restricting ourselves to an awareness of the fundamental problems, has already been dealt with (cf. pp. 316–17).

93. *NRH*, p. 82.

94. *WPPH*, pp. 23–24.

95. *Die Krisis der europäischen Wissenschaften und die transzendentale Phänomenologie* (The Hague: M. Nijhoff, 1954), pp. 99, 142, 149, 154–55.

96. *Ibid.*, p. 281.

97. "TS," p. 333.

98. *WPPH*, p. 89.

99. "Plato," p. 31. See the more elaborate discussion in *CM*, pp. 121–24.

100. "Plato," p. 59.
101. *WPPH*, pp. 36–37.
102. *Dialectic of Enlightenment* (New York: The Seabury Press, 1972).
103. *NRH*, p. 139.
104. *Ibid.*, p. 141.
105. *Ibid.*, p. 142.
106. *CM*, p. 28.
107. For the Aristotelian point, see *CM*, pp. 21, 27.

# Chapter 4

1. Cf. Paul de Man, *Allegories of Reading* (New Haven and London: Yale University Press, 1979), pp. 17 ("A literary text simultaneously asserts and denies the authority of its own rhetorical mode") and 58 ("But if reading is truly problematic, if a nonconvergence between the stated meaning and its understanding may be suspected. . .").

2. This point is clearly recognized by E. D. Hirsch, Jr., with respect to the understanding of the meaning of a text; see *Validity in Interpretation* (New Haven and London: Yale University Press, 1967), pp. 170, 203. Hirsch makes a very sensible criticism of theories claiming to account for the understanding of meanings, and thus too of Schleiermacher's canons. But his own theory of validation of interpretations amounts to the methodological defense of one meaning as more probable than another, which in turn rests upon the assumption that meanings of texts are at least "probably" objective. What Hirsch understands by this is evident from his first statement of the goal of his method, namely, "to reach a consensus, on the basis of what is known, that correct understanding has *probably* been achieved" (p. 17). This is not "Platonism," as Hirsch's position is sometimes described, but (at least practically) conventionalism, or in other words traditionalism of the same sort that Hirsch objects to in the case of Gadamer (p. 250). Hirsch does not explain what he means by a consensus. He takes it for granted that the objectivity of the meaning of a text is the same as its public accessibility by means of methodological devices. In the case of interpretations of humanistic texts (and especially of "eminent" texts or works of genius), a consensus is either worthless or worth no more than the persons who constitute it. And what method validates superior judgment?

3. Page references for Schleiermacher refer to Fr. D. E. Schleiermacher, *Hermeneutik*, ed. Heinz Kimmerle (Heidelberg: Carl Winter Universitätsverlag, 1959).

4. This has been correctly appreciated by Hirsch; see note 2 above.

5. Page references for Boeckh refer to August Boeckh, *Enzyklopädie und Methodenlehre der philologischen Wissenschaften*, ed. Ernst Bratuschek (Stuttgart: Teubner, 1966).

6. That is, the ontological basis ostensibly justifies a subsequent widespread misinterpretation of Saussure's correct doctrine of the arbitrariness of the signifier. Simply stated, it does not follow from the arbitrariness of names that they possess arbitrary meanings *apart from* those that have been conventionally assigned to them.

7. Page references for Heidegger refer to Martin Heidegger, *Sein und Zeit* (Tübingen: Max Niemeyer Verlag, 1977).

8. It should be noted that Alexandre Kojève announced the death of man a generation before Foucault (or Lévi-Strauss), but in the sense of the transformation of human beings into gods. For an interesting discussion of Kojève's influence on his successors in France, see Vincent Descombes, *Modern French Philosophy* (Cambridge: Cambridge University Press, 1980).

9. Page references for Gadamer refer to H. G. Gadamer, *Wahrheit und Methode* (Tübingen: J. C. B. Mohr/Paul Siebeck, 1960).

10. This point emerged from a conversation with David R. Lachterman, whose criticism of an earlier version of this chapter was very helpful.

## Chapter 5

1. *Schriften zur Literatur,* ed. Wolfdietrich Rasch (Munich: DTV, 1970), pp. 86, 107.

2. J. G. Fichte, *Zweite Einleitung in die Wissenschaftslehre* (Hamburg: Felix Meiner Verlag, 1954), p. 85.

3. *An Essay on Human Understanding,* ed. A. C. Fraser (New York: Dover Books, 1959), 1: 313, 315, 304; cf. 1: 330, 333, 344. G. W. F. Hegel, *Wissenschaft der Logik* (Leipzig: Felix Meiner Verlag, 1951), 1:20.

4. "Le cosmopolitisme sans 'émancipation'" (en reponse à Jean-François Lyotard)," *Critique,* 41 (1985): 578.

5. "Discussion entre Jean-Francois Lyotard et Richard Rorty," *Critique,* 41 (1985): 582–83.

6. "Der Spruch Anaximanders," in *Holzwege* (Frankfurt: Vittorio Klostermann, 1950), p. 311.

7. *Ibid.,* pp. 327–28.

8. *Op. cit.,* p. 583: "il est conversationnel; je suis tragique."

9. E.g., Aristotle, *De Anima* 433a7–8.

10. See Rodier's note to *De Anima* 431b5 in his edition, *Aristote. Traité de l'âme* (Paris: Ernest Leroux, 1900), vol. 2.

11. *Passions de l'âme,* 3:152.

12. *Ibid.,* 3:153.

13. *Op. cit.,* p. 30.

14. *Also Sprach Zarathustra,* in *Werke,* 2: 300, 318.

15. I put to one side Nietzsche's late (and in my view aberrant) intention to study physics in preparation for writing the projected volume(s) on the will to power.

16. *Philosophy and the Mirror of Nature* (Princeton: Princeton University Press, 1979), pp. 335f.

17. *Ibid.*, pp. 187, 340–41.

18. *Ibid.*, pp. 152–54.

19. *Ibid.*, p. 34.

20. *Ibid.*, pp. 12, 37.

21. *Ibid.*, p. 351.

22. *Ibid.*, pp. 372–73.

23. *Ibid.*, p. 174.

24. *Ibid.*, p. 379.

25. *Ibid.*, p. 377.

26. *Ibid.*, p. 369.

27. *Zur Genealogie der Moral*, in *Werke*, 2: 814–16, 819; cf. 2: 782–85.

28. "Le cosmopolitisme," pp. 576, 578.

29. *Ibid.*, pp. 570–71.

30. For an analogous dilution of an Enlightenment "narrative," see *Philosophy and the Mirror of Nature*, p. 377: "The edifying philosophers are thus agreeing with Lessing's choice of the infinite *striving for* truth over 'all of truth.' "

31. *Power/Knowledge*, ed. Colin Gordon (New York: Pantheon, 1980), p. 93.

32. *Ibid.*, pp. 81–83.

33. *Ibid.*, p. 88.

34. *Ibid.*, p. 79.

35. *Ibid.*, p. 93.

36. *Ibid.*, p. 119.

37. *Ibid.*, p. 133.

38. *Ibid.*, p. 133.

39. *Ibid.*, p. 1–36.

40. *Ibid.*, p. 36.

41. Pamela Major-Poetzl, *Michel Foucault's Archaeology of Western Culture* (Chapel Hill: University of North Carolina Press: 1983), p. 35.

42. Luc Ferry and Alain Renaut, *La Pensée 68: Essai sur l'antihumanisme contemporaine* (Paris: Gallimard, 1985), pp. 148, 152–53. The statements in question date from 1981–84.

43. *Ibid.*, pp. 156, 160–62.

44. *Ibid.*, p. 163.

45. *Reflections on Violence*, tr. T. E. Hulme (New York: Peter Smith, 1941), p. 71.

# Index